A. M. Murray.

Petticoat Pioneers

Petticoat Pioneers

NORTH ISLAND WOMEN OF THE COLONIAL ERA

Miriam Macgregor

A.H. & A.W. REED

WELLINGTON · SYDNEY · LONDON

First published 1973

A. H. & A. W. REED LTD
182 Wakefield Street, Wellington
51 Whiting Street, Artarmon, NSW 2064
11 Southampton Row, London WC1B 5HA
also
29 Dacre Street, Auckland
165 Cashel Street, Christchurch

ISBN 0 589 00771 8
Library of Congress Catalogue Card No. 72-97916

Typeset by New Zealand Consolidated Press Ltd and
printed by Dai Nippon Printing Company (Hong Kong) Ltd

Contents

CONTENTS

List of Illustrations

LIST OF ILLUSTRATIONS

LIST OF ILLUSTRATIONS

Introduction

Some of us find the search for information concerning our grandparents a difficult one, but this—if we are honest—is because we failed to listen to the stories of the old folk when we had the opportunity. Even more elusive are the tales of how or where our great-grandparents lived—and now it is too late. The old people have gone.

Snippets concerning some of the early settlers—the men—are to be gleaned from books of historical interest, but of the women there is seldom a word. The women who trudged long distances to live in a shack, bore large families, cooked in camp ovens, washed in the creeks, made bread, candles and soap, toiled beside their men in the bush, bent their backs cutting scrub and then sat up half the night mending torn clothes by candlelight, are scarcely mentioned.

When I began the task of offering a brief glimpse of these early women my first intention was to exclude the men completely; but this, I soon realised, was not feasible because it was the menfolk who led their wives and daughters into the wilderness.

Many were the first white women to settle in their particular district, and here we must remember that the various parts of the country opened up and became settled at different periods. Wives were taken to the Wairarapa and Hawke's Bay areas during the 1850s, while it was not until the 1870s that the Scandinavians arrived to tackle the Seventy Mile Bush. Further up towards the East Cape, settlement began at an even later date with women being landed by surfboats until well into the 1880s. A few of the women I have studied were not early settlers but were the first to be active in some particular field of their own.

Where possible information concerning them all has been collected from their descendants, but here an unforeseen difficulty arose through the fact that children and grandchildren belonging to the same family have different versions of what their parents or grandparents did and said. Some family contradictions were difficult if not impossible fully to reconcile.

It has not of course been possible to include every pioneer woman of the areas covered, but the fifty-four women studied are representative of the many omitted, for their lives ran in similar channels. This similarity posed a problem: though the women came from very diverse backgrounds, went up-country at different ages and led widely-differing lives, the basic way of life was in essence much the same—primitive homes and domestic equipment, lighting by slush-lamp or candle, cookery by camp oven, solitude and hard drudgery.

The detail of this could be repetitious, and I had to consider whether to omit it; but to have done so would have reduced the interest of the book for the descendants of the women concerned, and I decided that some repetition must be accepted. Physical descriptions of men and women I have included where possible, for the same reason.

I had also to consider the order of presentation, and chose the alphabetical order as having fewer disadvantages, for reference, than assembling the chapters on a geographical or chronological basis.

Where the histories are interlocked by marriage or other relationship, the names are cross-referenced by giving the number of other appropriate chapters in brackets. Quotations are set in italic and the style and presentation of the original have been followed.

In the appendix I have included some pioneer recipes to illustrate the type of fare that was served to a frugal pioneer household.

Throughout the work of compilation I have been given most generous assistance in the form of information and the loan of precious papers and photographs by pioneer descendants too numerous to list in detail. To all of them I offer my sincere gratitude.

Glengyle,   *Miriam Macgregor.*
Waipawa,
Hawke's Bay.

CHAPTER 1

Mother Mary Joseph Aubert

The Maoris of Hawke's Bay were indeed fortunate in 1871 when the dedicated woman who later became Mother Aubert joined the Meeanee Mission School. A full account of her life, giving details of how she evolved from one who was stated to have been the "ugliest child in the world" to the most wonderful woman in New Zealand, has been faithfully told in Pat Rafter's book *Never Let Go!*

Suzanne Aubert was born in France in 1835. Crippled at the age of two by an accident which left her apparently retarded and certainly disfigured, she grew up suffering humiliation and ill health. Unattractive in appearance by normal standards she may have been, but she had true beauty of spirit; a flame of sympathy for other people burned in her, urging her ever onward to fight for suffering human beings.

In 1860, at the age of twenty-five, she arrived in Auckland to begin what ended in sixty-six years of dedicated service to the poor and afflicted of all races and creeds in this new land which she adopted as her own country.

Eleven years of hardship, disappointment, frustration and failure faced her in Auckland, mainly because she was the most unorthodox Sister ever to have landed in the colony. In her own way she was a rebel, and the difficult years in Auckland seriously affected her health.

Little is known of her life as a teacher during her twelve years at Meeanee and most of it appears to have been in religious instruction and singing. She appears to have been more occupied with caring for the needs of the body and soul than with academic activities. Father Hickson SM wrote of her:

She became a tower of strength to the Mission, and the amount of good she achieved amongst both the white people and the Maori race was incalculable. All classes had the greatest confidence in her and, as she had many and varied qualifications, her services were of the greatest value. She could be a catechist, schoolmistress, physician, nurse, seamstress, choir-leader, organist, all by turns, according to the needs of the moment.

Wherever she went she travelled on foot, and she walked thousands of miles to visit Maori tribes, venturing where no white man would have gone unaccompanied. She was the only nurse working among the Maoris at that time and the only Catholic missionary in Hawke's Bay to whom the Maoris would listen and to whom they would show respect.

From 1868, as a result of the activities of Te Kooti and the spread of the Hauhau doctrines, many of the Maoris turned away from Christianity and the pastors who had

The Very Reverend Mother Mary Joseph Aubert (1835–1926). "The amount of good she achieved amongst both the white people and the Maori was incalculable."

been ministering to their souls. But where others failed Sister Joseph retained the confidence of the Maori: during this troubled period she baptised some two hundred of their children who were dying.

She became a missioner solely devoted to the Maoris and at this period she moved about the countryside wearing a grey skirt, plain blouse, a cape that reached to her waist and a straw hat with a veil. Under the skirt and tied round her waist were two large detachable pockets which she called her saddlebags; in one she carried a little bread and cheese, while in the other were three small books—a French *Imitation of Christ*, a Latin version of *The Little Office of the Blessed Virgin*, and a French *Catechism of the Interior Life* by M. Olier.

With her body and soul thus provided for she walked an average of 100 miles a week, covering the whole of the Hawke's Bay and Wairarapa districts. When she came to the rivers she swam, putting her clothes in a bundle on top of her head. On one occasion she was without food for forty-eight hours but then had the good fortune to find one potato. She ate half at once and kept the rest for the next day. She then walked another thirty-six hours without food, frequently stumbling and falling from utter weakness and at times having to crawl along on hands and knees to reach the Mission.

Many people sought her assistance at the Meeanee Mission. A letter written by her in 1874 noted *I love Meeanee because of the nearness of the Maoris, many of whom come every day for medicines. There were 1,353 sick people helped during last year.*

During her years in Hawke's Bay Sister Joseph developed many herbal medicines through personal experiments in pharmacy. She tried each one out on herself at each stage of the process, and once she collapsed when overcome by fumes. Fortunately she fell clear of the distillery equipment, but was unconscious when the housekeeper found her. In 1876 she successfully treated a Maori woman for leprosy, the report of the case being sent to London, where it was published in the *Lancet*.

2

In 1878, at the request of Bishop Redwood, she revised the Maori prayerbook which had been published by Bishop Pompallier in 1874. She had the work printed at her own expense in Napier and the following year produced a much smaller Maori prayerbook and catechism which contained only forty-eight pages. Its small size and low price made it readily available to all Catholic Maoris throughout Hawke's Bay.

In 1883 it was decided to restore the Maori Mission at Jerusalem on the Wanganui River. Sister Joseph was invited to accompany the Sisters to instruct them in the Maori language and to act as a nurse, caring for the Maoris.

In 1892 a new congregation known as the Daughters of Our Lady of Compassion was formed with Sister Joseph appointed as the Very Reverend Mother Mary Joseph Aubert. She was now a Mother Superior.

Mother Aubert, whose desire was to do only what God willed, declared that Providence was the bank in which she placed her confidence. She exhorted her Sisters to go in search of the unfortunate children abandoned on earth to all sorts of allurements and condemned to a life of crime and misery. The Sisters were to rescue those children over whom Jesus had wept, and for whom He had suffered; to go also in search of the aged and the sick, for they were the suffering members of Jesus Christ; to console, comfort, and help . . . Let the Sisters have only one thought, one ambition: to soothe moral and corporeal miseries, to save souls, to prevent sin and to promote the love of God.

To this end until her death in 1926 at the age of ninety-one Mother Aubert devoted her entire life, spending it also in the service of pioneering Maori education and social services. In her aims and ambitions for the relief of suffering and to provide shelter for the outcast of society, she simply "*never let go*".

CHAPTER 2

Susannah Barben

Susannah Barben arrived in Wellington in December 1840 in the ship *London*. She was accompanied by her husband Thomas and three daughters, the eldest of whom was about fourteen years of age. A letter written to her brother and sister in England provides us with a clear snapshot of the colony's early days:

Easter Sunday, April 11th, 1841.
My Dear Brother and Sister, I am sure you have many times wondered how we get on. We had a good voyage, as is said by those who understand sea voyages, but I assure you I did not like it very well except in fine weather; besides, myself and children could not eat the biscuits—we were nearly starved; but Barben managed it pretty well, and some of the people got quite fat—they had never lived so well in their lives.

We sailed past Van Diemen's Land for several days about a fortnight before we reached New Zealand. I assure you it touched our feelings to be sailing by the land where we had a brother without being able to see him after so many years since we saw him. However, I have written to him since I came to New Zealand by a person who was going to Hobart Town, but have not received an answer.

We landed at New Zealand on the Sunday week before Christmas Day. The Company has wooden houses for the emigrants where they stay till they build themselves houses or till another ship comes. There has been the ship London, *the* Stains Castle *with emigrants, the* Blenheim *from Scotland, and the* Lady Nugent. *Some of the people like here very well, and some do not. Some have gone back to Hobart Town in ships that bring provisions here—they give grand accounts of Hobart Town.*

We like it here very well. Our children are as happy as queens, playing out of doors nearly all the day. This place is entirely uncultivated, only where settlers have a spot here and there which grows potatoes, cabbages, peas, Indian corn, and other things abundantly.

I do not know how it is here in winter for it has been summer since we came, but the people who have been here a winter say there is very little difference, some nights quite frosty and the days scorching hot. Sometimes there are most powerful winds that last a day and a night, apparently enough to destroy the whole country, then the next day will be as fine as the finest day in summer. The people here are very healthy.

The natives are hardy, strong people. I was very frightened of them but have got to like them very well now. The houses are made of wood, and some of sticks plastered inside and out with mud, and thatched with bark of trees and covered with rushes. They burn wood on the ground—there are no coals in this part but there is plenty about thirty or forty miles from here but they say there is not capital enough to get them.

Port Nicholson, *circa* 1840. A sketch by Captain Owen Stanley

Port Nicholson is not as flourishing as is represented; there are no kinds of works yet—
it is quite an infant state. Plenty of work for carpenters at 10/- or 12/- a day; and for
sawyers at 12/- to 15/- a day; and for shoemakers, only they cannot get leather to go on
with. The New Zealand Company employs labouring men at making footpaths and horse
roads through the bush or woods at £1 a week and rations—10 lbs of flour and 10 lbs of
salt beef and pork. Barben has not had a regular situation since we came. They are not
ready for such as him yet. (Clerk).

We inquired for Stitchbury as soon as we came and heard he was working at Petone,
nine miles from here as a sawyer and doing very well. He was married to the person who
came after him and she was near being confined. Barben has been at Petone since, and
he had left to go to the Thames, about ten days' sail from here. Mr Gretton has taken an
eighth of an acre of land for three years at £2 a year; they have built two houses on it and
have plenty of garden ground, and he grew radishes this morning (Easter Sunday) nine
inches long and as tender as possible. We are living on them.

The natives will build a house for a blanket and 10/-, or a pair of trousers and so on.
They wear nothing but a blanket over them unless they get a shirt or anything for their
work or for their potatoes. They are very proud of our clothes; they get a deal of money
for their potatoes and some of them buy clothes off our people, then they go to any of our
people that they knew best to show themselves. I assure you we are very partial to some of
them and they are to some of us. They call a shilling one herring, a sovereign money gold;
they call vituals ki ki, potatoes are tiwers, a man is a tarney, a woman a wyena, gentle
folks are rangatiras, white people are pakehas and children are pickanninies.

Now for the price of the ki ki; Bread 8d for two pounds, (salt) butter 2/6 per lb, fresh
butter 4/- or 5/- per lb, cheese 2/6, beef and mutton 1/-, pork 7d per lb, rice 3d, beer

5

1/– a quart, gin, wine, rum 6d a quartern, bacon 1/7 per lb, sugar 4d, 5d, 6d and 7d per lb, tea (the best) 5/– a lb. Shoes for women, such as are 2/– or 2/6 in England are 7/– or 8/– here, men's from 16/– to £1 a pair, children, the lowest are 6/– and they are little use. There are no leather shoes for women and children and stuff ones are little use for there is no pavement—all hill and dale and the beach—the beach is the town.

We live about a quarter of an hour's walk from the beach and as much in the country as you can imagine. I hope you will take the trouble to write to us and direct to us at Wellington, Port Nicholson, New Zealand. The postage here is 3d. I don't know what you will have to pay. Now my dear sister and brother, we all desire our very kind love to you and your children, and hope you are all well and doing well. Our respects to the young man who lived with you. We remain your affectionate sister and brother,

Thomas and Susannah Barben.

While in Wellington they became acquainted with a widow, Douglas Mary McKain (26) and her four sons and daughter, Robina. In 1847 their eldest daughter, Sarah (47), married James Buchanan McKain, and that same year McKain's sister Robina (47) married a widower, William Villers. In 1850 these two couples and their children became the first families to settle at The Spit, now known as Westshore, and near what was shortly to become Napier.

A short time after the marriage of Sarah, Susannah Barben's second daughter married and went to live in Nelson, but it was perhaps Sarah's reports from Napier of a warmer climate in Hawke's Bay that caused Susannah to see little reason for remaining in Wellington. It was therefore not long before she moved with Thomas and their youngest daughter, Mary, to live in the infant settlement of Napier.

Thomas Barben died a short time after their arrival and was the first man to be buried in the Napier cemetery. For years the plot was marked by a wooden enclosure.

Mary Barben had been lame since infancy and had always used a crutch, but despite this disability she married James Hamshar, who took her to live at Wairoaiti along the Inner Harbour.

Susannah then spent her time living between the Hamshars and the McKains, the latter having gone to live at Petane in 1855. There were also times when Mary visited her mother and sister, the journey from Wairoaiti to Petane being made on a sledge drawn by a quiet old bullock named Stumpy because of his broken horn.

With other settlers these women knew fear during the Hauhau troubles of 1866 when, every evening, the Maoris at the nearby pa could be heard shouting their chants as they stamped round their flagstaff. Susannah's granddaughter, Robina Agnes Roe (*née* McKain) wrote later concerning the fight which took place at Eskdale on 12th October, 1866.

There had been a body of our men camping in the valley for some time, and on that day some more men, commanded by Captain Fraser, went to Napier from Wairoa and took all the men further up the valley as word had been received in Napier that a body of Maoris were coming down the valley. The two parties met opposite Captain Carr's homestead (later Mrs Beattie's) and a fight took place, at which, fortunately, our men were victors.

We at home heard the firing and supposed the men were just practising, However, presently a man came riding down with orders for all women and children to go up to where the men were. So off we all went, several families together, tramping up to the scene of the fight. But before evening we returned to our homes as there seemed no likelihood of further trouble for the present.

The Hamshars later took up land on the banks of the Waihua River, south of Wairoa, where Mary, despite her lameness, worked the ferry. During the days of Te Kooti when Hauhau rebels lurked in the surrounding hills, Mary and her daughter, Bertha, were forced to hide in the bush for at least a couple of days and nights. A letter written to Susannah at that period indicates the fear in which she lived.

Waihua, July 24th, 1869.

Dear Mother and all of you, I scarcely know how to write calmly. I little thought I should be in any more war. Nothing would ever have made me leave Napier if I had not thought it was all over. Dear mother, you will have heard that the natives have landed on the coast again, and are now, this very night, only 15 miles from Clyde, only three hours' ride. They have forced their way from where they landed first, and that was only three days' journey from us, and now so near. Some say they will go inland, or clear the coast before them.

Messenger after messenger we have put across to Napier for more men. One I put over the river yesterday (James had gone to town for flour). I knew by his headlong speed down a steep cutting near our house he was a messenger. I begged and prayed him to tell me if anything was up. I thought they were in town killing all the people and James with them. He said he was sent to get more men overland to meet them on this side, or by water, to land at Clyde.

Oh! what are the men doing? We were expecting to see troop after troop come by. Mr Richardson is the only one with a few men, Charlie Villers among them, and a few sawyers from Mohaka. What madness to send men in the steamers. They have gone to the wrong place. If some had come overland to Wairoa they would have done some good by meeting and preventing the natives either turning in the bush to join other rebels, or coming along the coast. Most of the men have left town to fight. The greatest indignation is felt by all that all those men were sent to a place where the wretches never have been nor likely to be, for they are now on the outskirts of the town.

The mailman is not back yet and it is 9 o'clock. He will not be here tonight. A man has just come from town and says that before he left a messenger arrived in town with the news that the natives had beat a party of our men and two killed. We shall know if this is true tomorrow by the mailman. Dear friends, you can think we are not very pleasantly situated. We are all well in health. I was so glad to see so many who had seen you on the Spit. It is now late. I can't say any more. My love to all. I trust God will guard us and the poor men who are now trying to protect us. Good-night. M. Hamshar.

Mary's daughter, Bertha, died a few years later.

Susannah spent her last years living in a room which James McKain built for her quite near to their house. At times she went from Petane to visit friends in Napier.

There were no wheeled vehicles, and as she could not be induced to ride a horse even if someone offered to lead it, she used to walk along the beach carrying her belongings in fairly large Maori kits.

She had strength to carry only one kit at a time, therefore she would take it a certain distance, sinking into the soft shingle at every step, leave it there and go back for the others. This meant she walked the distance three times, and this she did until she was over seventy years of age.

Susannah Barben spent her remaining years with her daughter Sarah McKain at Petane and was in her ninetieth year when she died. She was buried in the Eskdale cemetery.

CHAPTER 3

Mary Ann Bibby

Mary Ann Woodhouse was born in 1838 in Conder, Lancashire, where her father, a miller, owned a wind-driven mill. In 1860 she married Edward Bibby, also of Condor. The Woodhouse and Bibby families had been living in Condor since 1665, when they had left London to escape the results of the Great Plague.

In England Edward Bibby had been a cabinetmaker until sailing to Australia and then to New Zealand. After building a few houses in Napier he returned to England to marry Mary Ann Woodhouse.

She was a fairly short girl. Blue-eyed, her straight blonde hair was drawn back from a centre parting. She was intelligent and full of the indomitable spirit necessary to brave the long voyage in a sailing ship. This ordeal lasted 100 days, during which she had a premature baby which died. In 1862 she arrived at Waipawa in Hawke's Bay with Edward and lived on the northern side of the town which was then known as Sedgwick but is now known as Richmond Park. At that time Waipawa was known as Abbotsford, having recently been cut into township sections by the runholder, F. S. Abbott, from his Abbotsford station. By the end of 1861 Abbotsford township could boast an Anglican church, a courthouse, four hotels, two goods stores, two butchery shops, one blacksmith and a general store. There was nothing, as Mary Ann Bibby pointed out to her husband, for the women and children.

Edward, in the meantime, had been looking for land locally, but it had all been taken up. His heart had been set on the Poverty Bay district but Maori unrest and the constant scares in that area made land north of Wairoa a precarious proposition.

The inactivity while he went searching for land irked Mary Ann, and with his decision against the Poverty Bay area firmly settled she persuaded him to build a store on the bank of the Waipawa River. Accordingly he built a small shop with living quarters at the back. It was near the ford where people crossed the river, and the business, with Mary Ann in charge, opened on 2 July, 1862. From the beginning it was a success. In the meantime her husband did all sorts of work about the district, at the same time taking an active part in local body activities and in the organisation of the church.

Three months after the shop opened her baby, James, was born. Fifteen months later came Edward, and sixteen months after his arrival, Thomas was born.

The building was on ground above the river, but the well was on the lower level nearer the water. This meant that during the first years all the water for household use had to be carried up hill. Washing was hung out to dry over the bushes that grew where the Waipawa Mail Office now stands.

Then came the 1863 earthquake, described as a "terrific shake," which brought most

9

Mary Ann Bibby, *née* Woodhouse
1838–1910. She was "Pipi" to the
Maoris, by whom she was "very
much loved".

chimneys to the ground and made many homes unsafe for occupation. All the cooking had to be done out in the open, and these conditions lasted from February through the winter months.

Eventually the Bibbys had a family of eight children, four sons and four daughters, and life became very full. Mary Ann was not an accomplished needlewoman, but she did her best to attend to their clothes and with all this she also had to run the business.

By this time fear of Te Kooti and his Hauhaus had spread throughout the district. The local Maoris were friendly, but at any moment at attack could come from Te Kooti's forces. It was a time when men patrolled the streets all night, and it was necessary for all to be prepared for the worst. A small case of children's warm clothing was held in readiness to be snatched up hastily, and the little ones had been warned that if their mother came to them in the night they must rise from their beds without a word, dress in silence and follow their parents through the darkness to a place of safety. This could only be to the bush or to the blockhouse a mile or two up the river at Ruataniwha.

The Maori troubles subsided at last. Life became more normal and Mary Ann was able again to enjoy an hour's relaxation by riding with some of her friends, or by attending the Courthouse where "penny readings" were held. For this entertainment you paid a penny to sit and listen to someone reading from a book.

About 1866 a school was opened for the Waipawa children. Eighteen pupils were enrolled. Edward Bibby was secretary and treasurer, and afterwards chairman of the school committee, a post which he held for the next twenty-six years. His local body activities seem to have kept him fully occupied, for it was acknowledged by all that his wife was the real head of the business.

Mary Ann was also very much loved by the Maoris. They recognised her as being

10

The Bibby store, Waipawa, in the 1890s, had a lively mail-order business. "If Mrs Bibby will send som Patterns of what she as we can chuse from them."

the head of the firm, ceding to her the surname "Pipi", the Maori pronunciation of Bibby, but Edward was merely known to them by his Christian name, pronounced as "Eruwhitu". If a Maori admired a blouse she was wearing Mary Ann would take it off and sell it to him.

The paramount chief Te Hapuku was among her customers. While his wives squatted on the floor he would eye the pile of blankets for sale. "That one for this wife —that one for that wife—" he would decide, taking them from the pile and handing them to the fortunate women.

The people from Te Tapairu pa across the river found her most helpful in advising them on the outfitting of their children for school. Maori parents were anxious for their children to keep up with the Pakeha children, and brown feet that had never before worn boots were crammed into the leather contraptions.

The store developed into a tremendous business with mail orders coming in from as far afield as Ormondville, Kopua, Havelock North, Kuripapango, and the outskirts of the district. The confidence people had in her is shown by mail orders still in existence. They knew she would understand what they wanted, as the following letters indicate:

11

Ashley Clinton Makaretu, November 20th, 1878.

Mrs E. Bibby,
*Please send to me one turned down womens black hat as I want it for Mrs Folgier and if
you have not got a black one send one as you think will suit her. Three yards of broad
black ribben. Twelve yards of double width unbleach calico, three yards white table-
clothing. Please send these by Fridays train with invice, Mrs T. E. – – – –. I will be down
shortly and will settle for the same.*

The following mail order gives more extensive examples of the materials used by
women during that period.

Wallingford, May 4th, 1883.

Mrs Bibby,
*Could you kindly send me some things witch I put down as plain as I can. Mrs Gollon
of Wallingford recommends me to send to you. You will understand what I will need for
an infant. You will please send the things to Waipukurau railway station to Mr I. Gollon
to be called for. Mr Gollon is going down next week so he will get it for me the coach is so
expansive. If you will you will Oblidge
Yours Elizebeth H – – –
24 yards white calaco   6 strong greay calaco   12 y – – cheap greay calaco   12 y – –
flannell not more than 2 shillings per yards. 4y cross bard muslin   3 white roling binders
1 puff box   box fullers earth one box small safty pins, 1 card of trimming, the same sort
as I send. 1 pair of wimins lether elastic sides boots size 6 one pair of stockings cotton
2 pair of mens blue cotton socks. I do not want very expansive things. I herewith enclose
£2 two pounds as part paymint plese send the account with the things and I will send the
rest of the mony as soon as I can. P.S. 2 yards pink flanel for head flanels 3 reals white
cotton No. 24 3 reals white cotton No 40, 2 packets of dress hooks 1 white 1 black
you will Oblidge E. H. – – – –*

At times the orders were a little more difficult to decipher:

Arlington, May 10th

Mrs E – – – to Mrs Bibby
*Mrs E – – – is sory to year that her noot is mislaid as she is in want of the things wold
Mrs bibby oblige by sending 8 yards of lama like the Pattern to make the hole dress and
also 3/12 yards of Mersseler for Wight Jacket also som Pattern of narrow ribbon for
trimings to metch the lama rushing if you have it not plain ribbon and a wase ribbon to
metch if not the coller in wase band. Plain wide ribbon will do and also som ribbon to
trim the wight musling dress blue move or pink ribbon to metch for wase ribbon. If Mrs
Bibby will send som Patterns of what she as we can chuse from them. Also 3 yards of
round alascet for hare nets also 4 packets of hooks 2 wight and 2 black also som Patterns
of Musling for adress for young Person. If Mrs Bibby will get thes things ready it can
come up by the coch on Tusday next yours truly S.E – – –*

Early daybooks for the shop are still in existence, and notably through these books are records of charity items. The house was usually full. People travelling in from the backblocks knew they could always rely on a bed, or at least a meal.

By the 1880s the house and shop had become too small and as they wished to re-build on the same site, they bought a section across the road and bodily shifted the old house and shop over to it. This was done without their having to move out of the house, and as it was a slow process it meant they slept in the middle of the road. The task was achieved by slowly jacking the two-storeyed building and its adjoining cottage on to skids and gradually transferring the whole across to the new section.

When rebuilding began on the old site a fine two-storeyed wooden building with living quarters at the side and six bedrooms upstairs was erected. The hall was the length of a cricket pitch.

Life became easier for Mary Ann when her older boys left school and took over the shop. Although she never took an active part in church affairs she created a Christian home that not only built Christian character but a missionary spirit and an interest in both local and overseas mission work. In 1897 she took a trip to England and after that she retired.

By that time her boys had taken over the business. James managed the shop and Edward attended to the accountancy and office affairs, while Thomas took over the farm that had been taken up in the newly-opened bush country in the Blackburn district during the 1870s. This property eventually extended to 3,000 acres and became known as Lunesdale.

Mary Ann's busy life ended in 1910 when she died at the age of seventy-two years.

CHAPTER 4

Mary Glover Bibby

The well-known and much loved Mrs James Bibby of Waipawa was born Mary Glover Tod on 3 March 1867, in Kirkcaldy, Fife, Scotland. Her seafaring father sailed on ships plying mainly in Arctic waters, but lost his life in Tauranga Harbour during the only trip he made to New Zealand. Mary was three when her family moved to Edinburgh, and five when they moved to London. She spent her youth in London, attending the North London Collegiate School, but holidaying in Scotland or on the English south coast.

Mary Tod was of more serious mind than the average young person of her day. Her early ambitions veered towards missionary work but her health did not allow her to take this up. Eventually, after an illness, the doctors advised a long sea voyage. She was fortunate in having two uncles in New Zealand, Robert Tod of Braehead, Otane, and James Tod of The Park, Otane (in those days known as Kaikora). Mary sailed from London in the S.S. *Austral* in February 1891, and arrived at Kaikora at the end of April to stay with her Uncle Robert Tod, his wife Eleanor, daughter Nellie and son Rosslyn.

Mary Glover Bibby, *née* Tod, 1867–1937. "Nobody was surprised when her *Comrades and Friends* won the competition for the Country Women's Institute song."

Mary was a talented young woman and would have been an asset to any district. Short in stature, she had a nicely rounded figure. Her reddish-gold hair waved softly above a face noticeable for its rosy cheeks and bright blue twinkling eyes. She had a quiet sense of humour, she sang well, played the piano, and sketched and painted with competence.

Her paintings, now treasured by any fortunate enough to possess one, show good perspective and colour and the ability to record vividly what she saw. (Her pencil sketch of the old Patangata homestead is reproduced in *Early Stations of Hawke's Bay*.) The record of her voyage out and early days in New Zealand was faithfully kept in neatly-written diaries which, thanks to her acute observation, give vivid glimpses of the settlers and life in the district.

Nor was that life dull. Seldom a day passed without the arrival of a buggy bringing the Clarks, or the Howards, or the Dillons, or the Bibbys, or Uncle James Tod from The Park. There were picnics at Patangata, social gatherings, long walks over the countryside, even to Waipawa four miles away, while the two-mile walk to Kaikora for mail was an almost daily excursion. Usually, however, the longer distances were covered on horseback.

Four days after her arrival she wrote:

April 30th, 1891.

I walked to Kaikora this afternoon. A two mile walk along the country roads all by myself. The air was vocal with skylarks singing and it was strangely interesting to be continually reminded I was in New Zealand when I met folk riding their quiet long-tailed horses and when I met a strange wool-laden wagon drawn by eight great sleepy-looking bullocks. Kaikora is a modern village. After dinner Nellie and I went for a long ride to Waipawa. There and back was nine miles in a stretch and as I never had been so far before I'm very sore and stiff this evening. Still the ride was lovely through the hilly country and past lots of wooden houses with their verandas and gardens gay with chrythanthemums until we came to Waipawa. Waipawa is a flourishing little township made picturesque by the Maori inhabitants with their gay clothing and dark faces.

Saturday May 2nd, 1891. Nellie and I walked to the bush. What a difference between our woods and the New Zealand bush. Strange tangled growths on every side and not a plant familiar except the great pines which had conquered the undergrowth and rose up high and beautiful towards the sky. The bushes hang over with great festoons and tufts of lichen and snake-like creepers stretch from tree to tree and from the ground upwards. It is hard work to push your way through the thorny bushes but the whole scene is like a botanist's garden run wild.

On Friday May 8th, 1891 she gives us a view of early Waipawa and some of its inhabitants.

This afternoon Nellie and I rode to Waipawa, put the horses up at the Presbyterian Church paddock, and then walked to Mrs Rathbone's, climbed up to the house and took tea with them all. Mrs Rathbone was very pleasant, just looking as a young matron should, and the four little girls were very nice. The baby is just two months old but not pretty, and the eldest, Elsie, is a very well-mannered, good-looking damsel of ten. All the children were very talkative but they were all nice and not the old precocious colonials we hear so much about.

Then after that we did some shopping and then went to the minister's house and took tea there. Mr Johnston is a Scotsman of the quiet good sort, and his sister keeps his house. Miss Johnston is an elderly party, very plain and homely, but exceedingly good natured and very intelligent. She is as fond of cats as I am and three fine pussies made themselves at home with Nellie and me all the time. Miss Rosie, the school teacher called in the evening and we four went to the choir practice in the church at half past seven. We did our best at hymns and an anthem, the choir consisting of the organist, Miss Miller, the minister, three other young girls, Jinny, Nellie and myself. Miss Miller is the Rathbones' governess, a bright go-ahead girl who sings well and plays well, and Jinny is a little and very lively maid who lives with the minister and his sister, their niece, I think. We got home about ten o'clock and enjoyed a quiet ride in the starlight immensely, as we always do.

I forgot to say that Waipawa was swarming with Maoris even to a greater extent than usual. Every doorstep in the township had a group sitting on it and the roads seemed full of big Maoris, little Maoris, old Maoris, and young Maoris. Some young girls in particular looked very smart and even pretty, but most of the women were squatting about on the doorsteps looking rather untidy and decidedly uncivilised with their pipes and tattooed lips.

Her sympathetic nature is revealed after a visit to friends, the Howards.

May 28th, 1891. We got to the Howards in time for their dinner and we saw the whole family, four quiet sons and four noisy daughters. Also we saw the old grandmother. Poor old lady! I am more sorry for old women in the colonies than for anyone else. These bustling colonial homes aren't the ones for old people whose heart is in the old country, whose home is there and whose graves are there. The Howards' grandmother is a French-woman from Jersey, and although she can talk nice English, French is her tongue. A few commonplace polite words of greeting from me brought out a lamentation from her lips. "I wish I had never come to New Zealand. I wish to go home again," and much more in the same strain. " You'll have a scene," said the girls, "when you get on to that subject," but I did wish I could have been alone with her just to let her have as much crying for home as she liked. Mrs. Howard, her daughter, has only lately died of cancer after much suffering and this poor old lady has that awful memory too, as company. There she was, sitting in her armchair, with a din of laughter, music and conversation round her and no one speaking to or noticing her, while she looked the picture of weariness and desolation. I am sorry for old ladies who live with sons-in-law, or daughters-in-law, and especially for old folks away from home in the colonies.

A few months later, journeying to Woodville by train, she presents a picture of southern Hawke's Bay at that time. The occasion was a bazaar at Woodville which lasted for three days:

Wednesday, August 19th, 1891. This morning Nellie and I packed up and got ready for Woodville, and after having sent our bundles off to the station with Rosslyn in the cart we started off to Kaikora and caught the 12.27 train. We had a nice ride up in the train and as far as Waipukurau were in a carriage with about a dozen Maori men, women and children with tattooed faces and gay dresses. One woman had broad black ribbon pulled through great holes in her ears and a beautiful bit of greenstone attached to the ribbon by way of an earring. At Waipawa some more Maoris came in and the whole party pulled the most melancholy faces, uttering melancholy sighs and groans as they rubbed noses with the newcomers because there had been a death at Waipawa.

The scenery on our three hours ride to Woodville was very interesting. First the great plains like a flat grassy desert dotted over by sheep and with hills all round the plains, the beautiful snowy range of the Ruahines on the right, and the pretty plantations and green slopes round Sydney Johnston's house, Oruawharo. The house itself is a fine large building but painted red as it is and with a corrugated roof it looks decidedly strange.

Then we came into real bush country and past the towns of Ormondville and Dannevirke, such strange scattered wooden towns situated on land hewn out of the primeval forest. There are always three of four great well-built wooden hotels in these colonial towns, then two or three plain, wooden churches and a big, low-built schoolhouse. Then the other houses are of all descriptions but big, little, poor or rich they are one-storey little wooden houses to English eyes. Some are log huts, neither more nor less, but some are neat with nice gardens and smart verandas. Around these townships are forests of blackened stumps and blackened skeletons of trees, but some fields are sure to be there almost entirely free

Sydney Johnston's house, Oruawharo—a present-day photo. In 1891 Mary Glover Bibby described it as "painted red".

of stumps, and there sheep and cows are feeding. But many of these pastures are standing full of great trees, tall stumps and blackened fallen trees, and among these the horses and cattle rove. A scene of desolation.

It is indeed interesting to see as the train passes through the forest and stages of conquest—the Anglo-Saxon conquest of nature. There is the beautiful forest, the magnificent trees, the undergrowth of fair shrubs and the great tree ferns, just as it has been for a thousand years or more—but there is the settler's log hut and the few trees felled around it. Go a little further and there is a little settlement, three or four tiny wooden houses in an acre or two of clearing. There are children playing about the door and a few horses and cows graze around the houses. Then, as we travel on we come to the tiny township—the schoolhouse, the church and also the hotel. The railway station is there and also the general store, and across the country and through the bush runs the rough road leading to the next settlement. And so on until we get to the big townships like Woodville.

Still in Woodville she writes:

Saturday, August 22nd, 1891. In the afternoon Mr Crawford drove Nellie, Janet, Emily and me to the famous Manawatu Gorge. We drove over very rough roads to the entrance and then tied up our horse to a fence and walked through a gorge very much like the Pass of Killiecrankie. Then there were great hills all wooded with lush trees, bushes and qantities of tree ferns, and these hills went down, almost precipitously to a swift, fierce-looking river, the Manawatu. We enjoyed ourselves as we strayed for about a couple of miles along the coach road gathering ferns in abundance from the sides of the road, ferns such as our florists sell, of all sizes and kinds.

We returned home, but on the way came into a funeral procession and had to walk in it till we came to the Woodland Road where we turned off. A funeral in Woodville is a strange sight, especially when a well-known settler is being buried. This was the order of the return journey from the cemetery. First a group of horsemen, evidently chief mourners, then a few buggies etc., and then the band dressed in somewhat brilliant and fantastic costume. Then a crowd of children following the band and a large number of well-dressed folk walking on foot. Then the hearse, more traps and buggies, and more people on foot bringing up the rear. It was strange, but to look on it brought the same sad feeling as the orderly black funerals that we pass at home for it was someone being laid to rest in the hillside cemetery and someone had taken his last journey on earth.

In 1893 Mary Tod married James Bibby, the son of Edward and Mary Ann Bibby (3) of Waipawa and came to live in the house in Rose Street which is now occupied by her daughter, Miss A. H. Bibby. At the time it was considered quite a show place with its lovely view and with water running to the lead sink which had its own drain. Here they brought up a family of six sons and a daughter, their home being noted for its hospitality.

Mary became one of the best known church workers in the district, the house being visited by many of the world's well-known temperance workers and missionaries such as the famous W. E. ("Pussyfoot") Johnson and the leaders of the Salvation Army. She did a great deal of good as a Sunday-school teacher and Bible-class leader, and her influence meant much to a large number of people.

The Manawatu Gorge, *circa* 1885. "Very much like the Pass of Killiecrankie."

Mary had very modern ideas on child rearing and was one of those responsible for the opening of a branch of the Plunket Society in Waipawa. In fact the first Plunket meeting was held in the old Bibby dining-room.

Miss Jerome Spencer (41), founder of the Country Women's Institutes in New Zealand, was also a constant visitor, with the result that in 1925 the Waipawa CWI was formed with Mary Bibby as president. She held that office for nine years and was also a member of the Hawke's Bay Federation and the Dominion Executive.

Nevertheless she still found time to paint and to exercise her many talents, with a natural skill for the old fashioned game of "Squiggles", whereby a member of the audience drew a random line on the blackboard and Mary immediately developed it into a picture or animal.

It was in connection with the Band of Hope that she first tried her hand at writing dialogues for children, and later, when a suitable play could not be found for performance by the Women's Institute, it was no trouble to Mary to dash one off. On one occasion at a family wedding she did not think much of the hymns so wrote one herself.

In 1928 a competition was held for an original poem by an Institute member, the words to be suitable for an Institute song. Nobody was surprised when her *Comrades and Friends* was the winning entry. She also composed the music to which it could be sung, but the Central Executive decided that a tune which was more familiar such as the *Londonderry Air*, would be more suitable.

In 1935 Mary Glover Bibby's name appeared on the list of recipients of the King George V Silver Jubilee Medal for service in the community through the Country Women's Institute, Plunket and church groups.

She died in 1937 shortly before her seventieth birthday, but her Institute song lives on. Throughout the years the walls of country halls, schoolrooms and homes have echoed with the singing of the words, and as the voices rise there are still many who recall the bright blue eyes and smiling face of Mrs James Bibby.

19

CHAPTER 5

Kate Bourke

The place where Kate Bee was born in 1859 is now known as Ocean Beach, which is near Waimarama, a little south of Cape Kidnappers. Her parents, Francis and Ann Bee, arrived in Wellington in 1842 in the *London*. Her father, who had been a flour-miller in Nottingham, England, brought two millstones with him and built a flourmill beside a stream close to Wellington, but during a heavy storm the mill was washed out to sea and the millstones were lost in the mud and debris. In 1852 Francis Bee obtained a Maori lease of about 11,000 acres of hilly Hawke's Bay coastal land that was covered with fern but which had a few patches of bush in the gullies.

As a child red-haired Kate played on the beach with her nine brothers and sisters, but the family knew sorrow when one brother was drowned when he was swept out to sea while crossing the flooded Waingongoro River.

Education for the family was by tutors, but as tutors were not always available this became a problem, and at last the need for the children to attend school forced the Bees to move to Havelock North. Kate's education did not go far beyond standard two, but from an early age she became an avid reader, eagerly ploughing through the whole of Dickens and Macaulay by the light of slush lamps. In this way she educated herself.

On 14 October 1863 she was up early to be taken to the first Show to be held in Hawke's Bay. This forerunner of the district's present A & P Show was organised by settlers in the area and was held in Danver's paddock, Havelock North. Years later she recalled that she wore a new wincey dress for the occasion, the bodice long-sleeved, the hem well below the knees. She also remembered the bewhiskered gentry with their wives and daughters driving along in buggies and springcarts, the dashing young bloods racing down the dusty road on ponies, and the few even more gallant stalwarts on penny-farthing bicycles. The exhibits of the Show consisted of twenty-two horses, twenty-three head of cattle, eighteen sheep, six pigs, three dogs, and one lone hen.

By 1866 Kate's father had taken over the lease of the 14,000 acre Mohaka run about twenty miles south of Wairoa. The homestead stood on the bank near the mouth of the Mohaka River, which formed the northern boundary of the property, while directly opposite and across the river the cliffs rose up to a plateau inhabited by the Mohaka Maori population. White people in the district were few, but travellers passing up and down the east coast were able to spend a night at the Mohaka Hotel by run John Sim.

Once again Kate played on the beach with her sisters. They gathered driftwood shaking each piece carefully to rid it of katipo spiders, and during the summer they ate the ripe peaches that grew in profusion in the mild climate.

This peaceful existence was abruptly ended in 1869, when Hauhau rebels stirred the district into a state of terror. Te Kooti had escaped from the Chatham Islands and there were tales of the Poverty Bay massacre, to say nothing of other atrocities committed by his men. At Mohaka a blockhouse was hastily built, a tall, round gun-slotted building commanding a view of the river mouth.

Now, instead of driftwood, Kate and her sisters gathered shells which at that time littered the beach. These they sprinkled liberally round the blockhouse to serve as a primitive burglar alarm over which the lightest Hauhau be would unable to move unheard. She also tied a jagged broken bottle to a stick as her only defence against large, tattooed warriors.

One one occasion the girls, watching fearfully from the riverbank, saw a canoe laden with ferocious-looking men paddle their way past the settlement. Fortunately they continued out to sea, but it was later thought that this was the party who had murdered John Lavin and his family further up the river.

Kate's brother, George, was a member of the Armed Constabulary and the girls learnt all about the sending of smoke signals as warnings of danger. They also searched for and decided upon suitable hiding places in the bush, but it appears that when Te Kooti's men massacred the people at the Te Huki pa at Mohaka on 10 April 1869, most of the runholders had moved their families to safety.

During the 1870s their home at Mohaka was burned down, and a few years after this Francis Bee retired to live in Gisborne. By this time Kate had grown up to be a tall, slim girl with grey eyes, her red hair tending towards auburn. Straight-backed, she always stood erect and walked very smartly.

The annual social highlight in Gisborne was the military ball, which Kate usually attended with her sister Maria. It was always held on the Queen's birthday, 24 May, known as Victoria Day, and the two Bee girls with their heads of shining reddish hair never lacked for partners. It was at one of these balls that Kate met Charles O'Donel Bourke whom she married in 1888.

Charles was born at Te Aute in 1861 where his father, Peter Bourke, was postmaster and storekeeper at what is now known as Opapa. (Built in 1858, the old store is still in use near the Te Aute Hotel.) His parents, who had arrived in New Zealand in 1842, had come from Turlough, Castlebar, Ireland, and Peter Bourke was a civilian attached to a detachment of the 65th Regiment. At one time he was postmaster at Ahuriri, and at Napier when the office was moved there.

Charles was sheepfarming when Kate married him. They remained in the Gisborne district for a few years then moved to Meeanee in Hawke's Bay, where he still continued with sheep work.

When the great flood occurred in 1897 they were living in a cottage on the bank of the river. By that time they had four children, Harry, Dora, Molly and George. Charles was away sheepdroving at the time of the flood but Kate, watching the waters rise, saw the banks break opposite the cottage, and soon they were surrounded by rushing waters that came into the house.

She clambered up on to the table with the children, axe in hand ready to chop a hole in the roof to push them through if the waters rose any higher, but Charles arrived home before this became necessary and carried them all, one by one, to higher ground.

Kate Bourke, *née* Bee, 1859–1960, with a great-grandson. She was "the little girl who had been ready to stand up to tattooed warriors with a piece of broken bottle."

During the next few years they had three more daughters, Kitty, Nancy and Ellen, and some time later they moved to the Dannevirke district. Charles had a fertiliser works in Dannevirke as well as a butchery business, starting in one shop but moving to another nearer the town.

Tragedy struck on 19 January 1909 when the children went to the Manawatu River for a picnic. Molly and Nancy found themselves in difficulties in a deep hole and both were drowned. Molly was fourteen and Nancy only nine years of age.

In 1914 the Bourkes moved to Eskdale where they took up a 1500-acre property lying five miles up the Esk River from Eskdale. It was known as The Island because the boundaries consisted of the Esk River and numerous creeks and streams that necessitated twenty-four crossings.

The land consisted of hills and scrub, and as there were no buildings of any description Charles and his two sons had to set to work to build a home. All the timber was taken up the river as this was the only means of transport to the property, and in the meantime Kate and the girls lived at Eskdale until the new house with its verandah across the front was finished.

Years of hard work were put into developing The Island, where the stores came up the river only twice a year. Eventually, as Kate and Charles grew older, the farm was left in charge of Harry, their eldest son, and his wife, while they went to live between their two married daughters.

Kitty, who had become Mrs Charles Lee, and Ellen, who had married Gordon McAulay, both lived on the Kaiwaka Settlement north-west of Tangoio, twenty-two miles from Napier. Then, in 1937, Charles had a heart attack and died.

About fifteen years before she died Kate went to live with her unmarried daughter, Dora, who was leasing the small house situated beside the Eskdale church and known as Church Cottage. There, pottering between the tall hollyhocks in the old world garden, reading, knitting socks and doing the darning for the whole family, Kate spent her last years.

A great deal of her knitting was done without the aid of glasses, but as the years passed she complained that the light definitely wasn't as good as it used to be—and somehow she forgot to turn the heel of the sock so the leg just went on and on.

She died in 1960 in her 101st year and was laid to rest beside Charles in the Eskdale cemetery. Kate, the little girl who had been ready to stand up to tattooed warriors with a piece of broken bottle, was the first white child born in Hawke's Bay to attain her centenary.

CHAPTER 6

Heni Materoa (Lady Carroll OBE)

Heni Materoa, the daughter of Riperata Kahutia (23) and Mikaera Turangi, was born during the 1850s at Makauri in Poverty Bay. Her father was the son of Paratene Turangi, the man who ordered Te Kooti on to the boat when the rebel was being shipped away to the Chatham Islands, for which act Te Kooti later murdered him. Her mother, a chieftainess, was the daughter of Kahutia, a leading Poverty Bay chief.

Heni Materoa's early childhood was spent happily in the Makauri pa which lay seven miles west of Turanganui (Gisborne), but in 1864 came the news of Hauhau troubles and the advance of the rebels towards Poverty Bay. The people of Makauri were not in sympathy with the Hauhaus and it was thought advisable to move to a more inhabited part of the district.

The tribe therefore went to Turanganui and established a pa at the mouth of the Waikanae Stream where they were joined by the people from Te Arai pa. The men

Lady Carroll *née* Heni Materoa, *circa* 1850–1930. A press portrait, taken when she was a young woman. "She grew up to be an acknowledged beauty of the district."

24

then went out to work on surrounding properties during the day and returned to the
pa at night. Across the river at Kaiti was the pa of Hirini te Kani, and at that time
these were the only two large pas in the vicinity of what, in 1870, became Gisborne,
known to be loyal to the Pakeha.

Heni Materoa had little opportunity for education. She grew up to be an acknowledged beauty of the district with her dark, wavy hair, straight brows, full lips and the
moko delicately tattooed on her chin. To her friends and the family she was affectionately known as Te Huinga.

At that time there was no bridge over the river but Te Huinga and her friends used
to cross it in small canoes and spent many happy hours fishing and wandering along
the beaches. Nevertheless the elders of the pas were becoming increasingly concerned
over the fighting in Taranaki and the trouble caused by the fanatical Hauhaus.
In 1865 the Rev. Carl Volkner was murdered at Opotiki, and each day a few more
rebels crept into the district. In the April of that year the Williams family and people
at the Waerenga-a-hika mission station were forced to leave the district.

Bands of loyalitsts went out to join in the fray and at times the infant township and
the pas were thrown into a state of tension when the Ngati Porous came from
Tokomaru and Waiapu. When Henare Potae was in charge the Ngati Porous were
stationed at Hirini te Kani's pa, or further on where the Hardings' house later stood.

Te Huinga never forgot the excitement of watching the stalwart Ngati Porous come
into Turanganui, and then, with her friends, she would watch them go out again on
to the flats to chase and fight the Hauhaus. After the destruction of the Waerenga-a-
hika pa and the burning of the mission buildings there was the anxious time of awaiting
the return of those warriors who were so loyal to the white people.

The following year there were battles at Omarunui and Petane in Hawke's Bay,
after which Te Kooti was banished to the Chathams, returning later to murder
Te Huinga's grandfather Paratene Turanga.

On 4 July 1881 she married James Carroll, who was known as Timi Kara. He was
born in 1857 and was the son of Joseph Carroll, the first white man to take sheep
to Wairoa.

Joseph Carroll was born in Sydney in 1814, went to the Bay of Islands in 1841
and settled in Wairoa in 1842. He was of Irish extraction and it is believed that
Charles Carroll, one of the signatories of the American Charter of Independence, was
one of the family which, in the fifteenth century, was headed by the famous King
O'Carroll.

In Wairoa Joseph married Tapuke, a Ngati Kahungunu chieftainess who traced her
descent from Taraia, and when Timi Kara was born her confinement took place
under a cabbage tree which can still be seen in Wairoa.

At his birth young James Carroll received the attentions of the high priests, one of
whom severed his umbilical cord and threw it over a high cliff. It seems also that his
mother was unable to suckle him and this duty therefore fell upon two specially chosen
wet nurses. As a sequel to the special rites performed at his birth he was dedicated to the
Maori people and therefore carried away to a mountain fastness near the source of the
Ruakituri River, where he later became eligible for instruction in the Whare Wananga,

or storehouse of Maori religion, history and lore. He was about seven years old when he first saw a white man. This was his father, who had come to claim him.

Joseph Carroll had not set eyes on the boy since his birth and negotiations for his ransom now commenced. At first the tribe refused to part with its adopted child and young chief, but after long and serious talks in the meetinghouse the prior claim of parentage was recognised.

For various reasons he was then placed under the guardianship of George Richardson, an old family friend. He attended school until he was ten and then worked on his father's station, where he learnt to talk and debate with other musterers, some of whom were educated young men from England.

In 1871 he joined the Waikaremoana expedition against Te Kooti and for his bravery was mentioned in despatches and awarded the New Zealand Medal with a gratuity of £50. Later his ability caught the attention of Sir Donald McLean and led to the beginning of his parliamentary career. For three months in 1909 and for seven months in 1911 he was acting prime minister of New Zealand, and in the Coronation Honours of 1911 he was created KCMG.

Sir James had a placid nature. He was a tall, well-built man whose complexion, when he was young, was fair and showed little of his Maori blood. He spent much of his time away from home and during his many periods of absence Te Huinga, now Lady Carroll, stayed quietly in Gisborne. On her marriage she had accepted the Catholic faith at his request.

She became the leader of the Maori women of the district. and saw to the welfare of her people at the Awapuni pa, making sure they had plenty of food and clothing, and encouraging the younger ones in the crafts of the Maori people. There were no children of the marriage but she adopted her brother's eldest son, Whare, as well as two other boys named Toki and Joss, and later took in and looked after many others as well.

Despite her lack of conventional education she became an outstanding personality. Tall and stately and always beautifully dressed, she wore a chinchilla fur and was never without a hat on her dark, wavy hair. She loved good clothes and furnishings and, as a perfectionist, insisted that everything had to be of the best.

A wealthy woman through her mother's estate, she backed Sir James financially and built a large home in Kahutia Street where she entertained his parliamentary associates when they visited Gisborne. Under her supervision the people who worked for her in this home had to do everything well and live by the standards of her strictly Victorian morals. Once when one of her unmarried housemaids became pregnant she went to the boy responsible and personally thrashed him with a horsewhip.

Her garden was in the care of a Chinese whom she taught to plant kumara with the roots pointing towards Mt Hikarangi. Every fourth year she sent him on a trip home to China, herself paying his expenses. He worked for her for years and when he died she had his remains sent to China to be buried according to custom.

When Sir James was away she was driven about the countryside by one of her own people, nearly always being accompanied by her close friend and relative, Matehaere Halbert. In fact, during a lifetime of friendship, Matehaere was seldom far from her side.

Lady Carroll "became the leader of the women throughout the district."

Lady Carroll's home at Gisborne. "Anything for the advancement of the district . . . found a sympathetic place in her heart."

At times there were important decisions for her to make and one occasion arose after the death of Te Kooti when his followers of the Ringatu religion applied to her for permission to bring his remains to Poverty Bay. This request she firmly refused as the former rebel had murdered her grandfather.

As the years passed Lady Carroll became known to hundreds by reputation rather than personally because, although she could show bursts of fieriness when the occasion demanded, she was by nature a quiet and retiring person who delighted more in home life than in the glare of publicity. As an enthusiastic lover of Gisborne she had few equals. Anything for the advancement of the district, particularly if the Maori race was concerned, found a sympathetic place in her heart.

She gave £500 to the Kahutia Bowling Club, and the Carroll Shield for competitive games in ladies' hockey between Poverty Bay and Hawke's Bay. With her brother Pare Keiha she gave the land for numerous public buildings and churches, and in 1918 she was awarded the OBE for her orphanage work and fund-raising during World War I.

However, when the Duke and Duchess of York, later King George VI and Queen Elizabeth, visited New Zealand Lady Carroll refused the invitation to be present at the state banquet given in their honour at Wellington: this was because they had not previously been received on her own marae.

Te Huinga lost her Timi Kara when he died in Auckland in 1926. The people of Wairoa were anxious for him to be buried in the place of his birth but to this she would not consent, and his grave is in the Makaraka cemetery at Gisborne, the fine memorial being unveiled in 1929 by Joseph Ward.

Te Huinga died in 1930 and was placed beside Timi Kara in the vault beneath the memorial. When she died her most fervent wish was that her nephews and adopted children would carry on her work of caring for the old and young people of the pa.

After her death her brother Pare Keiha, who for years was one of Gisborne's champion golfers, set aside forty-five acres of their mother's estate for a golf course for Maoris only. The land lay just outside what was then the town limits, but unfortunately there were not enough Maoris to keep the club in operation so Pakeha players were allowed to join. The area was eventually bought by the city council for residential sites and a recreational park.

Te Huinga's large old home in Kahutia Street has since been turned into some twelve flats.

CHAPTER 7

Catherine Chamberlain

Catherine McKenzie, known to most people as Kitty, was born in Rossshire, Scotland, in 1847. Of a gentle nature and a sweet disposition which showed clearly in her face, she grew up to be of medium height, blue-eyed, and with brown hair so curly that it was difficult to control. She came to New Zealand in 1866 with her mother, Isabella McKenzie, her sister Jessie, and brothers, Evan, Murdoch, Roderick and John, and the family settled at Kuripuni, Masterton. Her mother, the widow of Colin McKenzie, had also been a McKenzie before her marriage, and had brought the family to New Zealand on the advice of her brother, John (27), who was already living at Whangaehu.

In the April of 1869 Kitty married Edmund Edinborough Chamberlain of Masterton. He was born in 1843 in a small hut on the Tinakori track, Wellington, and his father, Thomas Chamberlain (8), a dairyfarmer at Karori, had taken part in the first land ballot of the Wairarapa Small Farms Association. He had acquired sections on the Upper Plain for himself and five sons, and had also bought land allotted to Richard Kibblewhite. Edmund's portion of the latter became known as Rosswood.

In 1856, with his father, brothers and future brother-in-law, Brown Hunt, Edmund had assisted in getting the first wheeled vehicle across the Rimutakas. This was a

Catherine Chamberlain, *née* McKenzie, 1847–1933, as a young woman. Friendly Maoris made her house tapu to protect the family from Hauhau raiders.

bullock dray driven from Wellington to the foot of the range, where the baggage was loaded on to the bullocks and then taken over the hill to Featherston. The dray was then brought up to the top of the hill, taken to pieces and carried over the parts where the road had not yet been formed. Gangs were working in sections on the Featherston side but many stretches of road were still impassable. Altogether the dray was taken to pieces and put together again six times before Featherston was reached, and the journey to Masterton took twelve days.

After her marriage Kitty went to live in the Rosswood homestead, which had been built in the early 1860s. Their first child, Sarah Isabella, was born in 1870, and their son Roderick, in 1871. When she visited her mother and her sister Jessie, who had become Mrs Munro, Kitty rode a white horse. She usually carried small gifts of food to them, and both the white horse and its attractive rider were familar sights, not only to the settlers but to the Maori people, who soon learned to appreciate her many acts of kindness.

On Rosswood Edmund used Maori labour from the nearby Akura pa, and it was from these people that Kitty learnt of their custom of placing elderly, sick people out in an isolated whare to await their end. To let them die in the pa, she was told, would make the whole place tapu and therefore uninhabitable. She was also most disturbed to learn that as the old folk were expected to die in any case, food need not be wasted upon them.

She therefore developed the habit of taking food out to these ailing people, with the result that many of them recovered and were able to go back into the pa. In return the Maoris gave her such delicacies as they could afford, particularly eels, which they knew Edmund loved to eat.

Maori women formed the habit of bringing their weaving to the Rosswood verandah. There they would sit in silence, their brown fingers twisting the flax until Kitty took them each an egg-nog. After that they would beam at her, nod their gratitude and amble back to the pa. This treat was never refused them.

During those days there was unrest among the Maori population. Hauhaus, who had caused trouble in other parts, were making visits to the various pas of the district, urging an uprising against the settlers. Kitty and Edmund were not disturbed by the warnings and rumours until one day they realised that there was no Maori labour on the property and the Maori women were no longer coming to sit on the verandah. The eels, too, had ceased to arrive. It was then they learnt that Rosswood had been made tapu. In case of real trouble from the Hauhaus the Maoris had put this magic cloak of protection over the house and its inhabitants, and no Hauhau could go near while the tapu was in force.

Kitty's next baby, Catherine Susannah, was born in 1873, and then, in 1874, tragedy struck the household when Roderick was three-and-a-half. Both Sarah and Rodie had been out of sorts, and it was decided they were suffering from worms. Edmund therefore rode into Masterton to buy worm powder from the chemist.

On his return both children refused to take it. Sarah ran away and hid, but little Rodie was easily caught. Despite his struggles Edmund forced the child to take the powder while his mother held him, but as soon as it was down Rodie went into screaming convulsions of agony. As Kitty tried to pacify him he died in her arms.

Edmund leapt on his horse and rushed back to the chemist, who then admitted that by mistake he had put arsenic in the worm powder.

After this shocking incident Kitty was never the same happy person. She no longer rode the white horse, she seldom smiled, and for a time she became almost a recluse. Her next child, Florence Gertrude, was born in 1875, and 1876 saw the birth of Alfred Edmund. There was a spell of eight years before Rosa Adeline was born in 1884, and two years later her last child, William Edinborough, was born.

The tapu remained on Rosswood for ten years or more until a curious incident made it necessary for it to be officially removed. One morning when the family arose they realised that the house was surrounded by Maoris who stood watching the place from a discreet distance. Edmund called to them, asking the reason for their constant observation, and they replied that one of their number, having gone mad, had rushed from them and entered the house. Only a mad person would enter a tapu house.

Edmund assured them that there was nobody in the house but themselves, but the Maoris persisted in their belief. Therefore, to satisfy them, he said he would search

Right: Kitty Chamberlain with her mother, Isabella McKenzie, her son Alfred Edmund and grandson R. E. Chamberlain, who grew up to be a founder of the Golden Shears competition.

Below: Rosswood homestead, home of Kitty Chamberlain. "Maori women formed the habit of bringing their weaving to the Rosswood verandah."

Masterton, *circa* 1891. A watercolour by C. Aubrey. Edmund Chamberlain's flourmill is the four-storeyed building on the left.

the house. The man was found, fierce-eyed and gripping an axe, lying under the bed in which Kitty and Edmund had slept that night. He refused to move.

The Maoris were than asked to come and remove him, but this they refused to do as the house was tapu. But now that they were sure he was there they would do something about it: a messenger would be sent to the Papawai pa at Greytown for the services of an important tohunga, who at last arrived and with much chanting and ritual removed the tapu, so that the others could enter and take away the one who had gone *porangi,* or mad.

Apart from farming Rosswood's eighty acres Edmund was connected with the flourmilling and bakery trade and also farmed land at Mikimiki. The children attended the Fernridge school and later they all married except Catherine, who remained with her parents. Kitty's mother, Isabella McKenzie, often stayed with them and died there during a visit in 1904.

One morning in 1920 Kitty awoke to discover that she had lost the sight of one eye. In her usual reserved manner she remained perfectly calm and several days elapsed before she admitted this misfortune to the family. Ten days later she woke to hear Edmund moving about in the darkness and asked him why he was getting up before daylight. He answered that it was after eight o'clock and broad daylight, and it was then she knew she had gone totally blind. The rest of Kitty's life was spent in darkness.

She was attended to by her daughter Catherine, who declared she never heard her mother complain. Although blind Kitty said that in memory she could still see the beauty of the high, snowclad Tararua Ranges, the green trees and the stretches of golden grass in summer. In memory she could still see the faces of all her dear ones.

A further major misfortune occurred when she fell and broke her hip. Her days were then spent lying on a horsehair couch in the livingroom, still with never a word of complaint. Grandchildren would creep in to kneel beside her couch and touch her hand, but no matter how silently they came she was always able to name each child correctly. Each night one of them read the Bible to her.

In 1929 friends and relatives gathered at Rosswood to celebrate the diamond jubilee of Kitty's and Edmund's wedding, and despite the years her two bridesmaids, Mrs R. McGregor and Mrs M. McDonald, were again able to take their places beside her.

The final blow came in 1930, when she lost Edmund. She followed him in 1933, dying at the age of eight-six. In Masterton the old Rosswood homestead still stands in Kibblewhite Road, but it has long since gone out of the Chamberlain family.

CHAPTER 8

Susannah Catherine Chamberlain

In the days when secondary education was not so common among young women Susannah Catherine Bull and her sisters kept a school. Born in 1809, she married Thomas Chamberlain about 1831 and they lived in the boot manufacturing town of Daventry, Northamptonshire, England.

Thomas Chamberlain, born in 1806, came from a tall family. His grandmother, who had been an Edinborough, had been spoken of as "a giant of a woman", and when laid out after death was found to have been six feet two inches in height. The family was connected to the Parliamentary and screw-manufacturing Chamberlains, and there were some members who considered a lowly schoolteacher to be beneath their social level. They ignored Thomas after his marriage, treating him as an outcast and no longer one of the family.

Susannah and Thomas's first son, William Edinborough, was born in 1832, and their daughter, Sarah Ann, in 1834; Giles Edinborough was born in 1838 and Edwin Edinborough in 1841.

The few acres they owned jutted like a wedge into the neighbouring property of a titled person whose name is still known to descendants. This man was most anxious to buy their property and sent two of his agents to negotiate with Thomas.

Thomas refused to sell. He preferred to work his own land rather than to toil in the bootmaking factory. The agents persisted until, eventually, they offered generous terms for the lease of the land, the period to be until after the maturity of one crop.

This offer seemed to be too good to refuse, and at last Thomas agreed. The land was taken over and planted. When the young leaves appeared it was seen that acorns had been placed in neat rows, and as it takes scores if not hundreds of years for acorns to grow into oaks and reach maturity, the Chamberlains realised they had been tricked out of their land. They then decided to emigrate to New Zealand.

After turning every available asset into cash they made body-belts into which they thickly and closely sewed their small wealth of sovereigns. These belts were worn by Thomas and Susannah as they stepped aboard the sailing vessel *London*. Susannah's sisters had tried to persuade them to leave William and Giles behind with them to be educated, but the little boys sailed with their parents from Gravesend in the December of 1841.

The voyage was a nightmare of storms and sickness. Some fifteen people died, most of them children, and little Edwin was one whose body was slipped quietly over the side in its canvas shroud. Susannah was desperately ill and her body-belt was taken off and placed on William, who was nine and a half.

At last it was over and they arrived at Wellington on 2 May 1842. Passengers were put into open boats which were run as far as possible up the sandy beach. The women were then carried to dry land while the men waded ashore, and the goods also had to be carried ashore.

What is now Lambton Quay was then a sandy beach, and above high-water mark were a few shanties including some shops, all being primitive dwellings with thatched roofs of rushes and toetoe. Te Aro was mainly a large swamp, and where Luke's foundry was later built was then the site of a large Maori pa. Another pa stood at Pipitea Point, and the sight of so many dark, tattooed faces terrified the new settlers.

Susannah's first home in Wellington was a shanty on the Tinakori track opposite what later became Sydney Street, between St Mary Street and Lewisville Terrace. From here five-year-old Giles walked through the bush to attend an infant school opened by a Mrs Buxton. One day he did not return. Susannah and the family searched frantically through the bush, fearing he had been taken by Maoris, but it was later discovered that instead of going to school he had met the daughter of Henry and Mary Jones, who had taken him home to play with her brothers. When darkness had fallen he had been too frightened to walk home through the bush.

While living in the Tinakori track shanty Susannah's next baby, Edmund Edinborough (7) was born in 1843.

Thomas, during his early days in Wellington, took up bootmaking, but found that leather was almost impossible to procure. He then took up land at what was known as Parkvale, situated between Karori and Makara. It was all in dense bush and everything had to be carried in by hand over ground that was slippery and steep in places. Thomas carried a large oak chest into Parkvale on his back, and then trees had to be felled before they could build a house.

While the Parkvale house was being erected Susannah remained in the shanty with Sarah Ann and baby Edmund. Thomas walked between the two places at night, carrying back supplies of food for the next day. During his absence from Parkvale William and Giles spent the nights hiding in the oak chest in case Maoris came about the place.

The Parkvale house had clay walls and a clay floor, timber being pitsawn for the roof to carry the shingles. When it was finished their belongings were carried over the hills and through the bush, and Susannah moved to live there.

The bush felling continued and while engaged in this William had a leg crushed by a falling tree. Thomas carried the boy to Wellington to enable the leg to be given proper treatment by a doctor, and while there he rented a house in Mulgrave Street from a Mrs Hempleman, whose husband was captain of a whaler. It was found necessary to amputate William's leg, and this was just done with a saw and without anaesthetic— the leg was buried in Mrs Hempleman's backyard.

Susannah and Thomas spent three or four years at Parkvale before they decided to buy a portion of the hills at present known as Northland and begin dairyfarming. The house was situated on the hills west of what used later to be known as the Wireless Station Building, and the land stretched just west of this and almost to the Karori tunnel with one boundary crossing to the Botanical Gardens. Their baby Thomas was born here in 1847.

The following year the 1848 earthquake wrecked the house, but they rebuilt it and continued with the dairyfarm. Samuel was born in 1849, and in 1851 baby Susannah, but she died while still an infant.

In 1854 Thomas took part in the first ballot for the drawing of sections at the new settlement of Masterton and was successful in obtaining sections on the Upper Plain for himself and his sons.

In 1855 another earthquake completely wrecked their Northland house. The 1848 shake had been heavy, but was nothing in comparison with the violence of this one: the earth trembled at intervals for three weeks, with great rents being made in many places. It hastened their decision to move to Masterton.

The boys went first and built a house on their parents' section in readiness for their arrival. Ironically, considering past history, they called it The Oaks. William's section became Bellevue, Giles named his Starwood, and Edmund's became Rosswood.

It was 1858 before the dairy farm was disposed of and Thomas and Susannah were able to move over to Masterton. By that time a dray road had been built over the Rimutakas and they were able to take most of their goods and chattels over in a cart. Susannah was on board and Thomas rode. Their cottage, with its pitsawn timber and shingled roof, stood in what was later to become Edith Street, and despite the fact that the Chamberlain men were all over six feet, the doors were only five feet ten inches in height. Some of the cows had already been driven over to the Wairarapa so they were able to have milk and butter.

Their daughter Sarah Ann married Brown Hunt and also lived in Masterton. As a wedding present the family gave her their town sections. Wishing to turn them into money she sought advice from Henry Bannister, who told her there was no such thing as money in Masterton—everything was bartered. He told her that a man who had gone to Wellington to mortgage his section had asked him to sell him some ewes; when this man returned with the money and paid for the ewes he would pay Sarah £15 for her three sections. These town sections extended from the State Theatre to J. Bradbury's shop.

Susannah and Thomas had been in their new home only a year when Thomas died from a heart attack in the January of 1859. Susannah continued to live in The Oaks cottage, being visited by grandchildren and taking her part in the building of the settlement of Masterton. With Sarah she was one of the earliest members of the Methodist Church, attending the first meetings held in the home of Henry and Mary Jones.

Susannah had much in common with the Jones family as they also had come from Northamptonshire, had sailed on the *London* and had lost their youngest child on the voyage. In Wellington they too had faced much hardship as four months of salt meat and biscuits had left Henry too weak for much hard toil. Work, when it could be found, consisted of sawing timber, carting firewood and working on the roads that were being formed. Sometimes they had only two meals a day, these being potatoes and fish that Henry had caught in the harbour. At last, through perseverance, their conditions improved, and in the 1850s they made a move to the newly opened Wairarapa.

The effort of moving the Jones family over the Rimutakas began on 1 January 1856. A horse took their baggage in the early stages of the trip and by the end of the first

Karori, Wellington, *circa* 1846, where Thomas and Susannah Chamberlain lived for three or four years. At that time "it was all in dense bush".

Susannah Catherine Chamberlain, *née* Bull, 1809–1891. "Her health drinks such as senna tea were kept in little teapots which stood in a row on the mantelpiece."

The Oaks cottage, Masterton, built by Susannah Chamberlain's sons in 1855. It stood for some 115 years and was demolished *circa* 1970.

day they had reached the accommodation house at Mangaroa. The next day they crossed the Pakuratahi River and made their way to the summit, their belongings now packed on bullocks. The two young daughters were placed in packing cases balanced on either side of one quiet animal which made its way steadily along the precipitously rising track. The cases on the other bullock contained pots, kettles and a box of glass for the windows. On going down the hill one of the bullocks kicked over the traces, began backing, slipped off the track and rolled over and over until stopped by a log. Strangely, nothing was broken but the harness.

On the Wairarapa side of the range the family made for Burlings accommodation house, now the site of Featherston, where the meals were rough and ready. The next day they set out for Greytown where they stayed the night at the home of Mr and Mrs Kempton, and it was there that little Edward Jones made his first attempt at walking.

In those days the tracks lay to the east of where Greytown now stands and passed through the Maori settlement of Papawai. The Waiohine River, swift and treacherous at times, had to be crossed, and on the opposite bank they were met by their friend Charles Dixon, an early Wairarapa settler, with a horse and dray. The route then lay across swamps and the Taratahi Plain with its many boulders and morasses, until at last another mountain torrent, the Waingawa, was reached and had to be crossed. Another two and a half miles brought them to Masterton and homemaking in the Wairarapa began at last, but it was eight years before they could afford one dozen American chairs, for which they paid £4.

The first Sunday school in Masterton was held in the home of Henry and Mary Jones and Henry was its first teacher. Their work for the Methodist Church continued for some years and was carried on by their descendants.

Susannah Chamberlain took a great interest in those early Methodist Church beginnings and seldom missed a meeting. Another of her interests was the making of health drinks, such as senna tea and other herbal beverages, and these guaranteed cures for all aches and pains were kept in little teapots which stood in a row on the mantelpiece. Visiting grandchildren soon learned to keep very silent about their ailments when visiting Susannah, because they knew that a dose would follow immediately.

She died in 1891, but The Oaks cottage in Edith Street on the Upper Plain stood for 115 years. It eventually passed from family ownership and was allowed to become a dilapidated wreck, eventually used as a haybarn, and demolished about 1970.

CHAPTER 9

Elizabeth Colenso

Elizabeth Fairburn, born at Kerikeri in 1821, was the eldest daughter of William T. Fairburn, a carpenter and lay catechist of the Church Missionary Society. Her childhood was spent among the northern mission stations and she was educated at Mrs Henry Williams's boarding school for the daughters of missionaries.

In the isolated seclusion of the mission stations where she grew up, the chances of finding a husband of her own choice seemed quite hopeless, and as the years passed she became a capable Maori-school teacher. Some said she was austere by nature, but if this was so it was probably due to the severity of her young life.

By 1842 she was living at Otahuhu, where her father had charge of the mission station and where she taught the children at the school. She was then twenty-one and that year she received a proposal of marriage from William Colenso

Colenso, born in 1811, was the eldest child of Samuel May Colenso, a saddler and town councillor of Penzance, Cornwall. He was educated privately and at the age of fifteen became apprenticed to a local printer. By this time he had developed into a somewhat striking, sturdily built youth with handsome features and thick wavy black hair, and was taking much interest in all matters pertaining to religion.

After serving his time he went to London where he worked with Richard Watts & Son, printers to the Church Missionary Society, and as a printer and press were required for the Society's mission station at Paihia in New Zealand Colenso was engaged as a missionary printer. In 1834 he arrived at Bay of Islands where he immediately set up his press, becoming dedicated to a great output of work which became his first and only love. Nevertheless, by 1842 he had decided to take a wife.

He therefore applied for sabbatical leave for the purpose of visiting his parents in England and finding a wife among his own Cornish people, but this was refused and he was told to seek a wife among the daughters of the missionaries. It was then suggested that he should write to William Fairburn at Otahuhu, asking for the hand of his daughter Elizabeth.

Despite the fact that Colenso was a stranger to Elizabeth her father decided that she should accept this proposal of marriage. It was a year before Colenso went to Otahuhu to meet his future wife, who discovered him to be an outspoken man who made little or no effort to endear himself to people. From the outset it seemed obvious that any affection between them was unlikely to blossom, particularly as he had previously informed her in a letter that all he wanted was a suitable partner in his mission work.

The wedding was then postponed for a year, but these arrangements did not suit Bishop G. A. Selwyn who had plans for Colenso, as a married man with a wife who

In this building at Paihia William Colenso set up his printing press, 1834. Its "great output of work became his first and only love."

was a competent Maori scholar, to take over the Waimate mission in the north. Plans were then hastily made for the wedding to take place on 27 April 1843 and the ceremony was conducted by the Rev. J. F. Churton, the first Church of England minister at Auckland.

On arrival at Waimate Elizabeth found that her new home was to be a small house of two rooms previously occupied by the Rev. C. Preece. She soon settled into it and began the task of taking the sole charge of the boarding school for Maori girls which had been set up by Bishop Selwyn. He had previously seen her conducting a school for Maori girls at her father's mission station and had been much impressed by her intelligence.

But for Elizabeth it was a time of frustration. The long hours of endless and exacting work were made even more difficult by the constant interference of the Bishop and his wife. In the meantime William's work took him about the country and he was away on one of his journeys when Elizabeth gave birth on 1 February 1844, to her first child, Frances Mary. William arrived home a fortnight later to find her far from well after a difficult confinement. Despite the fact that both Elizabeth and William were devoted to little Fanny the baby's arrival drew them no closer together, but nevertheless he was concerned by her constant work with so much interference.

At the end of that year the Colensos sailed in the *Nimrod* for Ahuriri, where William, now admitted to deacon's orders, was to open the Waitangi mission station, and where Elizabeth would become the first white women to live in Hawke's Bay.

Others on board the *Nimrod* included James and Elizabeth (17) Hamlin, who were to establish the Wairoa mission, and Adam Keir who accompanied the Colensos as carpenter and general assistant. There were also Hamuera te Nehu, a young Maori who was William's personal servant, and Meretene Ripeka, (36) daughter of an East Coast man who had been exiled from his people. There were also five head of dairy livestock, being the limit allowed by the CMS to Colenso, and everything else necessary for the setting up of a mission station.

The ten acres granted by the Maoris for the mission lay somewhere near the Waitangi bridge at Clive. It was a swampy patch of toetoe, rush and flax, and very prone to flooding. Elizabeth's home in this waterlogged area consisted of a native-built whare without floor, door or windows, and with a square hole cut in the roof to serve as a chimney. Under these primitive conditions, at the age of twenty-three and with a young baby, she began the exacting dual routine of housekeeping and running a mission school. Her nearest white neighbour was Elizabeth Hamlin, eighty miles away at Wairoa who faced the same problems.

Elizabeth's second baby became due in the winter of 1845, and because she had suffered so much during Fanny's birth she longed to be near the capable assistance of her own white people. Therefore, at the end of July when seven months pregnant, she decided to make the long and hazardous trip of 130 miles to Mrs William Williams (51) at Turanganui (Gisborne). And as there was no chance of getting there by ship she had to walk.

This winter journey took them over rugged hilly country past Tangoio, Moeangiangi, Waikari and Mohaka to Wairoa. Fanny was carried by Maori bearers, and when the track made it possible for them to use a form of primitive open litter, Elizabeth was also carried, but for most of the journey she had to struggle along the tracks, clamber over bluffs and slither down slippery gullies to cross flooded rivers. The cold midwinter nights were spent under what shelter they could find. At Wairoa they had a day's rest with the Hamlins, and on 6 August they reached the mission at Turanganui. Unhampered, it took Colenso eight days to return to Waitangi.

On 23 September Elizabeth's baby was born, a son whom she called Ridley Latimer. Within a short time she returned to Waitangi to resume her duties and run the mission while Colenso went off on his everlasting journeys. Her loneliness was now accentuated by memories of the pleasant company at Turanganui, which was a much more populous centre than their own marshy flats.

In 1846 a more pretentious home had replaced their first primitive whare as by this time Colenso had realised the necessity of having the whole place raised up on piles because of the flooding. The floor was therefore lifted several feet above the ground by foundations consisting of entire tree trunks of kahikatea felled from Big Bush at

Elizabeth Colenso, *née* Fairburn, 1821–1904. A loveless marriage broke up in scandal, but she lived on to give fifty years of work devoted to social welfare.

Mangateretere and floated down the Ngaruroro River. The house, thirty feet by fifty feet with a verandah across the front, was still roofed by raupo and had a semi-detached kitchen at the back.

For the next five years Elizabeth coped with the ups and downs of the Waitangi mission until in 1851 an avalanche of scandal caused its doors to close. This exploded when the Maori girl, Ripeka, married in the latter part of 1850 to Hamuera, gave birth in May to a halfcaste son. Then, to Elizabeth's questions, she admitted quite frankly that Colenso was the father.

No doubt this came as a tremendous shock to Elizabeth but as there had never been any real love between the Colensos the admission did not come as a complete outrage to kill off her affection. For Elizabeth to leave the station was exceedingly difficult so, with studied forbearance, she continued to work in the school and managed the mission in the continued absences of Colenso.

Ripeka's son was called Wiremu, which is Maori for William. Colenso loved the little boy and Elizabeth found herself spending a great deal of the time in looking after the child.

In September 1852 Elizabeth's brother John Fairburn arrived to take her two children, Fanny and Latimer, back with him to Auckland where they could attend school and learn to speak their own language. Elizabeth could have accompanied him but decided instead to remain until the Bishop had made his decision concerning her husband's lapse from morality.

It had, of course, been necessary for Colenso to confess to higher authority that Ripeka's baby was his son, and at last news came in November when James Hamlin of

Wairoa brought a letter from the Bishop stating that Colenso had been suspended from his holy orders as a deacon. The Bishop also stated that Elizabeth was to return to her family and take with her the little boy, Wiremu, over whom there was much argument between Ripeka and Colenso.

She left for Auckland on 30 August, the first stage being overland to Wairoa as there was still little shipping from Ahuriri and vessels left more frequently from Wairoa. On her arrival at Otahuhu Wiremu was refused admittance to the Fairburn home and was eventually boarded out at £12 per year, first in a European home and then through Maoris to the Bay of Islands.

From 1854 to 1860 Elizabeth taught the pupils of the Maori boardingschool attached to the Taupiri mission station in the Waikato, and then in 1860, she went to England with the children.

During the period in England from the early 1860s she lived on the outskirts of London, spending much time translating tracts into Maori and proofreading the sheets before their final printing. Her 1862 diary shows that she became busily occupied with church affairs and through the Church Missionary Society she came in contact with many Maoris who had travelled to England.

She spent much time assisting these people, helping them to obtain suitable clothes for the English climate and showing them the sights. Many of them were entertained by Royalty, as one diary note indicates:

. . . the New Zealand party with whom I went on Wednesday last to Plymouth by command of Her Majesty the Queen, whence Her Majesty's yacht awaited them and took them over to the Isle of Wight where the Royal carriages were in waiting and conveyed the party to the Palace at Osborne where a most gracious and condescending reception was granted them by the Queen who permitted them to address her while Mr Jenkins interpreted, They were highly delighted. The Queen and Princesses gave them their portraits. They had lunch in the Palace and afterwards were taken back in the Queen's yacht to Portsmouth and then were taken to visit the large ships of war and the fortifications etc. We got home from seeing them by the last train at 12 midnight.

Some of the Maoris to whom she showed places of interest and took on the underground railway in 1863 were Wharepapa, Horomona, Hirini and Rukana. She also came in contact with the artist, Mr Strutt, who painted several of her Maori friends. Also in 1863 she presented the chief Pomare and his wife and child, (10) to Queen Victoria.

Elizabeth returned to New Zealand in 1866 and lived in Paihia, where she taught Maori children as well as some of the missionaries' children. In 1870 her daughter Fanny was married at Paihia to William Henry Simcox. The young couple left at once for England where they remained until 1874 when they returned to Paihia with three children.

In 1875 Elizabeth was asked by Bishop John Selwyn (the son of Bishop G. A. Selwyn) to go to Norfolk Island, the headquarters of the Melanesian Mission, to help the girls who were at school there. By 1876 she was deeply involved in this mission-school work, the daily routine consisting of chapel, school, sewing classes and the cutting out of materials, cooking, and then more school and more chapel. She spent twenty-two years at Norfolk Island, at times returning to New Zealand for holidays.

In 1880 she was again in Hawke's Bay which was by then a very different district from the one she had known nearly thirty years earlier. On 5 January she was in Napier visiting the Williams family, the Rev. Samuel Williams (53) of Te Aute being there also. On that day she wrote:

A lovely day. Settled to go with Mr Samuel Williams to Te Aute today and from thence to Otaki. Mr S. W. told me my box was too high to go by coach so Mrs Williams (51) and Emma W. drove me in their carriage to town and I bought a portmanteau for 50/– and a tin bonnet box for 9/– which we took back with us and drove round a different road home and I packed my things.

We went before dinner to see the school buildings close by. After 4 pm Mrs Williams and one of her daughters most kindly drove me to the station and saw me off. Mrs Bourke was also going to Mrs S. Williams's – – – her little boy had gone to the wrong station and was left behind. We got to Pakipaki station and found Mr W's buggy waiting for us. We stopped at a native village on the way for Mr W. to see a sick man and I renewed acquaintance with some old Maori friends here and got to Te Aute rather late. It was very cold. Mrs S. W. (54) received us most kindly.

Tues. 6 Jan. 1880. Very fine. We went to see the school buildings and to call on Mrs Thornton the wife of the schoolmaster. Late in the afternoon Desmond Bourke turned up to Mrs B's great relief as she was getting quite anxious about him. Mrs Allan Williams and Mr and Mrs Thornton and one or two other young people called during the evening.

Wed. 7 Jan. 1880. A fine day. Mr W. kindly drove me to the point where the train stops at a given signal to pick up Te Aute passengers and I went by train to Kopua, and coach to Woodville where at 3 pm we got a good hot dinner and coach and horses were changed as we were soon to enter the Manawatu Gorge. A fearful looking road was cut out along the face of the cliff and only just wide enough to admit the coach, the outer wheel often appearing to be only a few inches from the edge of a sheer precipice down into the Manawatu River.

I should have said that at Waipukurau station a party of play actors (some juveniles) entered the train and went by coach. We were glad enough to get off that fearful looking road. We reached Palmerston North by 7 pm, had some tea at the hotel and at 8 o'clock went to await the train to Foxton (due at 8.30) at the station, but after an hour's delay they telegraphed and found that the train had gone off the line somewhere so we had to lie down on the seats in the waiting-room and defend ourselves as best we could against the voracious mosquitoes. At 11 pm the train at last appeared and we went on, arriving at Foxton at 1 am and went to bed at White's Hotel. A Mr London from Wellington and a widow lady were fellow passengers from P.N. to Foxton and were put into one bedroom.

Breakfast at 5.30 am and at 6 the coach started along the sandhills to the beach for Otaki, the tide low and the beach hard. We changed horses half way and reached Otaki at 9.30 am. I stole a march on them as they did not expect me till tomorrow. Found all well and the children much grown but Fanny looks thin having been much tired out for want of servants.

Elizabeth remained at Norfolk Island for more than twenty years, the long period being broken by several trips to New Zealand when she stayed with her daughter and friends. She left Norfolk Island finally in 1898 and lived with the Simcox family at Forest Lakes, Otaki, until her death in 1904.

During the years from 1898 to 1904 Elizabeth translated the *Book of Common Prayer* into Mola, the common language used by the Melanesian Mission at Norfolk Island and by the missionaries in the islands. By that time she was much crippled by arthritis.

At the age of eight-three Elizabeth died and was buried in the Simcox plot in the churchyard of historic Rangiatea at Otaki.

In Hawke's Bay near the Waitangi bridge at Clive a small stone monument commemorates the fact that William Colenso's mission station was situated somewhere within the vicinity. It is quite inconspicuous and few of the people passing realise it is there; it does nothing to indicate the hard, demanding life lived there by Elizabeth Colenso, Hawke's Bay's first white woman.

CHAPTER 10

Elizabeth Colenso and Hariata Pomare

In the last chapter it was stated that Elizabeth Colenso (9) assisted many Maoris when they visited England and it is through her diary that we learn of the presentation of the Pomares to Queen Victoria.

In 1863 Elizabeth writes that she was visited by Hare and Hariata Pomare; she had known Hare's father in New Zealand thirty-two years earlier. The young Ngapuhi chief and his pregnant wife were staying at the Asian Hotel, where it was impossible for Hariata to have her baby.

As the time for the birth drew nearer officials at the Colonial Office sought Elizabeth's assistance in making arrangements for Hariata's confinement. Elizabeth, who had done so much for so many Maori visitors to London, at once set about the task of finding a room in which the Pomares could stay and in which Hariata could have her baby.

After much trouble she found a place and soon had the Maori couple settled in it. Their board was paid through the Colonial Office, the account being 6 gns for two weeks. The exact date of the baby's birth is obscure because Elizabeth herself was ill at this period, but it appears to have taken place somewhere between the middle of October and the beginning of November.

The baby boy's arrival was reported to the Queen and evidently caught her interest. Elizabeth then received a visit from Mr Dealtry of the Colonial Office, who said that the Queen had stated she would be the child's godmother and wished that he be christened Albert Victor.

The present sent by Her Majesty was a handsome green morocco case containing a beautiful gold cup bearing the inscription *Albert Victor Pomare from his Godmother, Queen Victoria, November 1863.* There was also a gold knife, spoon and fork with the same inscription on the knife, and a present of £25 for Hariata.

Mr Dealtry went on to say that the baby was to be baptised on Thursday 3 December at St Paul's Cathedral, at 1 pm. There were also letters from the Duke of Newcastle's secretary which said that the Queen wished to see her godson at Windsor on Friday, and that if Elizabeth were willing it would be as well for her to go along also as an interpreter. Then, on 2 December, a letter came from the Duke's secretary confirming Mr Dealtry's arrangements.

Elizabeth bought herself a new pair of boots and a hood and cloak for the baby. She ordered a fly (one-horse cab) to be at the door at 8.30 on Friday morning to take them to Paddington station, and she informed Mr Dealtry of the day the baby would be baptised. Her friend Mrs Johnston, who lived nearby, kindly suggested that

46

the christening breakfast should be at their home, and it was arranged that all should go there after the ceremony was over.

On Thursday 3 December 1863 Elizabeth wrote:

Sunny but blowing tremendously. Mr Dealtry, Mrs Dealtry and Mr Birch came in a fly about 12.30. Mrs D. and Mrs Kerry (the nurse) with baby went to the church in the fly and we, Mr Dealtry, Mr Birch, Hariata and I followed on foot. The church was half full of people. Hariata was churched before the christening, the Rev. Mr McSorley asked me to kneel with her and translate the service – – – which I did – – – after which the child was baptised Albert Victor according to the Queen's command.

Here Elizabeth is referring to the thanksgiving service of women after childbirth commonly called the Churching of Women! According to the old (1662) Church of England Prayer Book the woman, at the usual time after her delivery, shall come into the church decently apparelled and there shall kneel down in some convenient place as hath been accustomed or as the Ordinary shall direct, and then the Priest shall say unto her etc. etc. She continued:

We then repaired to Mr Johnston's where there was a splendid cold collation laid out at which were Mr and Mrs Johnston, Mr Dealtry, Mr Birch, the last two were Godfathers to the baby, and Mrs Dealtry who stood proxy for the Queen. Rev. H. McSorley, Mr and Mrs May, Pomare and wife, Mrs Hall, Mrs Howell and myself. Wines, champagne etc in plenty and cake etc. etc. I had some fun pulling the crackers and reading the mottos inside. After the first lot had dined the table was filled again by the Misses Johnstons for some young friends, Mr Johnston and Mr Howell, who were too late for the first. The London folk returned home after dinner but we all stayed for the evening party. At this there was dancing and other young people present with the baby in great request among the ladies.

Fri. 4 December. 1863. A most lovely day. Hare Pomare, Hariata and child and I started at 8.30 this morning in a fly for Paddington station. Took train and, changing at Slough, reached Windsor about 11 am. Took a cab to the castle where we were ushered into a warm cosy sitting-room where refreshments were brought us, tea, coffee, bread and butter, cakes and wine. Sir Thomas came in to see the baby, and many ladies. After a time the Queen sent the Honourable Mrs Bruce to say she wished to see the baby but first inquired what time we had arranged to go back. I told her Mr Dealtry had named 4.30 pm.

Mrs. B. went back to Her Majesty and then came and said that the Duke of Newcastle had requested that they might not be detained late for fear of cold etc. I said they were often out at parties in the evening and as we had a fly I did not think they could hurt but that of course we would do whatever Her Majesty wished. Mrs Bruce went and returned, saying that the Queen did not wish on any account to alter the arrangements which had been made etc. So we stayed till 4.30pm. Soon after this [conversation] Mrs Bruce came and took us to see the Queen.

We went along a magnificently ornamented winding corridor, full of paintings and statues etc. with soft seats at intervals and splendid carpet. We waited some minutes in the corridor as the Queen was not quite ready. The housekeeper then proposed taking us to see the drawing-rooms and dining-rooms full of rich and beautiful and costly furniture. In the second drawing-room was the table where Her Majesty takes her coffee and the etiquette is for the gentlemen to stand and on going into the second drawing-room they may sit down.

We walked all round the Royal family's dining-table which was laid for dinner and was resplendent with gold and silver plate. The Queen's seat was pointed out to us in the middle of one side opposite a magnificent gold (or gilt?) flower vase filled with flowers. We admired the view from the windows and now we were hastily recalled as Her Majesty was ready to see us. We were led into an audience chamber adjoining the drawing-room and stood waiting our Monarch's approach.

She came preceded by attendants opening the doors and was followed by four of her daughters, the Princesses and the interesting little Princess Beatrice about five or six years old. The Queen came forward with a sweetly! sweetly! smiling face bowing to each of us in turn. We bent the knee and bowed to our gracious Sovereign.

The Queen came and kissed the baby and admired his healthy fine appearance and said how pleased she was to see him. She spoke of the war in New Zealand and said how much it troubled her and she earnestly hoped it would soon be over. She said she should always feel a great interest in the child and hoped he would be a good man etc. etc.

I interpreted to Hare Pomare and he made a suitable reply and then returned grateful thanks to the Queen for all her great kindness to them and also for the splendid present to the baby and £25 to Hariata.

Her Majesty smiled most graciously. Baby then began crying lustily and the Queen and Princesses retired. They turned around two or three times and smiled and bowed goodbye till out of sight.

We were then shown by the housekeeper all through the state appartments. Arrived at the banqueting hall an attendant came up with Prince Leopold, an interesting and pleasing looking boy, but who seemed rather bashful. He wished to see Baby who was shown to him and kissed by him. We then proceeded on our tour of inspection through the rooms which were most magnificent.

We saw Mr Frith painting the picture of the Prince of Wales and the Princess Alexandra's wedding, also the room the Princess occupied before her wedding, the Waterloo room, the rooms containing the celebrated Bayeux [sic] Tapestry – – most beautiful– – the whole history of Queen Esther in the Bible portrayed in beautiful needlework. We saw a splendid doll's house which had been presented to the Princess Royal when a child by her nurse– – – cost about £400.

At length we got back to the large banqueting hall where Prince Leopold saw the baby. I forgot to say we saw the hall where Her Majesty bestows the Order of the Garter in which hangs a full length picture of the Queen in the dress worn by Her Majesty on such occasions. At one end of the room is the throne– – – a raised armchair, ascending by steps, made of most beautifully and elaborately carved ivory which came out of the exhibition of 1851. We each sat for a minute or so in it and Hare laid the baby in it.

As soon as we had returned to the corridor from whence we had set out an intimation came from the Queen that she wished to see the baby again. We waited till the Hon. Mrs Bruce came, who said we were to wait a little as Her Majesty was not quite ready. In the meantime, while crowds of Her Majesty's female attendants came to see and nurse the baby the attendants and children of the Crown Princess of Russia (Princess Royal) and the Princess Beatrice with her brother, Prince Leopold, holding the hand of his little nephew, Prince William, were all there. The four children came round the baby, the Princess Charlotte, a pretty little thing in white, took hold of his hand and said, "What a pretty little hand he has– – – what pretty fingers."

I ventured to ask if I might kiss the little one year old Prince's hand (Henry) and was permitted to do so.

Mr Bambridge, formerly of Waimate, Bay of Islands, now appeared, having received the Queen's command to take Hare Pomare's likeness, which he did, taking him away with him for the purpose.

The Queen now sent for me with the baby to her private audience room and received me most graciously so that I felt at ease immediately. Her Majesty made many inquiries as to Hariata's health, both before and since her confinement. She then inquired how long I had been in New Zealand. I told her I was born there and well remembered the times of cannibalism. The Queen lifted her hands saying, "Good gracious!" and looked at Mrs Bruce. She then asked how long I had been in England and when would I return. I answered nearly three years and I thought of going back in October next. She then said she supposed I could speak the New Zealand language well. I said yes– – – better than English.

The Queen smiled very sweetly and said she should always feel a great interest in the child and that I must write from time to time to let her know how it got on. Mrs Bruce asked the Queen to take it in her arms and try its weight which she did and said it was the finest child of his age, six weeks, she had ever seen. She gave me back the child and smiled most sweetly, wished me goodbye and retired. I returned to the room where Hariata was and Mrs Bruce appeared and conducted us back to the room we were first received in.

The housekeeper then came and refreshments were ordered for us. A messenger then came to ask if two ladies and my lady Canning could see the baby. They came and pronounced the universal opinion, "the finest child of his age they had seen".

Hare returned and a cab being ordered the housekeeper saw us safely into it, giving me the address and name, she having promised to show Fanny and Latimer and myself the private rooms in the spring or summer if I write and let her know a day or two beforehand.

On 6 December further messages came via Mr Dealtry from the Queen. The Pomares were to be taken to London to be photographed by Mayall, 224 Regent Street. Further, they were to be outfitted with necessary clothing.

So, at Mayall's on 10 December, by command of the Queen, Hare, Hariata and young Albert Victor had their likenesses taken in various positions, in groups and separately. Elizabeth's photo was also taken gratuitously by Mr Mayall. Then, after consultation at the Colonial Office, a list of suitable clothing was made. Hare was taken to the tailor while a cloak, dress and shoes were purchased from various shops for Hariata.

Other presentations consisted of scarlet woollen leggings and jacket for the baby, a necktie for Hariata and a handsome silver hunting watch and chain for Hare, a gift that quite overwhelmed him.

Hare and Hariata Pomare with their son, christened Albert Victor at the request of his godmother, Queen Victoria. "The Queen took the baby in her arms to try its weight, and she said it was the finest child of his age, six weeks, that she had ever seen."

Through the kindness of Elizabeth's friends the Pomares were well entertained in England, being taken to the cattle show at Agricultural Hall at Islington and to other places likely to interest them, and one acquaintance, Mr Moon, provided Hare with a horse to ride. But at last their visit came to an end and right up to the last Elizabeth saw to their welfare, attending to their packing and carefully folding the extra gifts that kept arriving for the baby.

On 22 December she was engaged all the morning with Hare, supervising the writing of his letter to the Queen.

On 24 December she wrote:

Cloudy but mild. Baby and I in fly with luggage. Off by 8.30 am. Called at Mrs Johnston's to say goodbye, also at the Miss Taylors' who gave Hariata a bag of fruit and nuts. Called on various other friends to say Goodbye and took train to Gravesend at 10.40. Reached Tilbury Street at 12 and crossing in railway steamer to other side took boat and went on board the Statesman *where Hare was glad to see us. Unpacked and repacked into a large box fixed in the cabin the things brought with us, separating and marking each package and with the help of Mr Cooper (from Emigration Board) put all to rights for them.*

Dined on board. The captain (Marshall) seemed a very nice man. At 5 pm I bid them a last farewell and went on shore, crossed to Tilbury, got to French Street, took a bus to Shoreditch station, train to Park and got home after 8 pm quite tired out.

And so the Pomares sailed home to New Zealand with Queen Victoria's godson, Albert Victor, and within a short time Elizabeth Colenso had taken other Maoris under her protective wing, guiding their steps round the bewildering city and being their friend in a strange land.

And what happened to little Albert Victor? He grew up and years later it was rumoured that he had been lost at sea.

CHAPTER 11

Sarah Ann Cripps

Sarah Ann Rigelsford, born in London in 1822, was an educated girl of good family. Blue-eyed and of medium colouring, her figure was inclined to be short and plump. She trained as a dressmaker and soon acquired her own business with her own billheads. In 1844 she married Isaac Cripps, a large, bearded young police constable who had been born at Sevenoaks in Kent. Their first child, Mary Ann, was born in 1845, their son Isaac in 1846 and their daughter, Emily, in 1848.

By the end of 1849 Isaac had resigned from the London Police Force with a good-conduct discharge. He had signed a contract with Charles Enderby's whaling company, which had plans to form a settlement in the Auckland Islands and to establish a whaling base there.

Sarah was not pleased with these arrangements. She had no wish to leave England but had to pack their worldly possessions and to sail with her husband and three young children in the brig *Fancy*. She little knew of the bleakness of their destination.

The Auckland Islands, consisting of a group of one larger and five smaller islands, lie approximately 200 miles SSW of Stewart Island. The climate is cold, wet and windy. Scrub, tussock and sub-antarctic meadowland cover the lower levels and the soil is peaty, waterlogged and sour. For the whole of the long voyage Sarah was so desperately seasick that at one stage she begged the sailors to throw her overboard.

The small band of settlers were not impressed with the Auckland Islands where the wind blew the vegetables out of the ground, but they set about erecting the prefabricated houses provided by the company. Sarah's next child, Harriet Sophia, was born there, at Port Ross, in 1851. She was baptised on 31 March 1852 by G. E. Carwithen, chaplain of HMS *Calliope*, when the ship called at the Auckland Islands. The certificate of baptism was a sheet of ordinary notepaper.

With the scarcity of right whales the new colony was a failure. It lasted only until 1852. Most of the settlers, tired of the cold days, the dark, lowering skies and howling gales sought a warmer climate in Australia, but the Cripps family came to New Zealand.

They sailed for Wellington in the brig *Kitty*, arriving there with £5 in coppers, all that was left from Isaac's salary of £52 per year, from which expenses for food had been deducted. In Wellington they settled in Tinakori Road where, in 1853, their son George was born. Times were hard and Isaac spent the next eighteen months labouring about Wellington for wages of 2s 6d a day. Fears of Maoris caused him to sleep with an axe beside the bed.

In 1854 brighter days came when Isaac was engaged by the Wairarapa runholder, John Valentine Smith, to work on his Mataikona property. Once more Sarah packed their belongings, and again they sailed on the *Kitty*, this time round Cape Palliser and up the east coast of the North Island to Castlepoint. From the ship the land appeared to consist of endless hills and deep gullies.

At Castlepoint they were lowered into boats and rowed inshore to where they could be carried through the surf. John Valentine Smith was there to meet them with a pack bullock to transport their belongings to Mataikona. They camped for the night, then set out next morning on the nine-mile coastal journey.

It was February and the day was hot. Progress was very slow as they trudged along the beach. Sarah and Isaac each carried a child, the youngest of the five now being ten months old and the next a toddler of not quite three years. Hot and weary they arrived at Mataikona pa in the evening. A hangi had just been opened and the white people were immediately offered food. In later years Isaac and Sarah were often heard to declare that they had never tasted potatoes like the ones that came out of that Maori oven. Nor did they ever forget the Maori hospitality they received on that February evening.

John Valentine Smith's Mataikona block consisted of 17,000 acres which were defined as rugged fern hills with little grass, grazing 1,000 ewes. Sarah and Isaac remained with Smith for two years, during which time their daughter Caroline was born, in 1855. Their next move, in 1856, was to Henry Buxton's Whareama station where Isaac was to work as a shepherd, and this time the move was made in the relative comfort of a bullock dray.

At that time Whareama, now known as Langdale, consisted of 16,729 acres, carrying a mere 2,700 sheep. Sarah and Isaac lived in a slab-and-thatch shanty on the banks of the Whareama river a little below the Ica ford. Here, in September 1857, while the flooding river was causing concern, the twins Ellen (16) and Sarah were born. Both mother and river had to be watched at the same time.

One night four months later, in January 1858, they awoke to discover the rushing waters of the river up to their door and still rising. It was a matter of getting the little ones out at once. Fortunately there was a deserted Maori whare on a small hill half a mile away, and with the rain beating about them they set off through the darkness to reach it. In some of the hollows the water was waist deep and the children had to be carried through it. They reached the whare safely and spent a wet and miserable night in it, but next day the flood waters had receded sufficiently for them to return home.

Those were the days of early settlement in Hawke's Bay. People made their way there by following the coast from Wellington, or by crossing the Rimutakas to the new settlement of Masterton and then making their way to Castlepoint. The way was arduous and long, the accommodation houses few, and the travellers became so numerous that they were a burden on the young wives of settlers. Blairlogie station was on the main route, and it is said that it was Thomas Telford of Blairlogie who first suggested to Sarah and Isaac that an accommodation house near there was badly needed.

It was also said that in 1857 Telford assisted Isaac to acquire 40 acres near the main route, not far from Blairlogie. The land cost £20. A wattle-and-daub house was built in Isaac's spare time. The walls were a foot thick, the roof thatched with toetoe or raupo, the chimneys were of stone blocks set in clay. Divisions between the rooms were of sacking and the floor was of hard trampled clay; the large fireplace held a backlog to last a week. They moved in on Good Friday, 1858, and called the place Sevenoaks.

It was not long before the accommodation house was in full swing, nor was it long before Sarah had earned the reputation of being an excellent cook and a superb hostess. Her delight in caring for people and making them happy and comfortable acted as a magnet, bringing travellers hastening across the hills and rivers to Sevenoaks. To the joy of the settlers she also opened a shop and a post office. Mail and stores came up the coast.

Isaac found it necessary to devote half of February and all of March to getting in sufficient stores to last the winter. From his homestead to Castlepoint was a distance of fifteen miles and involved fording the Whareama at Hikurangi, and crossing the Trooper to the coast. Isaac would start in the early morning driving a sledge drawn by two bullocks, and return the next day with his load. While he worked the small farm Sarah toiled hard to run the shop, feed the guests at the accommodation house, clothe and care for the children. Education for the latter was also a problem which she attended to herself until several of the settlers arranged to procure a tutor who stayed for a week with each family in turn and left sufficient lessons to keep the children occupied until his next visit.

Their son Thomas was born at Sevenoaks in 1860, and in 1863 their daughter Margaret arrived. It was a sad blow when Margaret died of appendicitis at the age of fourteen.

As the years passed and Sarah's figure became more rotund she bore a strong resemblance to Queen Victoria. Her hospitality and kindness became legendary and when help was necessary—from Kahumingi Station to Castlepoint—the cry was for Granny Cripps.

Perhaps it was her skill as a midwife which brought Sarah her greatest fame. When babies were arriving—the nearest doctor was at Masterton, twenty miles away beyond the hills and unbridged rivers—the plea for Granny Cripps was really urgent. Nor did she ever refuse a call: the moment word came, off she would go, hail or shine and whatever the hour. But one stipulation she made—whoever came for her had to lead her horse while she sat on the side-saddle gripping her bag, because Granny Cripps hated riding. In September 1880 she was a passenger in the train that was blown from the Rimutaka hill line at a point known as Siberia. Three adults were injured and three children killed, but Sarah's own time had not yet come. It was twelve years later in 1892 before her life of unselfish pioneering service ended. It is not surprising that she was known as "the best loved woman from Wellington to Ahuriri".

Sarah Ann Cripps, *née* Rigelsford, 1822–92. At her accommodation house near Blairlogie she " . . . delighted in caring for people and making them happy and comfortable, earning the reputation of being an excellent cook and a superb hostess."

Sevenoaks accommodation house, built by Isaac Cripps in 1858. Here, "to the joy of the settlers", his wife "also opened a shop and post office."

CHAPTER 12

Elizabeth Crosse

Elizabeth Thorby was born in 1829 on the Essex side of the Thames, England. In 1840 she sailed with her parents in the *Lady Nugent*, arriving in New Zealand in March 1841. They first set foot ashore in Wellington at the spot which later became the lower end of Tinakori Road, but which was then a very fine beach. They found the place populated by only about 700 white people as many of the colonists who had come out under the New Zealand Land Company Scheme had already ventured on towards the Hutt Valley.

The family lived for five weeks in the Company's barracks which had been provided to house immigrants, but her father finally built a home on the steep slopes of Bolton Street at the back of the Sydney Street Cemetery. He opened a store at Thorndon, but as soon as a road had been made they moved to Karori, which was then covered in native bush.

Elizabeth was of sturdy build. She had lively blue eyes, a fair complexion and fair to reddish hair. She grew up among Maori children and soon learnt to speak their language fluently. In 1853 she married Charles Grant Crosse.

The name Crosse originates from the days of the Crusaders when ancestors of the family were cross-bearers during the Holy Wars. There has been a Latimer George Crosse in almost every generation.

Charles was born in Essex in 1825. According to family recollections he spent a short period in the Merchant Navy on the England to China run, and was also in the Colonial Service of the Indian Army. In 1853 he decided to settle in New Zealand.

The first eighteen months of their married life were spent at the Hutt and they then decided to go farming in Hawke's Bay. By that time Elizabeth's first baby, a daughter whom she called Elizabeth, had been born. In 1854 they went to Napier by schooner and were delayed there for some time before they were able to lease a property, but eventually Mangamaire, seven miles south of Porangahau, became available. From Napier it lay over 100 miles away by Maori tracks, and to get there was the problem because by that time (1855) Elizabeth was again well advanced in pregnancy.

Maoris were at last engaged to convey them and all their belongings by boat as far as Patangata on the banks of the Tuki Tuki River, but the first stage of the journey involved walking from Napier, ploughing through the heavy shingle along the ridge flanked on one side by the sea and on the other by the lagoon, and then through scrub and swamp to a point near the present Black Bridge at Haumoana. This difficult walk of nine miles took them a whole day, with Elizabeth in her delicate state having to carry baby Elizabeth who, now almost a year old, was no longer a lightweight.

Napier as it was in the 1860s. When Elizabeth and Charles Crosse passed through
in 1854 it was less impressive than this.

The mouth of the Tuki Tuki is at Haumoana, and here they camped on the bank
for the night and next day were taken up the river by flat-bottomed boat. That journey
was something Elizabeth never forgot. She was one of four women in the party,
Mrs Newman of Arlington station being one of the others.

In those days the Tuki Tuki was much narrower and deeper than it has become
during later years and it took the Maoris six days to navigate the heavily laden craft
as far as Patangata. By the time they arrived there they were out of food and very
hungry. At Patangata pa Elizabeth's time came and she gave birth to a son whom they
called Thomas Ezekiel. The other women assisted her during the confinement, and for
most of the people of the pa this was their first sight of a white baby.

When she was fit to travel once more on they went, with the Maoris carrying their
belongings overland to Pourerere on the coast. At one place an old chief offered
Elizabeth 1,000 acres of land for the baby. She asked him what he would do with the
little one, and he replied that it was when they were cutting their teeth that they tasted
the sweetest.

After traversing the many hills and gullies between Patangata and Pourerere they
walked along the beach and met the first white man they had seen since leaving Napier.
This was Sam Onyons, who was looking after sheep for Northwood and Nairn, the
owners of Pourerere station. At last they reached Blackhead and here they were forced
to wait for low tide because at high tide the four or five miles of jagged rocks were
covered to a depth of three feet of water. Walking now became most difficult, especially
carrying a new baby.

After negotiating the rocks they came to the mouth of the Porangahau, where they
were met by a Maori canoe and paddled up to the site of the present Porangahau

township. Here they camped for the night on the river bank, Elizabeth weak and exhausted from her recent confinement, the long trek over the hills and the scrambling over the rocks. Nor had she been asleep long when an unexpected flood arose in the middle of the night and swept most of their belongings away down the river and out to sea. The Maoris did everything they could to assist, giving them hospitality until their own hut could be built on Mangamaire Station. This was constructed from poles cut from the bush, slabs of bark, pressed clay, and toetoe for the roof. Elizabeth then found herself to be the first white woman living in that part of the district.

The block of Maori leasehold they had taken up was approximately 19,500 acres. They had no horses to begin with, and the sheep, when they eventually arrived from Sydney, had to be mustered on foot. By 1860 they had 1,127 Merinos on the property, the wool being taken fourteen miles whence it was shipped from Blackhead.

The next baby to arrive was Catherine, and then came Latimer George, who was followed by Fanny, May, Samuel Grant, Clara and Charles. During confinements she was no doubt assisted by the Maori women who called her Peti (Betty), or by Sarah Lambert (24) who lived near Porangahau, or by Sarah Herbert (19) who lived some miles to the south at Wainui, now Herbertville.

It was ten long years before Elizabeth emerged from Mangamaire and only on rare occasions during that time had she seen another white woman. Her nearest white neighbour was seven miles away, this being Sarah Lambert whose husband was managing Whangaehu station for the St. Hill brothers. Elizabeth was never slow to admit how much she owed to the Maoris for their kindness towards her.

Education for the children was divided between what they could be taught at home and by attending the "settlers' school" opened at Porangahau in 1867 by Mrs Hirtzel where each child paid 6d a week. Emma Hirtzel was the daughter of Sarah Herbert (19) of Wainui. Later the boys went to William Marshall's school at Napier while the girls attended the Ladies' College, the principals of the latter being Mrs and Miss Shepherd.

Elizabeth lost Charles when he was killed in 1871. His horse shied at a pile of telegraph poles stacked on the riverbank near the present Porangahau bridge and bolted under some trees, the lower branches sweeping Charles out of the saddle, causing him to break his back.

Elizabeth was then left to fend for herself and the children. At times she had scares—on one occasion a man calling and demanding food and a bed, threatening her with violence if she refused. She shouted for one of the children to bring her the gun although in fact she did not possess such a thing.

For a while the Mangamaire station was carried on by Elizabeth and her sons, and the 1873 sheep returns place the flock at 3,348 sheep. In 1874, after nineteen years on the station, she took up residence in Napier for the sake of better education for the children and then as the years passed, she moved from place to place. In 1891 she went to Palmerston North, then moved to Wanganui on account of the health of a daughter. After three years in Wanganui she went to Dannevirke, finally returning to spend her remaining years in Palmerston North.

On her 100th birthday she was still brightly alert and could recall the early days in Wellington when she was taken to the first official race meeting on Petone beach, and attended the first church service in Mr Hornbrook's store in Mulgrave Street. She could remember when the hills of Oriental Bay were George Duppa's sheep run, and Te Aro flat and Thorndon were barren wastes dotted with a few flaxbushes.

By that time she had lost the sight of one eye, but except for an occasional backache she was fit and well. She was a very exacting old lady who always wore a lace cap, a cape embroidered with jet beads, while her hands were kept warm in a muff. In her long widowhood she became Grandma to thirty-eight grandchildren, from whom she always expected the best of Victorian behaviour in her presence, though this was often relieved by the humorous twinkle in her eyes.

Her income was never large but she was by nature generous and always had a small gift of some sort to give away. Anything she could spare was given to the Willard Home in Palmerston North. She held her authority to the end of her 101½ years, never giving up the reins. She died in 1931 and was buried in the Palmerston North cemetery.

Elizabeth Crosse, *née* Thorby, 1830–1931. "She was never slow to admit how much she owed to the Maoris for their kindness towards her."

CHAPTER 13

Catherine Buchan Dahm

Catherine Buchan Ramage was born in 1872 at Limavady, County Derry, Ireland. She grew up to become a capable young girl, olive complexioned, with large brown eyes and beautiful black hair. To her family and friends she was known as Cass.

Her father had always been delicate and because of his poor health her parents decided to emigrate to a warmer climate. In 1883 passages for New Zealand were booked on the *Tongariro*, but when the time for departure came Mrs Ramage found it necessary to remain with her own ailing mother. She kept the youngest child with her but insisted that Cass should sail with her father and three brothers.

On the voyage the family became friendly with a Mr and Mrs Jones, the latter being a kindly woman who took a particular interest in Cass. This couple took over a hotel at Tuparoa on the East Coast. Mr Ramage found a home for the family in Auckland and Cass, at the age of eleven, went out to domestic service. Back in Ireland, however, it was not long before the grandmother died and Mrs Ramage then came to New Zealand, but unfortunately she too died a short time after her arrival.

Mrs Jones, who had kept in touch with the family, eventually took Cass to live with her at Tuparoa. It was an isolated place without roads, the only access being by sea, and it was at Tuparoa a few years later that Cass met John Thomas Dahm, a short, thickset man with fair hair and bright blue eyes. She was eighteen when they were married at Waipiro, which had the nearest church, in August 1894.

Tom, as he was known, was born in Otahuhu in 1858. The son of a sea captain who had retired to that place, he had been apprenticed to a saddler but had later taken up road contracting, although his ambition had always been to have a farm of his own.

Access to their cottage at Tuparoa was along the beach at low tide and it was here in 1895 that a Maori woman assisted Cass when Minnie, her first baby, was born. Minnie, as a toddler, had snowy white hair which frightened the Maori children, who had never before seen a white child. At her approach they ran and hid. Cass's next baby, Edward, arrived in 1897 and again a Maori woman walked along the beach to assist the young Pakeha mother.

They were still at Tuparoa when her father died in Auckland and the articles sent to her from the family home came by sea. Tom went along the beach with a sledge to collect them from where they had been landed by ship, but he was caught by the tide on the return journey and everything, even the sledge, was lost in the sea.

Later they moved to the Gisborne area as Tom went wherever there was work, and they were at Waerengaohika when William was born in 1898. They were at Ormond when Corless arrived in 1900, and at Waerengaokuri when John was born in 1901.

60

It was while she was pregant with John that Cass assisted Tom to make a hencoop; as he cut the wire netting a tiny flake flew up into her eye, causing her to lose the sight from it. There was no doctor and she could do little more than keep a dark shade over it to exclude the light.

Frederick was born in 1903 when they were at Te Arai, near Manutuki, and by this time there seemed to be always two babies in the house—the old baby and the new baby—yet despite the growing family Cass and Tom saved hard to buy land.

In 1903 they went to live at Hangaroa, about twenty-three miles south-west of Gisborne. Transport was not easy but Tom harnessed the horse to the sledge upon which Cass packed their food and belongings, the old baby, the new baby and the fowls. The rest of the family walked over the rugged country, little Corless being only three. All went well until the fowls escaped and the cork came out of the yeast bottle, which meant the loss of that most important commodity for making the family's bread.

At Hangaroa the heavy bush came right up to the back of the house and Cass warned the children not to enter it for fear, not only of getting lost, but of wild pigs. Tom's work took him to Papuni where he saw a farm he hoped he might buy, but this was soon sold to a Miss Baker who suffered from a cleft palate and whose only wish was to live in a little hut, isolated and alone in the backblocks.

They had been at Hangaroa for two years when Tom purchased a place in the Ruakituri Valley. The children helped pack their belongings on ten packhorses and they set off on a four-day trek to what would at last be their own farm. There were no roads into the valley and the trip was made along Maori tracks, over bushclad hills, down gullies and across rivers through Papuni. Two cows and their calves formed part of the cavalcade, one being a young bull calf and the other a steer.

The first night saw them camping in the outstation hut of a large property. The second night found them sleeping out on ferns under ponga trees. On the third night they put up a tent, and all the children crawled into one bed. On the fourth night, as it was now raining, they sheltered in the house and sheds of an elderly couple, Mary and Alex Mills, who were living out in the backblocks. Mary Mills was a little grey-haired woman, very neat and tidy as she stood beside her white-bearded husband.

By this time heavy rain up the valley had caused the rivers to flood, making it necessary to wait two or three days for the fords to become passable. At last, tired of waiting for the waters to recede, they made a long detour over hills and through scrub and fern until they came to their own place.

The property, fifteen miles from Te Reinga, consisted of some 1,400 acres of rough outback land which stretched into a long area of rolling hills, few flats and much heavy bush at the back part. It had been purchased from a Mr Worsnop, who had left standing the walls of a small hut from which he had removed the corrugated iron roof. Tent flies were thrown across the walls for protection and they also put up tents. Cooking was done over an open fire, and also in a camp oven, while water was obtained from a nearby well.

They lived in this state until Tom had built a cottage. The trees had to be felled and pitsawn in the bush and the timber was then packed out on horses. Bushmen came later to cut and burn a large block of trees and then grass was sown. Sheep were brought and had to be swum across the river, but as bracken soon sprang up in the new pasture, and there were no fences, the children had to hold the mob together to eat the fern before it grew too large.

One day Tom went to town and bought an unbroken racehorse with the registered name of Glendower. Unfortunately he came to a sad end, being badly injured after falling into the swimming pool in the creek. They called the property Glendower in his memory.

Great expectations were built round the first wool clip. Tom sent the wool to be sold in England, thinking we would get a better price by doing so, but instead of receiving a cheque the envelope contained a bill for the expenses. It was a bitter disappointment.

For years Cass cooked only in camp ovens and sewed for the family on a little hand machine that seldom worked, but at last a new treadle Singer was brought in by packhorse. She attended to the vegetable garden and soon had the cottage surrounded by gay flowers. The nearest neighbour was nine miles away and there were times when Cass was called out at night to assist a new baby into the district. Away she would ride on Parker, a surefooted old horse who seemed to know his way through the bush in the dark. Visitors were rare, the main ones being dark-skinned Assyrian hawkers whose wares and outside news would brighten a dull day.

Education for the children was also a problem as they were many miles from a school. Cass taught them their ABC and how to write from copybooks, and then Tom took over, setting out lessons for the day. Between them they educated the family to the best of their ability until the Waikatea school opened.

Cass Dahm, *née* Ramage, 1872–1963, with her husband and family. "The annual outing was a picnic that usually lasted a couple of days."

Catherine and Thomas Dahm with daughters Corless and Nancy. "The last of her nine children, Nancy, was born in 1916 and for the first time Cass knew the comfort of a nursing home."

Within a few years the district began to open up for closer settlement. Cass and Tom realised that a store and post office would be necessary to serve the new settlers, and they knew, too, that a more central position than their present home was needed. With this project in mind Tom built a six-roomed house with store and post office at what was known as the front end of the farm. He also made the furniture and installed a colonial oven where the old black kettle sang on the hob and pots of soup hung from the hooks above the fire. Washing was now done near the well, where two large tubs sat on a bench while the copper was set in the bank on raised bars. On Saturdays the tubs were taken into the kitchen for baths, hot water being carried from the copper. On Sundays the children were always tidy and neatly dressed.

In 1906 Andrew was born, and in 1908 another son, Joseph, arrived, yet despite the growing family Cass continued to run the store and post office. Her eldest son rode to Te Reinga to collect the mail, and stores came twice a year, hauled across the river in a cage.

The annual outing for the family was the Te Reinga sports meeting. During early years they rode, taking a packhorse laden with a tent and blankets, but later, when the road was put through, they were able to go in a buggy. Tom and Cass sat on a seat in the front while the children filled the back, the bumping eased by cushions. It was a picnic that usually lasted a couple of days.

Cass spent many years in the back country coping with the store and post office, the numerous swaggers of those days and the Maoris. To the latter she was always a good friend, making many articles of clothing for the women and constantly supplying soup to anyone she considered in need of it.

The last of her nine children, Nancy, was born in 1916 in Wairoa and for the first time Cass knew the comfort of a nursing home. Then, as the years passed, she formed the habit of going to Wairoa once a year to buy the necessary bolts of material to make clothes for the family. There would be grey flannel to make petticoats for the girls and warm shirts for the boys, materials for dresses and blouses, towelling and bolts of tough unbleached herringbone sheeting. From the fifty-pound flour bags, of which she used one a week, she made tea-towels, table cloths, pinnies, and lined the boys' pants. Nothing was ever wasted.

When Nancy was due for secondary school Cass took her to live in Wairoa while Tom spent periods between Wairoa and the farm. He died in 1940 at the age of eighty-two.

Cass spent her last years living with Corless in Wairoa. During her long and useful life she had never been in hospital until the night before she died—this was in 1963—and then it was only because the doctor considered it would be better for her. She was then ninety-one.

CHAPTER 14

Emily Gates Eaton

Emily Gates Deadman, the daughter of James Deadman of London, met Edward Farmer Eaton when she was nineteen years of age. Born on 30 June 1828, she had developed into a brown-eyed girl of short, roundly-built figure. She had an affectionate nature and a strong leaning towards religion. She married Edward on 22 December, 1851, and two weeks later they sailed for New Zealand in a chartered vessel, the *Stag*. Also on board were Edward's brother, James Eaton, and his wife Maryann, who was Emily's sister.

Edward was a short, fairhaired man. Born in 1827, he was the son of Daw Eaton of Tovill-Maidstone, Kent, and came from a family whose silver bore its monogram. He was a Latin and Greek scholar, had studied architecture, and could turn his hand to the more practical side of building. Notes in an 1850 diary indicate that he had spent much time at carpentry work.

The *Stag* arrived at Port Cooper, as Lyttelton was then known, on 17 May 1852, and Emily and Edward walked over the steep Bridle Path to the infant Canterbury settlement. After spending four weeks there they left for Wellington on 15 June, arriving there on 17 June, and there they remained until January 1855.

Brief entries in Emily's diary suggest that the time spent in Wellington was not a happy period for her. She was often pregnant and not at all well, suffering continually from bad headaches. She did not care for social life and among the few friends mentioned are Mrs Kinnisborgh and Mrs Iggulden, the latter losing one of her twin babies.

Emily was fortunate in having Maryann living near her although, like most of the other people mentioned, Maryann is "poorly". This, no doubt, was because she was pregnant. Emily was with her when her baby arrived, this, she admits, being her first experience of such an occasion.

She writes that in Wellington in 1852 measles were prevalent among children, causing many to die. The wind blew unceasingly and there were numerous earthquakes (She records these on 7 and 8 April, 29 May and 11 June.) Her first baby, Edward Augustus, whom she called Teddy, arrived on 2 September some three weeks premature, and no doubt Maryann was with her at this time.

Time was then spent sewing, not only for the baby but also for Edward, whose work trousers and waistcoats she made, and who was working for a firm known as Jeffreys. To do her shopping she walked down the Beach, now better known as Lambton Quay.

Her second baby, whom she named Henry James Deadman (Jim) after her father, was born on 10 May 1854, arriving six weeks before he was expected. Maryann nursed her but almost immediately her own children became ill with the measles and Edward was obliged to stay at home. However, four days later Emily was able to struggle downstairs.

The Wellington climate did not suit her and she was told by Dr Monteith that she would never be well while she remained there. She continued to miss her mother and her own family, and she probably suffered from bouts of intense homesickness. She attended chapel regularly, admiring the preaching of Mr Creed and Mr Watkins, but found it almost impossible to get Edward along to chapel. It is this fact, perhaps, which causes the reader of her diary to sense an undercurrent of unhappiness between them, and things certainly come to a head when on 28 May she states: *One of the most miserable days with Edward I ever spent. Never spent one like it with him before. Hope I never spend another like it.*

However, three months later, on 28 August, she writes: *My dear Edward joined me in prayer for the first time. Nothing could have given me more consolation, having felt more happy since Sunday, tho' I feel I am a great sinner and need to be always watching, but I know I cannot without God's assistance which I know if I seek I shall find.* From that time onward she refers to him always as "my dear Edward" and from between the lines one senses an improved atmosphere and the affection she feels for him.

Emily Gates Eaton, *née* Deadman, 1828–1901, with her husband Edward Farmer Eaton. Despite illness and earthquakes, a happy marriage.

By that time Edward had left Jeffreys to work on his own account and was taking an interest in the Wairarapa. Emily's diary note of 10 October 1854 states: "*My dear Edward started for the Wairarapa. Hope the Almighty will preserve him and direct him aright. Oh how I miss him. I long for him to return. The days are like months.*

Teddy then became really upset with teething trouble and the baby too was quite ill. Emily was thankful to see Edward return but on 13 November he started again for the Wairarapa and she found herself in very low spirits during his absence. Again the baby was ill with a great deal of fever and to combat this she put him in tepid baths. At the same time she knew she should be packing their belongings for the move to the Wairarapa.

Edward meanwhile was doing his best to prepare a home in the new settlement that was to become Masterton. According to a letter he wrote years later, he came across Charles Dixon and his son David, then aged about thirteen, who were sawing in the bush near their home. He asked Dixon to sell him timber to build a small house and Dixon said he would supply him only on condition that he built *his* house and this Edward felt compelled to do.

Some of this timber had previously been pitsawn by Henry Jones (8) and his son John, who had had trouble with Maori owners over its payment and, returning to the Hutt, had left it with Dixon to sell.

The Dixons had been living all the winter with their ten children, in a primitive whare composed chiefly of bark and with a slab-and-clay chimney. For himself Edward therefore hastily put up a mere shell of a place measuring ten by twenty feet and divided into two rooms, the floor loosely laid, the walls unlined and the windows of calico. There was no chimney until some time later. Then, after building Dixon's house, he returned for Emily and the two little boys.

On 8 January 1855 Emily wrote:

Monday. Started for the Wairarapa. Firth took us in his cart to Browne's. Expected Burling would have sent their horse and mule to have met us there but they did not. Ed had to fetch them but they could only spare the mule. He returned on Wednesday. Started on Thursday for Hodder's [a hostelry on the route]. *I walked ten miles, the longest distance I ever walked.*

January 12, Friday. Started for Burlings. I had to walk thirteen miles. Poured with rain all the way.

January 13. Started for Masterton which is twenty-six miles. I rode the mule and the children were on the horse (in hampers), a long tedious journey. Did not arrive till after tea at night. We went to Mrs Dixon's. She kindly gave us some tea and a bed.

January 14, Sunday. A beautiful day. My poor baby very poorly.

January 15. Still beautiful weather. Very uncomfortable. Our things have not come. The house is unfinished.

Their goods, which had been sent ahead weeks previously, still sat at the top of the Rimutakas awaiting the pleasure of Mr Burling, who lived on the Featherston side and who was to see to the cartage from that point.

On 30 January Emily recorded: *Just finished supper at about half past nine when we were visited by a fearful shock of earthquakes. Our house seemed to be riding along with the greatest possible fury. I took one child and Edward the other, we going down to*

Dixons' met them with their ten children making for our house. Their chimney had fallen and the house unsafe to remain in. They were all in their night clothes.

The night was very dark and shock followed shock with only brief periods between, while at times the rumbling noise sounded like a gale of wind. They put all the children to bed and some of the adults lay down while others walked about outside. Twenty-two people sheltered that night in the tiny cottage.

Joseph Masters (29) was among those present and at some time during the night he served a tot of brandy to each adult. At that period he was engaged in building a slab house which was later to become Richard Iorns's (30) store.

The earth quivered for many days but at last settled down and Emily began to think she would like the place, which she considered small but pretty. Living conditions in the hut were primitive for a long time, the furniture consisting of a few blocks of matai for seats and a table and bedstead of rough scantling and boards. The house became known as Ivy Cottage.

Wheat, potatoes, and sometimes wild pork were purchased from the Maoris, the wheat being 15s a bushel. Beef was bought from Mr Donald of the Manaia run at 6d a pound, and sheep from Richard Collins of Te Ore Ore at 30s, but before long most of the settlers had sheep and cows of their own. There was a great deal of bartering

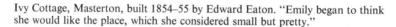

Ivy Cottage, Masterton, built 1854–55 by Edward Eaton. "Emily began to think she would like the place, which she considered small but pretty."

as money was scarce, and Edward gave work to the value of £17 for their first cow. Corn was ground into flour by handmill and with yeast made excellent bread which Emily baked in the camp oven.

In 1848 her father died, presumably in London. In 1857 her mother came to New Zealand, arriving in Wellington and then joining them in Masterton. In July of that year Edward's brother James went to Melbourne, and on 2 August Emily wrote, sadly, that Maryann had sailed with the dear children on the *Marchioness*. Also on 2 August the Rev. Mr Ronaldson christened her new baby, whom they had decided to call Emily. Her health appears to have improved and she had more babies, the next two to arrive being Maryann and William Farmer.

They left the Wairarapa in 1863 when Edward decided to go to Dunedin, mainly on account of the children's education. Auckland at that time was beset by Maori troubles, the wind blew in unceasing gales at Wellington, and as they had disliked Christchurch there was only Dunedin left.

Their next son, Samuel Pearce, was born in Dunedin, but sorrow also awaited them there. Jim and little Emily both died from what was call malignant scarlatina when all six children had scarlet fever at the same time. Later the remaining little ones became ill with diphtheria, which caused the death of little William. The next four children born to Emily and Edward were Alfred Freemantle, Ellen Jane, Percy Seymour, and another baby who died.

Emily's mother, who had gone to the South Island with them, died in 1871, and in 1874 came the sad news of Maryann's death in Melbourne.

Emily and Edward remained in the South Island for the rest of their lives. Despite their former dislike of Christchurch they appear to have returned to that place because Emily died there on 12 December 1901, and Edward too died there on 14 April, 1907.

In the Wairarapa their little home Ivy Cottage, to which a small addition had been made, stood for 107 years before it was partially wrecked and moved to become a wash-house at the rear of another house. It was the first home in Masterton to be built of pitsawn timber.

CHAPTER 15

Harriet Fletcher

Harriet Lomas, born in the February of 1849 at Brinksway, Lancashire, was the eldest child of Joseph and Elizabeth Lomas, a couple who had spent years of their lives working in the cotton mills. In 1856 when Harriet was seven she emigrated with her parents, brothers William and George, and sister, Mercy, to the kinder climate of New Zealand. As they walked towards the Liverpool docks the snow was over the tops of their boots. Joseph Lomas paused to turn and shake his fist at the tall, smoking mill stacks, declaring that he hoped he would never see them again.

They sailed on the *Alma*, a fast clipper which did the voyage in three months. On board they became friendly with James and Sarah Peers and Samuel Fletcher, the latter being the son of Sarah Peers by her first marriage. They disembarked at Wellington and from there Joseph Lomas took his family to settle in the Hutt Valley where he had decided to begin farming. The severe flooding of the Hutt river forced him to abandon this plan and he then went back to Wellington where he found employment as a gardener at Government House, his family living in a cottage at one of the bays.

Harriet grew up in a Wellington that had been disrupted by severe earthquakes. Blue-eyed, with dark brown hair, she developed into a fairly short young woman with a plump figure, and on the day after her seventeenth birthday she married Sam Fletcher. Over her wedding dress she wore a beautiful, large paisley shawl.

Sam, born in 1839 at Clitheroe at the foot of Pendle Hill, Lancashire, was the son of John Fletcher and his wife who had formerly been Sarah Wharmby. His parents owned a small pub known as the Bird In The Hand, the sign indicating, his father used to explain, that in this poaching Lancashire village a bird earned honestly was worth at least a dozen caught illegally in the forest. Yet despite these convictions John Fletcher found it necessary to leave hastily for America when his best friend and brother-in-law, William Wharmby, was wrongfully accused of poaching, and warning came that he also was about to be arrested.

John Fletcher died in America and his widow married James Peers, a man with a hard mouth and bushy side whiskers. Life became a more serious affair for young Sam: hard work was now the order, and gone were the days of wandering over his beloved Pendle Hill. He was seventeen when Peers and his mother decided to emigrate to New Zealand, and until then Sam had been working in the cotton mills.

In Wellington James Peers obtained a position as overseer of the chain gang of prisoners at Mount Cook gaol, the job suiting him admirably. Sam worked for six weeks at roadmaking for 6s a day, then, realising that his mother no longer needed him, he sailed for Hawke's Bay where he learnt to handle sheep and cattle. Seasons were spent shearing and years were spent driving bullock wagons from Napier to Forest Gate, a station lying about eleven miles west of Waipawa and owned at that time by J. Russell Duncan and Colonel Herrick.

There were thirty-six bullocks to be looked after. Three teams of twelve to a wagon would wend their way along the flats of the Tuki Tuki and Waipawa riverbeds, continually crossing and re-crossing. If one wagon became stuck it took the other two teams to haul it out. The trip usually took three weeks and at Forest Gate time was spent splitting totara logs for bridge building, railway sleepers, posts and rails which were loaded on to the wagons and taken back to Napier.

And so for six years Sam toiled with bullock wagons between the totara forests and Napier. He was now a thick-set and well-built young man whose reddish hair and beard glinted in the sun. His hobbies were wrestling and boxing, and none could shift a load with his ease and speed. One day in 1862 while in the Wakarara district the outline of a hill made him stare in near-disbelief; then, with Harriet in mind, he applied for 144 acres of this land which had been newly opened by the Government. The rent was £55 per year, the value was £1 per acre. He bought three cows from Forest Gate and left them on it.

After their wedding Harriet and Sam sailed from Wellington to Napier on the *Lord Ashley*. At Napier their belongings and stores to set up a home were loaded on to one of the wagons and the journey began along the shingle ridge from Napier towards the Tuki Tuki River. After about a week the slowly plodding bullocks turned along the Waipawa, heading towards the ranges as far as what is now the Evertree property which at that time was owned by William Fannin.

The journey from Napier to Evertree took two weeks with the nights spent camping along the riverbanks. In the daytime Harriet, sitting up on the bullock wagon, carried her best bonnet most carefully until they reached the place in the forest where they would live in a slab and totara-bark hut. Using this as a base, Sam worked for other people, at the same time cutting a track through the bush to their own property, and longing to show Harriet what had caught his fancy.

Harriet, in the meantime, spending her days alone in the slab hut tried not to be depressed by the gloom of the forest. One day she was baking bread when several large tattooed Maoris arrived at the door and demanded her newly baked loaves. She threw the bread at them then slammed the door and waited trembling in the darkness for Sam's return. After that she refused to stay alone. Each day she went into the bush with Sam until at last the day came when she stood with him on their own property.

Puzzled, she stared about her, endeavouring to discover why Sam should be so excited about this desolate remote place with its stretches of manuka, its tall dark rimus and totaras. It was all so lonely and wild, and only seven miles away was a pa containing some 300 Maoris. The Ruahines loomed closely and, silhouetted against their blue was a long green hill. Looking at its undulating contours she suddenly understood: it was Pendle Hill! Nor could there be any other name for their property.

That night they slept on bracken strewn under the bullock dray, and the next day Sam felled timber to form the rafters for the roof of a clay hut. He borrowed a barrow to wheel raupo from Holden's Swamp, which was several miles away at Tikokino, while the clay itself was dug near the site of the hut.

The walls, two feet thick and four feet in height, kept it warm and cosy beneath the thatched roof. Harriet knew that much hard work lay ahead of them; trees to be felled and pitsawn, ground had to be dug, wheat to be planted and eventually ground by hand into flour. Everything had to be done to make a home from standing bush with little more than their two hands—and at that stage she could not know she would bear a family of thirteen children.

The first-born was Elizabeth, who arrived in the February of 1867. Harriet returned to her mother for this first confinement, travelling back to Napier along the riverbanks by bullock wagon and then by ship to Wellington. While she was there her mother died in giving birth to another baby, a little girl named Elizabeth Ann, whom they called Annie. When Harriet returned to Pendle Hill she took not only her own baby but her baby sister Annie as well, declaring that if she could look after one baby she could look after two. But Annie was sickly from the beginning and lived for only six months. She was the first to be buried in the private cemetery on Pendle Hill.

After a short time Sam's mother and stepfather, with two sons and a daughter, came to live at Pendle Hill, and the clay hut was extended to form a double unit wherein the families lived one at either end. Granny Peers was therefore in attendance when Eliza Ellen was born in 1868, Joseph in 1870, Sarah in 1871 and Ellen in 1872.

During those early days water was carried from the river and cooking was done in the camp oven or in an outside clay oven in which a fire was built and the bread put in after the hot embers had been raked out. One day, after heavy rain, Granny Peers's oven collapsed when it was full of pastry.

Harriet made their end of the hut very cosy and gay with muslin curtains which had been dyed a rich orange with onion skins. Moleskin for the children's clothes was dyed reddish-brown with rimu bark and all sewing for them was done by hand. Her next baby, Albert, was born in 1875, and then Herbert came in 1876.

By that year enough land had been cleared to carry 195 sheep, and apart from toiling on his own property Sam was still working for other people in the district. To collect their stores he rode twenty miles to Waipawa, first crossing the Waipawa which, in winter, became a raging torrent that scoured holes and was full of rolling boulders. In fact the river was a dangerous hazard and Harriet dreamed wistfully of a bridge.

The private cemetery at Pendle Hill, where Annie Lomas was the first to be buried. A modern photograph.

Her next babies were twins, George and William, born in 1878, then came Edward in 1880, Jane in 1882 and Annie in 1884.

Education had somehow to be arranged. Their first child, Elizabeth, had no schooling and was taught to read and write by Sam. Eliza went to school for a short time at Waipawa, boarding with a Mrs Bennett. There was no school for Joseph, but Sam taught him to read and write. Sarah attended school for a while at Onga Onga in what is now the little museum. Ellen and Albert went to Waipawa and stayed with Mrs Bennett. Herbert and George went to the Blackburn school but the latter's twin brother William was sent to Waipawa and Mrs Bennett. Edward, Jane and Annie also went to the Blackburn school, these children having to walk seven miles each way through rugged bush country. In later years they rode horses.

At various intervals Sam bought in land from neighbouring properties until he had 1084 acres. Shearing was difficult because the woolshed was across the river at a place known as Fern Flat and the sheep had to be driven through the Waipawa twice to get to the woolshed to be shorn. At one stage from twenty to thirty cows were milked, and a great deal of cheese was made.

If Harriet went out to visit a neighbour she rode side-saddle on horseback, and on the rare occasions when the settlers held a picnic she took her little ones in a box nailed to a bullock sledge. Visiting clergy held church once a month at Pendle Hill, friends sometimes stayed for a meal and Harriet made her famous batter pudding with twelve eggs. Life moved along happily but changes were at hand.

In 1900 Harriet's daughter Eliza died and was buried in the private cemetery. In the beginning of 1892 she was again pregnant and by that time James and Sarah Peers had moved away to their own property. In the April of that year Sam caught a bad chill. After becoming over-heated when threshing grass seed he stood talking for too long in the cold night air. Joseph Rhodes, of the Springhill property took him to the hospital at Waipukurau, but it was too late: pneumonia set in and he died on 21 April 1892, aged fifty-four, and was buried at Pendle Hill.

Six months after his death his son, Samuel James, was born. At this confinement Harriet was assisted by Mrs Dust who lived with her daughter, Mrs Joseph Reeves just across the river from Pendle Hill.

The Pendle Hill homestead, where Harriet Fletcher lived for many years. A modern photograph.

By the time Sam died his sons had acquired interests in various properties. Between them the boys ran Pendle Hill for their mother, but under the supervision of the trustees, Jonathan and Thomas Holden, and from about 1905 George and William Fletcher leased the property from the estate.

The old clay hut was replaced by a new house built by the boys, and Harriet lived there for years, her daughter Sarah, who married George Douglas, living with her. The river was still troublesome in winter and the bridge was still a dream. At last, about 1920, Harriet wrote to Sir George Hunter about the need for it, explaining that in time of flood they were unable to leave the place.

Through the efforts of Sir George permission to build a swing bridge was finally granted in 1925, but by that time Harriet had left Pendle Hill to live at Brinksway, the property owned by George and William at Onga Onga. Her health had deteriorated and it was necessary for her to be nearer a doctor, or at least in a place where the doctor's visits were not obstructed by the river.

Yet, despite the illness that gradually became worse, Harriet did her best to help with the daily chores and household jobs right to the end.

She died at Brinksway in February 1926. Her coffin was placed on a small truck and taken across the river to Pendle Hill where she was buried beside Sam. She was seventy-seven years of age.

The swing bridge was built in 1931—five years too late for Harriet, the first white woman to live in the Wakarara district, to be carried across it.

Harriet Fletcher, *née* Lomas, 1849–1926. From a portrait printed on her memorial card. The unbridged Waipawa River ruled her married life

CHAPTER 16

Ellen Franklin

The night Ellen and Sarah Cripps were born, the waters of the Whareama rose perilously close to the slab-and-thatch shanty standing on the bank of the river. That was in 1857, when their parents, Isaac and Sarah Cripps (11), were working on Henry Buxton's Whareama station. The following year the Crippses opened their Sevenoaks accommodation house and post office store, and the children always had before them the example of a hard-working mother.

Ellen grew to be an energetic girl. She had light brown eyes, brown hair and was of medium height. About 1880 she married Robert Franklin of Wainui. Born in Melbourne in 1855 he had landed at Porangahau in 1865 with his parents, Samuel and Mercy Franklin, who had settled at Crispin Grove. Ellen's first home after her marriage was at Wimbledon, where they built and opened the first store for the settlers who were beginning to make their way inland from the coast.

After Wimbledon opened it was not long before others looked towards the country further inland and Bob Franklin took a fancy to the land just past Titree Point. He tendered for sections and got the first blocks for 30s an acre. By this time he and Ellen had three sons, Sam, Jim and Fred.

During the winter of 1887 a block of bush on the front of the section was felled and then burnt in the February of 1888. The smoke could be seen nine miles away at Wimbledon and, pointing it out, Ellen explained to her small sons that Father was burning the bush so that they could live on the farm. It was Victoria Day, 24 May 1888, when they packed up and moved to the new home where she was to be the first white woman to live in that area.

Sam and Jim, aged five and four years respectively, rode on a platform mounted on a pack-saddle with ropes to prevent them from falling off, while three-year-old Fred rode on the front of the saddle of a man named Pike who was working for the Franklins. Their father attended to the bullock dray. Their mother was pregnant with their next brother, who was to be called Walter.

The route to the property followed a narrow bush track through cuttings and deviations. Winding between trees it climbed up and over what was later known as the Blue Papa Cutting, then descended to a flat before rising to more ridges and falling to more gullies. Spurs were negotiated until at last they climbed the final hill to the selected building site.

The house, built by Ellen's brother, Isaac Cripps, was far from finished when they arrived. Most of the timber was pit-sawn on the place, the rough boards being planed at night by the light of slush lamps. Cooking had to be done in a camp oven in the open fire. There was no sink, no wash house, no tanks for water, which meant that every drop had to be carried up the hill from a well until 1891, when two 800-gallon tanks were installed.

On their arrival the seed that had been sown after the bush burn was showing up well, especially the rape that had been sown down with the grass seed. But that winter, owing to difficult access, it was impossible to get stock in to graze. The rape took control, turning the land into a mass of yellow flowers which gave them the name of Bloomfield. When the rape seed ripened some tons were cut and threshed by hand, then carted to Cape Turnagain by bullock dray and sent to Napier to be sold.

Bob Franklin had a team of twelve bullocks and a dray, his team being acknowledged as the best in the district. He was the first to take a bullock team from Titree Point to Dannevirke, a distance of thirty miles, the trip taking three days to get there and three to return. The country was bushclad and hilly.

Their son Cliff was born in 1892, and in 1895 they had another son, Cyril, who lived only nine months. In 1897 Ellen at last gave birth to a daughter whom she named Sarah Ann after her own mother, the ever-popular Granny Cripps. Six week's after Sarah Ann's birth Bob Franklin died of pneumonia. He was forty-two years of age.

Ellen Franklin, *née* Cripps, 1857–1934, with her son Cyril, who died at nine months. "A fine and capable woman to whom others went when they needed help."

Where many would have lost heart Ellen decided to carry on. She managed the house and family while Sam Crosse, who was shepherding on Bloomfield at the time, took over the management of the property until her sons Sam, and then Jim, were old enough to take over. That was in 1902, and at that time she bought a block of land which squared off the property and brought Bloomfield to over 4,000 acres. She became known in the district as a fine and capable woman to whom others went when they needed help. Her home was ruled with a firm hand and when she said a thing had to be done the boys knew it *had to be done* and that at the same time she was always scrupulously fair.

At Bloomfield everything ran to a strict routine with the clocks being always kept twenty minutes fast to give the household more daylight. On Monday, wet or fine, Ellen arose at 5 am to boil the copper for the washing which had been left to soak on Saturday. It was out on the line before breakfast. Tuesday was both ironing and pastry-making day because the Potts's irons could heat up on the stove that had been made hot for the pastry. Wednesday was cleaning day with the big kitchen to be scrubbed out. Thursday was bedroom day. All floors had to be washed, and all the bedroom china. Friday was baking day with cake tins to be filled. Saturday saw the washing of the floors all over again. Down on her knees. No mops.

On Sunday there was no work done, the Sabbath being strictly kept. Services were held some distance along the road in the Rabbit Board office and after it the minister came to lunch. On Sunday evenings there were Bible readings when Ellen sat in a large chair and the family gathered about her to listen.

As more settlers came the Rabbit Board office was also used as a school but before this happened the young Franklins had a governess. Their mother was blessed with good health and never suffered as much as a headache. Every night she sat at her desk faithfully to record the day's happenings in her diary, also attending to accounts and lists of stores to be ordered. The latter came up the coast and then inland by bullock wagon. Sewing for the entire family was done on an old Worthington hand machine: Horrocks's herringbone material turned into shirts for the five boys, grey flannel made into vests bound with tape.

As time went on the house was enlarged until it had a billiard room as well as the four bedrooms, kitchen, and large living-room and hall. A safe was kept in the billiard room, the key to it being always hung beside the clock in Ellen's bedroom. Lighting was by gas manufactured by their own plant, which was kept in a nearby shed. The benzolene to run it was also kept out in the shed.

At last the road to Dannevirke was completed, and after the packhorses and coaches came the motors, the mail now being delivered three times a week. In 1912 Ellen had the property surveyed and paid gift duty to divide it up between her family. She continued to live in the homestead but retained 50 acres which had been cut off for her. The rest of the homestead area was owned by her son J. R. Franklin, who put a manager on and went to live in Wanganui.

In 1934 J. R. Franklin's son, James Wylie Franklin, was managing his father's property. He lived in a manager's cottage that had been built and had working for him a man named Joblin, who lived in the shearers' quarters. There was also Michael O'Shea, a cowman gardener employed by Ellen Franklin, who lived in the men's whare. Ellen, at this period, had a companion help living with her. She was Miss Effie Laton Smail, aged about forty. She was a gentle person of refinement, quietly spoken and very attentive to Ellen, who by that time was seventy-seven years of age.

Throughout the years Ellen had remained a woman of habit with most of her acquaintances knowing that she invariably rose at 6 am, breakfasted at 7.30 am, had dinner at noon, tea at 6 pm and went to bed at 9 pm.

On Sunday 6 May 1934 this routine would have been carried out as usual, but on that particular evening Jim Franklin, having played a hard game of rugby the day before, went to bed straight after tea because he felt tired and unwell. He was soon deeply asleep. That evening O'Shea took his lantern and walked along the road to visit a friend and as he passed the window he saw the two women sitting at the tea table. By then Effiie Smail had been at Bloomfield only eight weeks.

Another settler, Rangi Churchouse, happened to be out visiting that evening and was on his way home when he saw the glare of a fire at Bloomfield. He left his motorcycle at the gate and rushed up the hill to find the house a mass of flames and nobody to be seen. He entered Ellen's bedroom through the open window but was driven out by the heat and smoke. Next he tried the kitchen door but had to close it against the flames and heat. He then ran round the house to find fire breaking out of every window in the front portion giving a strong impression that it had been lit in several places. He then raced back to his motorcycle and rode to give the alarm.

Joblin, in the meantime, according to his later statement, had sat by the fire in the manager's house for about half an hour and had then gone to bed in his own quarters. While lying in bed he had noticed lights flickering on the wall and had got up to discover the homestead to be ablaze. He had gone at once to awaken Jim and they had hurried over to the house but had been unable to get in on account of the smoke and flames. Jim had therefore hastened away on his motorcycle for help. Half a mile along the road he had met Churchouse returning with a party to help fight the fire.

The Bloomfield homestead was a furnace and nothing could be done. Ellen's sons watched it helplessly, each knowing that had the two women escaped they would have been there with them. At daylight they began searching among the still smouldering ruins for the bodies. They found the charred remains of their mother just out of the passage and into the kitchen, while all that was left of Miss Smail lay in the hall near the diningroom door.

There was nothing to show what had started the blaze that had engulfed the place in so short a time, nor was there any apparent reason why the two women had been unable to get out of the house through the nearby front and back doors. There was no indication that they had tried to fight the flames. It was too early for them to have retired to bed; and the moment a fire broke out they had had the necessary equipment at hand in the form of a fire extinguisher hanging near the front door. What had prevented Miss Smail from running to Jim for help? His cottage was only 600 yards away.

This question and many others concerning the Bloomfield fire have never been satisfactorily answered. Were the two women murdered? The family consider this to have been a fact.

It is possible that some person, knowing that the key to the safe in the billiard room hung beside the clock in Ellen Franklin's bedroom, entered through the window that was always left open except when an easterly wind was blowing. It would be natural for anyone knowing of the safe's existence to suppose that money was kept in it, and with the key already in hand it would be an easy matter to return later when the two women were asleep. A glance through the livingroom window would also give the intruder a view of them both safely seated before the fireside, allowing a quick entry to obtain the key.

It is not hard to imagine that Ellen had been disturbed by some sound, or that some reason had taken her away from the fireside and towards the kitchen at the critical moment. The kitchen and bedroom doors were close and she would see the man in her room. She would have stood up to him exactly as she had faced up to everything else in life. He had perhaps lost his head and knocked her senseless. She had fallen just through the kitchen door. Miss Smail had then come into the passage to investigate the disturbance and had been dealt with in a similar manner. As he was no doubt known to these women the intruder had then set fire to the house to cover his deed.

Is this what happened to prevent the two women from leaving the house before it became a raging furnace? We shall never know. What we do know is that Ellen Franklin, who had spent her life in developing fine character in her family and in helping others, and who was respected by all who knew her, had met with a most tragic end.

CHAPTER 17

Elizabeth Hamlin

Elizabeth Hamlin arrived in New Zealand in 1826, a mere five years after the Ngapuhi chief Hongi Hika had returned from England and Australia laden with muskets.

Born in England in 1804, she was Elizabeth Osborne before her marriage to James Hamlin. Early photographs do not indicate that she was a tall girl. They show a sweet face and suggest that she had blue or grey eyes and perhaps a slight wave to the dark hair drawn back from a centre parting.

Her husband James Hamlin, born in England in 1803, was trained as a flax dresser and weaver. Drawn towards missionary work he came to New Zealand with the Rev. William Williams, (51), sailing on the *Sir George Osborne*. They arrived at Sydney on 17 December 1825, and left that colony the following 18 March, reaching The Bay of Islands on 25 March, 1826. The New Zealand that greeted them was a place of bloodshed with the wars of Hongi Hika raging through the countryside.

Six weeks after her arrival Elizabeth's first child, James, was born. The following year in October George was born and in 1829 came John. George, unfortunately, was born with a hare lip.

During those early days they lived at Kerikeri. Elizabeth's home was a primitive hut which was later improved by a window and cupboard built by James. His diary note of August 1830 says that he built a door for his house.

Except for James and the very few nearby missionaries Elizabeth lived with only Maoris around her and soon learned to speak their language. Nor was James always at home. His work as a lay catechist and his earnest endeavours to spread the Gospel took him about the district. There was the site to be chosen for the Waimate mission, the nine-mile road to it to be formed and a bridge to be built over the Waitangi River. Fellow missionaries Clarke and Davis assisted in these projects, and in fact James Hamlin's 1830–34 diary indicates that he was very seldom in Kerikeri.

During his absences Elizabeth was never idle, for the wives of the missionaries also had their duties. From daybreak till breakfast time and in the evenings she taught in the mission school for girls and women. For the rest of the time she was occupied in training Maori girls in the simple domestic accomplishments of cooking, laundering and sewing. And she had her own young family to care for.

It appears too that her health was not always good. On 31 August 1830 a brief note in her husband's diary states: *Took Mrs Hamlin down to Paihia.* And on 4 September: *News arrived that Mrs Hamlin very poorly at Paihia consequently I packed up my things and set off with Mr W. Williams and remained there till Thurs. when Mrs Hamlin got a*

80

little better when also I left and returned home. One wonders if Elizabeth lost a baby on this occasion.

In the January of 1831 a man-of-war called in at Paihia. Elizabeth and her husband took little George to have his hare lip examined by the ship's doctor, hoping that something could be done about it. The doctor and his assistant performed a painful operation on the little boy, who was then three years and three months of age. The lip was apparently cut and then pinned together and tied with a silk thread round the ends of the pins. A plaster was then put on which remained until the following Friday when it was taken off and replaced by fresh plasters. On the Saturday these plasters were also replaced and one of the pins removed. There was no anaesthetic for little George.

When the Waimate mission opened in 1831 the homes for the Hamlin, Clarke and Davis families were far from complete. Built on similar lines they were two-storeyed with verandahs running across the fronts and with three dormer windows tucked beneath the shingled hipped roofs. When Elizabeth moved into her home there was neither ground nor first floor, the stairs had not yet been built, the roof leaked and draughts blew through the walls. The place for the chimney had still not been decided. When she looked outside she could see nothing but high fern from which Maoris emerged to peer inquisitively through the gaps where the doors and windows would later be placed.

The well was another troublesome factor: at fifty-three feet only seven feet of water had appeared. The chimney, when it was eventually constructed, smoked badly, but with its erection cooking could be done at the huge open fireplace which had a bread oven built alongside. Stores came by ship to Kerikeri and were then carried inland. Pork was served day.after day.

That year James's diary note of 22nd September states *A little after 12 Mrs Hamlin was taken poorly and delivered of a son.* This was Osborne.

By 1833 the house was still incomplete, but by this time the two elder boys were being taken to school at Paihia. Then on 4 March James's diary briefly recorded that: *On Monday morning about half past four Mrs Hamlin was through the mercy of our Heavenly Father safely delivered of a son.* This was Edward. And again in September 1834: *Mrs Hamlin was through the mercy of our Heavenly Father safely delivered of a son.* Frederick had arrived

With all these babies toddling about her feet Elizabeth had no option but to bear the inconveniences of the mission house; but in 1835 a move was made to Mangapouri on the Waipa River. They left the Bay of Islands on 30 April but through Maori unrest and fighting were held up at both Tamaki and Puriri, while at Thames some Maoris threatened to follow and strip them. It was the end of June and midwinter before they reached their destination, the children crying from the bitter cold.

In that wild and desolate country Elizabeth was right back to the primitive raupo-hut stage, waiting for mud bricks to be made to form the fireplace and chimney. And now there was the added fear of living right in the midst of the most bloodthirsty of the tribes, who gave ample evidence of the eating of human flesh. The most terrifying of these was the cannibal chief Awarahi, of the Mangapouri. The Maoris coveted Elizabeth's poor cooking utensils and would demand anything that caught their fancy, offering a few potatoes in return. It was under these circumstances that her son Henry Martyn arrived, and he seems to have been the first white child born in the Waikato.

In the spring of 1836 the Maoris left Mangapouri for Manakau, so it was decided to move the mission station to that place. They left on 8 September and proceeded to Moeatoa, a headland projecting into the inlet of the Manakau which runs up to present-day Waiuku. Here the performance of building a house began all over again, the lack of a chimney causing all cooking to be done outside while constant rain made it impossible to keep stores and clothing dry. January of 1839 saw the birth of Josiah Pratt, and in June of the same year the mission was moved to Orua Bay, nearer the Waikato Heads.

At Orua Bay, in 1840, Sophia was born, and the following year Elizabeth had a miscarriage. James was away from home on missionary work most of the time and Elizabeth, left alone with the children, was suffering once again from poor health. In September 1841 James returned to find she had been ill but had recovered. He is off again, returning in November to find her in a very weak state having been again dangerously ill during his absence. In the February of 1842 both Elizabeth and little Sophia were desperately ill with fever, but in 1843 Elizabeth was well enough to give birth to Jane Elizabeth.

In the June of 1844, barely two months before the birth of her next baby, Ebenezer, Elizabeth experienced the distress of a flood in the house. Caused by an exceptionally high tide, it came on a cold winter's night to deluge the house and leave more than two feet of water covering the floors. The children were in bed and had barely had time to get out and find dry clothes before wading through the water to higher ground not far distant. The beds, light boxes and furniture floated about the room, while seventy volumes of James's precious books spent the whole night under water. All the linen in the house, and their half year's supply of potatoes, flour, sugar, tea and other eatables were, according to their nature, badly damaged or lost altogether. Several successive tides broke through the house, making it impossible for the family to return for at least five days, and then there was endless repair work to be done before even the doors could be closed.

Until 1844 James had been a lay catechist in the Church Missionary Society but on 22 September of that year he was admitted, with William Colenso, to deacon's orders. The ordination was performed by the Right Rev. Bishop Selwyn at Auckland. At the end of that year they left with their eleven children for Wairoa, on the East Coast, where James was to establish a mission station. Also on board the *Nimrod* were William Colenso, his wife Elizabeth (9) and small daughter Fanny, who were bound for Waitangi in the Ahuriri district where another mission station was to be established, eighty miles to the south.

Poverty Bay was reached on 24 December, and after spending Christmas Day on board Elizabeth and the children were left with the Rev. and Mrs William Williams (51) at Turanganui while James and his eldest son went on to Wairoa to see about a house for the family. The house they were to have occupied at Wairoa had been built for the Rev. W. C. Dudley, who had fallen ill before he could occupy it. It was leaning on all sides, and the raupo had been pulled to pieces by pigs. While it was being made

Elizabeth Hamlin, *née* Osborne, 1804–58. In 1835 she was living in a chimneyless
raupo hut and surrounded by cannibal Maoris.

habitable Elizabeth remained with the Williams family for seven weeks, then left on the 12 February for Wairoa.

As the Wairoa Maoris had been anxious for a missionary to live among them a party of thirty travelled to Turanganui to help the Hamlins complete the remaining sixty miles of their journey. The family walked all the way via Mahia with certain Maoris allotted to look after each child. The journey lasted several days and took them through the shadowed stillness of deep silent forests. At times they skirted extensive swamps, climbed over high bluffs or slid down steep cliffs until at last a stretch of sand led them to the mouth of the Wairoa River. In the meantime their cases had been landed at Wairoa, the boxes containing the linen being soaked through from top to bottom.

The early years at Wairoa were disappointing and frustrating, with difficulties that loomed in all directions. James left Elizabeth almost at once to tour his large district and, strained and lonely, she had trouble with the Maoris. During his absence the store was broken into, the wheat mill was stolen, and it was obvious that the Maoris were acquiring drink from the whaling stations established along the coast.

The Maori population was numerous, and while many of them had learnt of the benefits of Christianity from others and accepted it readily, there were bitter quarrels which resulted in two chapels and two bells ringing at the same time for morning prayers in opposition to each other. James's services were held in a large Maori whare at Te Uhi.

For Elizabeth the work of making a home began all over again. Conditions were even more primitive than they had been in the north, and by 1845 James was still building a chimney. Her life was a routine of everyday tasks such as instructing Maori women in the arts of writing, reading, cooking, washing, cleaning and anything else that could be useful. Sewing depended upon what materials were available, and clothing was usually a problem. At the same time her own children had to be clothed and taught everything that was within her scope. The nearest white women to her were sixty miles to the north or eighty miles to the south.

On one occasion when James was away a chief who had complained about his head rushed out of morning prayers and was later found drowned in a creek. The news soon spread and the incident brought forth horrid yells and indecent gestures exceeding anything Elizabeth had witnessed since her arrival in the country. Muskets were continually fired in all directions with bullets falling near the house.

In May of 1846 she was once again "taken poorly", which resulted in another miscarriage; and less than a month later she was laid up with what was termed a "putrid sore throat". In April 1847 her twelfth and last child, Mary, was born, and about a fortnight later, with Elizabeth still very unwell, every Maori girl in the house ran away, so that she was left without help of any kind.

A tough time then followed for both Elizabeth and James: in June and July of that year there was a very bad epidemic of whooping cough and fever, with many children dying. Sophia became dangerously ill and at the same time Elizabeth and James were both suffering from inflammation of the eyes.

After they had had nearly three years of existence in the primitive shack a man named Cooper came from Turanganui to build them a house. By this time relations with the Maoris had improved, but now James's health had begun to deteriorate with much head and eye trouble, and trouble also from poor diet while travelling round his district when he ate only pork and potatoes when obtainable, and fernroot at other times. It was months before he could get a passage to Auckland for medical attention.

In 1851 Elizabeth, whose own health had continued indifferent, also headed for Auckland for medical treatment. The long hours of toil, which included baking seventy pounds of flour into bread each week for the mission school, were beginning to prove too much for her diminishing strength. She returned seven months later in the middle of May 1852 and was put ashore at Mahia whence she had to walk to Nuhaka, a matter of some fifteen miles, and from there ride horseback to Wairoa. Such a journey in her poor state of health, was far too much for Elizabeth.

In 1853 she was again very ill and her husband's diary tells of epidemics, earthquakes and floods, the latter being caused by heavy rain for seventeen days on end, the worst downpour they had experienced during their eight years in Wairoa. A great number of totara trees, native huts, and whole stacks of wheat came down the river and were washed out to sea. Crops of corn, potatoes and kumara were all destroyed.

In December 1854 they actually had a holiday when, with the family, they went to Waiau to spend Christmas, Elizabeth having long since promised to visit the Maoris there. For the Christmas feast a temporary house of about eighteen by twelve feet was erected, the roof covered with calico. In this the food was laid out in two long rows of which they partook without any noise or the least disorder. This, wrote James, was keeping Christmas as it ought to be kept.

By that date their eldest sons had spent several years developing land at Otahuhu, previously taken up by James and known as Waipuna. Perhaps to be nearer medical attention, Elizabeth appears to have spent most of her remaining years there.

On 11 April 1858 James wrote that he embarked in the *Zillah* for Auckland and arrived there six days later. On leaving Auckland he went to Waipuna, where he found Elizabeth very ill. On 1 January he sailed from Auckland and was met in Turanganui by Archdeacon and Mrs William Williams and others: he was by then wearing a black armband.

At some period between April 1858 and the end of that year Elizabeth Hamlin, the first white woman to live at Wairoa, had died and been buried at Otahuhu.

CHAPTER 18

Sophia Louisa Harris

Sophia Louisa Crail was born at Akitio in 1860. She was the daughter of Robert Crail who had run away from his Border-country home in England when only nine years of age. He had gone to sea and after some years of sailing had left his ship to settle in New Zealand. He spent several years in Wellington, where he married, and by the mid 1850s had brought his family to live in Hawke's Bay where he did shepherding work.

Sophia Louisa was known to her family and friends as Louie. She went out to work as soon as she was considered old enough to do so, and by the time she was fifteen she had spent some years in the employ of Mrs J. D. Canning of Oakbourne station in the Porangahau district. Her father in the meantime had taken up 500 acres of land at the foot of Gentle Annie, about twelve miles out of Gisborne on the Tiniroto Road. He moved there with the rest of his family in 1870, but Louie stayed on with Mrs Canning.

She developed into a capable girl. Brown-eyed, with dark wavy hair, she was a tremendous help to Mrs Canning, who had had indifferent health after the death, at an early age, of her little daughter. There were also two young Canning boys to be cared for and much work to be done in the station homestead. It was not long before Louie's happy nature caught the interest of Thomas John Harris, the head ploughman at Oakbourne.

Born in Cornwall in 1856, and usually known as Jack, Harris had come to New Zealand as a young man. He had landed in Auckland and had then spent a period in Avondale before moving to take up his position with the Cannings in Hawke's Bay. He was a kindly person, his handsome bearded face indicating a strong character, and although he was not tall he had a big chest. He was determined, careful, and a great worker.

Louie married him in 1878 when she was eighteen years of age.

J. D. Canning, at this time, was involved in financial difficulties and in 1878 was bearing the extra burden of having to send his wife home to England to consult medical specialists. In an effort to pay Jack the £300 owing to him for wages he offered him draught horses to the value instead of the money. Jack refused, pointing out that he needed the money in cash as he wished to strike out on his own, and in some way the money was then found. Louie packed their belongings and they left Oakbourne to go to her parents' home at the foot of Gentle Annie.

At this period the Hangaroa district was being opened up. The rough hilly country lying twenty-seven miles from Gisborne, via Tiniroto, was cut up and balloted for in

500-acre sections. Jack drew a section, then followed the Maori tracks out into the back country to inspect it. He found it to be covered in red manuka and flax, and with patches of light bush, but with a good clearing on the bank of the Hangaroa River which would enable him to graze his first stock.

Louie stayed with her parents for a year and during this time her first baby, Albert Ernest, was born. Jack, in the meantime, erected a tent on the property and began to build a totara-slab whare with shingled roof and a clay floor. When it was finished Louie, carrying the baby on her back, rode out to live in it with him.

They called the place Avondale. By this time it was 1880 and Louie found herself to be the first white woman to settle in the Hangaroa district, and in fact she was the only white woman living there for the next ten years.

Cooking was done in the camp oven and water was carried from the creek. Their stores came from Gisborne, which meant going there on horseback to fetch them, Louie riding side-saddle and Jack leading a packhorse. The journey took three or four hours each way, and every time they rode the twenty-seven miles and back they broke off riding whips of willow or poplar from trees they passed on the way. On returning home the whips were planted as cuttings on the property. The cuttings thrived, and most of the willows and poplars of the district originate from cuttings taken from these original trees.

After the birth of Louie's second child they each carried a child when they went to town, but the arrival of the third baby made this impossible. It was five years before Louie went to town again, and by that time she had five children, the eldest being able to look after the little ones. Eventually they had ten children, five boys and five daughters, and as the birth of each baby drew near Jack rode more than twenty miles to Patutahi for a midwife. During her last five confinements Louie was attended by Mrs Lynch of Patutahi.

The slab hut was added to as the family increased. The first six children were educated by governesses, while the last four went to school at Patutahi where board was found for them. There were no idle moments for Louie, who worked endlessly to cook their meals and make their clothes. Pillows and mattresses were stuffed from pigeon and pheasant feathers, while pigeon fat was boiled down to lubricate saddles and bridles. A sportsman's paradise, the birds were there in their thousands. Wild pigs also were plentiful.

During the early years Jack worked by contract and bought in stock when he could afford to. He began with Lincoln sheep, then crossed them with Romney, eventually finishing with purebred Romneys. His first cattle were Shorthorns but he changed later to Aberdeen Angus. He had an endless fight with the manuka which kept recurring, no matter how much it was cut back, but being a progressive farmer he gradually added to the property until he had expanded the 500 acres to 5,000.

They continued to live in the slab hut until about 1900, when a new house of seven rooms, surrounded by front and side verandahs, was built. There was no bathroom, but the family bathed in a tin tub in an outside wash-house and saddleroom, where the copper was boiled for hot water. The old slab hut was then used as a woodshed.

A seven-stand woolshed was another acquisition to the property in 1900. It was burnt down in 1902 and replaced in 1903. Machines were installed in 1906, the starting of the engines becoming a day's highlight for young and old. By that time the district had become more populated and winter stores were able to reach them by wagon, usually about March or April before the new, roughly-formed roads became bogged by winter rains. Church services were also being held at the various homes in turn.

Louie, with her own children off her hands, was always doing something for somebody. Each day she prepared food for five extra people because, she always declared, someone might be waylaid on the road and need food and a night's shelter. When neighbours were in need she went to them with a basket laden with necessities. When people became ill she took them nourishment and stayed to nurse them. When a new baby arrived in the district she was there to assist. Sewing for the poorly clad children of the roadmen also kept her busy. She became, in fact, known as the mother of the district.

One confinement almost got her into trouble. It occurred when the wife of a roadman gave birth to a stillborn child and difficulty arose in knowing what to do with the tiny body. One thing was certain—it had to be removed from the sight of the grief-stricken mother. Louie rose to the occasion by placing the babe in a large cornflour box and burying it in the garden. Six months later she had a visit from the police, who had come to make inquiries concerning the child; she explained that she had had to bury the baby and they complained that she should have reported it.

Bereavement came in 1908 when Jack died at the age of fifty-two. After his death Louie lived on at Avondale while her son, Thomas John junior, managed the place until 1916. Sam Lyons then managed for her until 1918, and then Thomas managed it again until Henry Edward took over the running of the property in 1923.

In 1923 Louie went to live in Irenui Road in Gisborne, and in 1925 a trip to England with a daughter came as a reward for a lifetime of labouring for others. On 6 June 1937 this "mother" of the Hangaroa district died at the age of seventy-six and was laid to rest beside Jack in the Patutahi cemetery.

Of the first settlers who took up land at Hangaroa the Harris family is the only one now remaining. The Avondale property, which grew from virtually nothing but flax, manuka and bush is now 7,000 acres of English grass. It is divided into three blocks that are farmed by the third generation of Louie and Jack's descendants, and today the land winters 18,000 sheep which clip 700 bales of wool, and 2,800 head of cattle, the surplus all going off fat. The last hill on the inland road from Gisborne to Wairoa is still known as Harris's Hill.

CHAPTER 19

Sarah Jane Herbert

Sarah Jane Woods was born in 1814 at Farnham, Surrey, England. A short girl with a small figure, her straight, dark hair, parted in the centre, framed a face with blue eyes. When she married Joseph Herbert of Reading, Berkshire, in 1833, she became known as "little Mrs Herbert". Their son Jesse was not born until 1840, and in 1841 they sailed in the *London* for New Zealand, arriving in Wellington on 1 May 1842. They settled in Petone, where Joseph took up carting and the building of roads.

One of his major contracts was the formation of a road between Wellington and Petone above the high-water mark as the existing track was impassable at high tide. He had just started the job when the earthquake of 1848 destroyed half the settlement and caused many colonists to turn their backs on New Zealand and head for Australia. However it was an ill wind that blew somebody some good because it also raised the shoreline several feet and saved the contractor half the expected work. The earthquake of 1855 raised the shoreline yet higher.

By 1854 their family had increased by the additions of Emma, Charles, Thomas, William and John. During that year Joseph took up land at Tautane, south of Cape Turnagain, and in the spring he sent 600 Merino ewes to the property. The sheep were driven by his son Jesse, then aged fourteen, and a young companion, and Sarah watched the two boys set off on foot with only one dog to help them. They were to pick up another 400 sheep at Castlepoint and it is said the young drovers lost only three or four sheep, which died through overeating wheat grown by the Maoris at Papuka.

Joseph and Sarah intended to follow immediately with their five other children but the cutter was delayed by bad weather. The two boys lived on alone at Tautane, running out of food and relying on help given to them by Maoris and on what they could shoot for themselves.

At last the cutter arrived and anchored a little to the south of Cape Turnagain. With her children Sarah was lowered in the boat and rowed towards the shore where Maoris stood watching their arrival. As the surf slapped the boat she was picked up and placed on the shoulders of a burly Maori who carried her to the sands. She then learned that she would be the only white woman within miles.

Their first clay hut was no more than primitive, but at least it sheltered the family. The camp oven was put into use and water was carried up from a stream. Stores had to be conserved as they came only once a year and were landed on the beach.

Sarah's next baby, Jane, was the first white child to be born in the district. Eventually Sarah had twelve children, ten of whom lived, the later arrivals being

89

Alice, Arthur and Alfred. One of her main problems was to keep them all properly clothed.

Soon after their arrival there was trouble with the Maoris because the area they were occupying had been marked off as a Native Reserve of 1,000 acres. The land, a mass of toetoe and fern, lay between the Wainui and Tautane Rivers with small clearings on the spurs round the Maori pa. The Maoris objected so forcibly to their presence that in 1856 Joseph wrote to the Land Office, asking that his boundaries be adjusted in the register to the south of the Wainui River. This was done and they moved to what was then known as Wainui.

At that time and for many years later the main track between Wellington and Hawke's Bay ran through what was to become the Wainui settlement. It soon became obvious that travellers would need an overnight stopping place in that vicinity and Joseph quickly enlarged their clay home into a wayside accommodation house. The clay ovens that were built outside during those days were also capable of baking more food than the camp ovens and made excellent bread when the hot embers had been raked out. But bread could not be made until the wheat had been sown, ripened and ground into flour.

We no longer know exactly why they had so much friction with the Maoris, but for some reason the Natives continued to object to the Herberts' occupation of the Wainui land across the river. They stole sheep, threatened to drive away the cattle, and refused to let them cultivate the land. The all-important wheat crop was in constant danger of being deliberately ruined, and the Maoris pulled down a flag that Joseph had erected as a notice to travellers.

In 1857 Joseph again wrote to the Land Office, complaining that despite his receipt for 80 acres the Maoris still claimed the area was theirs, and that any day he expected his wife and family to be without a home. However, they managed to remain there and Sarah's days were filled by the cares of feeding her growing family and keeping them clothed. All sewing for them was done by hand out of whatever materials she could procure, and she also made Joseph's suits.

There were many travellers to be accommodated and fed, and in fact so numerous did these people become that Joseph found it necessary to build a second accommodation house. He also built a store and several cottages in the growing settlement of Wainui. In 1860 he was issued a run of 4,050 acres with the Wainui River as the northern and eastern boundaries, and in the November of that year he paid for 160 acres of the run by the Wainui village. Then in 1863 he went to the Land Office to freehold more land but discovered that his intended purchase had already been bought without his knowledge by neighbouring runholders. He then retained only the 280 acres to which he had title, relinquishing his interests and rights to the rest, and turned his efforts to the building of the Wainui township.

The running of the two accommodation houses took most of Sarah's time, the children, as they gew older, assisting with all that had to be done. In common with other settlers of the period she made and used slush lamps, rose at dawn and retired long after darkness had fallen.

She became an experienced midwife and, with so many children of her own, knew what to do in time of sickness. She was always ready to hold out a helping hand and it

Sarah Jane Herbert, *née* Woods, 1814–76. "She became an experienced midwife . . . and on one occasion walked fifteen miles through the dark bush to a confinement."

is not hard to guess that it was her willing assistance to Maori women which eventually improved their relationship with the Maoris who had previously been so hostile.

Sarah seldom left home except at the call of another woman. On one occasion she walked fifteen miles through the dark bush when Mrs White, the wife of the head shepherd at Oakbourne station, was confined. The Whites named their son Herbert in recognition of Sarah's long walk and her timely assistance. Herbert White was later a well known runholder in the district.

Her route to Mrs White was along Maori tracks through a valley known as Doctor's Gully. At the head of the gully a track, later called Finger Post Road, went down to the Mangamaire stream and then towards the present Porangahau-Waipukurau road.

There were times as she grew older when she rode on horseback, but only if one of her sons walked ahead and led the animal.

Sarah died in 1876 at the age of sixty-two. She never knew that Wainui, the place where she had worked so hard, and helped so many would become known as Herbertville.

CHAPTER 20

Annie Hunter

Annie Guthrie, born in the Isle of Wight in 1838, was the eldest child of Thomas Guthrie and his wife, who had formerly been Ann Groves. In September 1839 she sailed in the *Adelaide* with her parents who were emigrating to New Zealand, and they arrived at Port Nicholson in the March of 1840·and were landed on Petone Beach.

Thomas Guthrie was descended from one of the Dukes of Fife, and at some time his forebears had moved to the Isle of Wight. In Wellington his name appeared on an early burgess roll, his place of residence being shown as Upper Willis Street, his occupation that of stockholder. By 1847 his family had been increased by the arrival of Thomas, Jane and little Catherine.

During that year he negotiated with Maori owners to lease land at Castlepoint on the East Coast, his yearly rental being almost £200. When he bought portions of the property it was mainly by cash transaction. Castlepoint station was estimated to contain 24,960 acres, which did not include the Whakataki Native Reserve of 6,000 acres, and for this he arranged grazing rights with the Maoris. In March 1848 he purchased stock and in the April drove 700 sheep and 150 head of cattle to the property. Tradition relates that when the first of Guthrie's cattle appeared over the ridge the Maoris, not having seen cattle before, performed a haka of welcome.

During his absence his wife Ann had a desperately anxious time with twelve-months-old Catherine, and when he returned she sadly reported that the baby had died. A few months later, with Annie, Thomas and Jane, the Guthries went up the coast by ship. They were rowed ashore, were carried through the surf and became the first white settlers at Castlepoint.

For £11 the Maoris had built them a small raupo thatched homestead close to the seashore. William Colenso later reported it to be strong and commodious, contrasting it unfavourably with the neglected Maori chapel for which there had been no financial inducement. However, in the earthquake of October 1848 the chimney collapsed and the house was badly damaged. It was replaced by a more comfortable dwelling.

In 1851 Donald McLean, Land Purchase Commissioner, reached Castlepoint with his party. He later recorded in his diary that they *had a good dinner and kind reception from Mr Guthrie who with his wife appear to be kind industrious people. Mrs Guthrie was a particularly good-natured, clean English woman whose attention and politeness speak volumes in her favour.*

Relations between the Guthries and the Maoris were always good, as they soon recognised Ann's ready willingness to assist them in any troubles or ailments. In return she received much assistance from them.

The lighthouse at Castlepoint, where Annie Hunter's father leased some 30,000 acres from the Maoris in 1847. A modern photograph.

During those days the only possible transport was on horseback, and travelling about the countryside was difficult on account of the many unbridged rivers. In the 1850s travellers along the coast route became so numerous that Thomas Guthrie found it necessary to open an accommodation house. It was situated on the seafront about 400 yards from his own house and was approximately half way between Wellington and Ahuriri, as Napier was then known. In 1855 it was leased to Ann's brother John Groves, who had come with his family from the Isle of Wight.

Annie grew up at Castlepoint where there was nothing but hills beyond hills and the sea stretching towards the horizon. She was a tall slim girl with a bright, intelligent expression, blue eyes and straight brown hair. Her education was given to her by her parents and by tutors, among them William Marshall, later of Napier, who arrived at Castlepoint in 1853 to teach the Guthrie children.

Courtship came to Annie during the 1850s when William Henry Hunter drove sheep up the coast to the Porangahau station which had been taken up by his brother, George Hunter junior, and the representatives of the late Kenneth Bethune. William was managing the property with his brother David, and they lived in two houses which had been brought from Wellington by ship, landed at Blackhead, and then carted to the station and erected about six miles from the Porangahau pa.

William and David were the sons of George Hunter senior who, in 1840, had brought his wife and children to New Zealand in the *Duke of Roxburgh*. William, born in London in 1830, was a handsome man with a long dark beard.

Annie and William were married at Castlepoint on 5 November 1860 by the Bishop of Wellington. After the ceremony and its following festivities they rode to the new two-storeyed home, with its early-type colonial oven, which had been built for them at Porangahau.

The district was peopled mainly by Maoris, but having grown up among Maoris along the coast Annie understood them, spoke their language and knew their needs. And of course news travelled. The Porangahau Maoris knew perfectly well that Annie was the daughter of the Pakeha woman down the coast—the one who for so many years had given so much assistance to their people. Small parties therefore soon formed the habit of coming to the house seeking her help in their sickness, injuries or other troubles and exclaiming, "Annie, Annie . . . Where Annie? Where Annie?"

William's brother David married Polly Monteith, the daughter of Wellington's first doctor, and she became Annie's neighbour.

Annie was an excellent horsewoman who taught many young people to ride. On one occasion an unbroken horse was brought in: two shepherds held the rearing animal while she mounted, and after a long day's ride she brought the tamed horse quietly home. Her side-saddle was treasured by the family for years.

The first of her babies to arrive was William George, then came Thomas Henry who was followed by Arthur Clement, who died of typhoid when he was about eighteen years of age. Robert was born next, and then Helen, Annie Constance, and Harold Graham. They were educated by tutors or a governess, the boys later going to Napier Boys' High School where two of them were dux. A small family church was built on the edge of the garden and at times William Colenso preached in it when he walked along the coast.

In 1869 unrest among the Taupo Maoris, together with the activities of Te Kooti in the Urewera country, made necessary the establishment of a number of military posts in the Taupo district. These posts were supplied with stores and equipment from Napier, 100 miles away, and this long line of communication, through very difficult country, was protected by blockhouses erected at strategic points along the route.

William Hunter was one who drove stock to feed the troops, the tracks winding over the hills along which they slowly made their way later becoming the Napier-Taupo Road which, in 1874, was opened for coach travel. Annie, waiting at home with the family, knew many anxious weeks until his return.

In 1868 her father, Thomas Guthrie, sold his Castlepoint station to G. M. Waterhouse and retired to his Whakataki property. When the Guthries left the people of the district made them a presentation of a canteen of silver, the plaque on the lid inscribed with the words: *Presented to Mr and Mrs Guthrie by the settlers of Castlepoint and District. In the name of hospitality.* Thomas Guthrie was a strong man who always made light work of lifting 200 lb bales of wool into the surfboats. He died in 1876.

That same year, with her youngest child still under two years of age, Annie lost William. He was buried beneath a large karaka tree on the property. Then, in 1879, her mother, Ann Guthrie, died when she was with Annie at Porangahau.

With both parents and her husband gone Annie was left to cope with the bringing up of seven children. She did her best to make their childhood and home life happy, attending to their religious upbringing by reading a chapter from the Bible to them every morning after breakfast.

To take them to the dentist in Napier she rode six miles to Porangahau, leading a horse which carried the small children in panniers on either side. From Porangahau, in the mid 1870s, she could take the mail coach to Waipukurau, and from there continued the journey by coach to Napier. For these necessary periodic visits rooms were kept permanently booked at Napier in the Criterion Hotel.

Annie's brother-in-law George Hunter, who owned Porangahau station, died in 1880. The property was inherited by his sons, George (later Sir George) and Paul(21) and by that time both George and Paul had arrived to take over the running of the station.

About 1890 Annie and her seven children, who were all grown up by that time, went to live at Otope, some fourteen miles south-east of Dannevirke. This small bush-covered property was worked by her sons, and there she lived in a single-storeyed house while a two-storeyed house was built for her son Thomas, who married eighteen-year-old Florence Annie Price, the daughter of A. H. Price of Motuotaraia station.

Annie did not live at Otope for long. She moved to a large old home in Edinburgh Street, Dannevirke, where she remained for the rest of her life and where, in her later years, she was cared for by her niece, Miss Ethel Wishawe, who was the daughter of her sister. Annie died of pneumonia at the age of sixty-seven in 1906 and was buried in the Dannevirke cemetery.

Annie Hunter, *née* Guthrie, 1838–1906. "Small parties of Maoris formed the habit of coming to the house seeking her help in their sickness, injuries and other troubles and exclaiming 'Annie? Where Annie? Where Annie?' "

CHAPTER 21

Edith Blanche Hunter

Edith Blanche Morrah was born in Australia in 1862. Her father, Edward W. Morrah, the son of an English doctor of Irish descent, emigrated to Australia as a member of the staff of the Bank of Australasia. He married in Australia, his wife belonging to an old Tasmanian family who had emigrated there in 1823.

During the late 1860s when he was managing the branch at Ballarat, banking losses in New Zealand were serious enough to warrant investigations. He was sent across the Tasman to make a special report and later, due to his forceful and aggressive personality, he was appointed to direct the Bank's operations in New Zealand.

He brought his family to Wellington in 1870 and they lived in a large two-storeyed house on the corner of Aro Street and Upper Willis Street. Their family numbered thirteen, some born in Australia and some in New Zealand, Edith being third in seniority.

In Upper Willis Street, nearly opposite their house, was the home of Robert Hunter who, at times, was visited by his nephews, George and Paul Hunter (20), and it was there that Edith met Paul. By that time she had grown into a young woman of medium height. Quiet and shy, she had large brown eyes and straight black hair drawn back from a centre parting to be gathered in a bun at the back of her head.

Thomas Paul Hunter, born 1860 in Wellington, was a tall young man with fair hair who gave promise of developing into a large man. He was the son of George Hunter who had arrived in New Zealand with his parents in the *Duke of Roxburgh* in 1840. Paul's grandfather, the first George Hunter, was the first mayor of Wellington, and before leaving London he had been appointed a local director of the Union Bank, which intended starting business in Wellington. His son George (Paul's father), who married Margaret Paul, took up land in Wellington and owned a farm extending from Island Bay to Athletic Park.

Also, without leaving Wellington to view it, he took up land at Porangahau on the East Coast and placed his two brothers, David and William, in charge of it. In fact he never saw his 32,000-acre Porangahau property. His son George (later Sir George) arrived at Porangahau in 1877 to take over from his uncles, and about three years later he was joined by his brother Paul. After the death of their father in 1880 they owned the land in partnership.

Edith and Paul were married on 6 January 1885 by the Rev. F. E. Telling-Simcox, the first vicar of Porangahau, who made the journey to Wellington to perform the ceremony. Their honeymoon was to Rotorua where they visited the Pink and White Terraces. Later they travelled by coach to Waipukurau and drove the twenty-eight miles from there to Porangahau by buggy. The road leading towards the coast wound over steep hills, dropped to boggy patches and was little better than a bullock track.

On the station a new house had been built to receive the bride, a two-storey straight-up-and-down box which, in later years, was twice built on to; and although there was much work to be done with plenty of staff to handle it, life was lonely for Edith. To one who had been used to having her friends and family about her, the station, situated on the coast six miles north of the small Porangahau settlement, was isolated. Most of the land was fern-covered with a small amount of manuka, scrub, and considerable amount of toetoe and flax.

By 1900 there were some 51,000 sheep on the property with up to 3,800 being put through the thirty-stand woolshed on a good day's shearing. The wool was taken seven miles to Blackhead where it awaited shipment in the wool storage shed. At Blackhead the reef gave reasonable shelter provided the sea was not too rough, and neighbours south and west also used this so-called port, some 3,000 bales of wool being shipped from there each year. At times there would be fifteen bullock drays on the beach in one day, which would have made a total of over 200 bullocks.

Stores came by ship to Blackhead twice a year and were brought in by surfboat. A bullock driver with a picked team then drove out into the sea and met the boat, collected the stores and brought them back to the wool storage shed, and from there to a vermin-proof storing place on the station. Flour came in 2-hundredweight sacks and tea in 50-pound chests.

The garden was developed over a large area, protected from the gales by a high macrocarpa hedge. There was an orchard which produced an abundance of all types of fruit, while vegetables were grown for the house and the men's whare. There was a large staff of shepherds, fencers, bullock drivers, cowboys, carpenters, and house servants, all of whom had to be housed and fed.

Edith's seven children were all born in the homestead, the first being Jessie Edith in 1886. Then came George Edward in 1888, the twins, Cyril Paul and Thomas Percy in 1890, and Helen May in 1893. After a gap of seven years Allen Maxwell (Joe) was born, but he died from tetanus two months before his tenth birthday. Lastly there was Eion Leslie, who was known as Jim.

During her confinements Edith's general health was watched by the Rev. F. T. Telling-Simcox, who was greatly interested in medicine. Universally known as Parson Simcox he became a legendary figure during the forty-three years he moved about the Porangahau district attending to the spiritual, medical, dental and sporting needs of his flock.

Until 1898 when a small dairy herd of Jersey cows was brought from Taranaki, butter was rarely made and, like most country people, they used dripping instead. When the herd allowed butter to be made it was kept in a large drainpipe sitting on bricks and buried in the ground. Cream to be made into butter was kept in enormous stoneware jars with lids. The butter churn was wooden, the clap-clap of the butter pats slapping the butter on to a large wooden tray, grooved to allow the buttermilk to run off, was a familiar sound. Later the cream was kept in cream cans in a concrete-lined cupboard in the side of a bank near the dairy on the south verandah.

There were fowls and chickens of all kinds on the property, a duckpond nearby and

Edith Blanche Hunter, *née* Morrah, 1862–1940, of Porangahau station where she went on marriage to Paul Hunter in 1885. Despite having servants, she was an indefatigable worker.

turkeys further out on the run. There was no butcher's shop in Porangahau, but pukeko, wild duck, quail and pheasants, pigeons and hares made good food for a man with a gun.

Edith's house had a large square wooden bathtub which was capable of taking young George, Cyril and Percy all at the same time. The water had to be heated at the kitchen range and then carried to the bath. At first she had a colonial oven, but later a Shacklock Orion stove, made in Dunedin, was installed. It had an oven on either side of the centre firebox, hotplates right across the top and a hot-water cistern set at the back.

As the children grew their education was attended to by a governess, but later the boys went to the Porangahau school and then to boardingschool in Wellington or Wanganui Collegiate while the girls went to Chilton St James in Wellington. When they were at home, transport about the countryside was in a yellow wagonette drawn by two horses, or sometimes three or four horses for heavy loads. There was a seat in front for the driver and one other person while the children and others climbed in the back and sat facing each other on long seats.

Edith went to Wellington once a year to stay with her parents, shop, and to visit the dressmaker. The journey meant a day's drive to Waipukurau, the night spent there and the next day by coach, later by train, to Wellington.

The Tavistock Hotel, Waipukurau, in the 1890s, where Edith Hunter would stay overnight on her annual visit from Porangahau to Wellington.

Highlights also came with visits by train to Napier, the first stage being to the Tavistock Hotel at Waipukurau where they would stay the night and leave the buggy in the stables. Next day they would take the train to Hastings and stay at the Carlton Club Hotel, or to Napier to stay at the Masonic Hotel.

Race meetings, which were grand affairs, would be attended. The women wore large hats and dresses to the ground, the frills and flounces of their skirts going down the centre front and continuing round the hem. A parasol completed the outfit in grand Edwardian style. Hunt balls were attended and friends were visited over a stay of several days before returning to Waipukurau, where they would be met at the station with the horses harnessed and ready for the journey out to Porangahau.

In 1904 a severe earthquake brought down all the station chimneys and caused much inconvenience in the preparing of food for so many hands.

In 1907 Paul Hunter brought the first motorcar into the Porangahau district—a six-cylinder red Minerva, very smart with acetylene lamps and a large brass horn, and with dickey seats to hold the large family. Ladies who rode in it wore fawn tussore silk dustcoats, scarves and veils to hold their hats on and to keep the wind from spoiling their complexions as they raced along at fifteen miles an hour.

Despite the fact that she had servants, Edith was never idle. She compiled a knitting book written in her own hand and containing the instructions for balaclavas, Kitchener socks, shawls and long petticoats for babies in complicated knitting and crochet patterns. She knitted for soldiers during the Boer War and World War I, for orphans, the Red Cross and for returned soldiers at the Pukeora Sanatorium, which was then newly opened.

There was her family to knit for too, and an endless amount of mending to be done. Ironing was a tremendous task where irons heating on the stove were carried to the table to cope with huge damask tablecloths, tablenapkins, calico camisoles and frilly petticoats. There were the stiff collars for the men, and nightgowns and nightshirts with frills and tucks.

In 1908 Paul and George Hunter decided to separate their interests and, after a partnership of twenty-eight years, divided the station, each taking 16,000 acres. As the first and original homestead was on the portion taken by George he retained the name of Porangahau station while Paul's became known by the old Maori name for the district, Papakihau.

Paul, who was public-spirited to a high degree, took an interest in most committees and projects which concerned the advancement of the district. He died in 1926 and was buried in the private cemetery at Papakihau.

Edith lived until the age of seventy-eight years when she died on 5 March 1940 at Waipukurau and she too was buried at Papakihau. The land is now farmed by their descendants.

CHAPTER 22

Te Aitu Jury

Te Aitu was a young Maori girl of high rank. Noted for her beauty and her cloud of dark hair she was the daughter of the Wairarapa chief Te Whatahoro of Ngati Kahungunu, who was also a close relative of Wiremu Kingi. Her home was near Tauherenikau, about four miles eastward of Featherston.

One day the pa where she lived was overcome by a surprise raid from the Ngati Toa chief Te Rauparaha. Her father, Te Whatahoro, who was quietly inspecting his kumara patch at the time, was easily captured. As he was about to be slain he demanded the chieftain's privilege of being dispatched by his own mere, this being regarded as the most honourable means of death for those of high rank.

Te Aitu then experienced the horror of witnessing her father's head being split open with his own greenstone weapon, after which, with others, she was taken as a captive to Kapiti Island. She was living on this island fortress of Te Rauparaha when John Milsome Jury saw her, fell in love with her and, to use his own words declared that she had "the loveliest face he had ever seen".

John Milsome Jury was born in Great Towers Street, London, in 1814. He was a restless lad whose nature was full of the need for change, and leaving home at the early age of fourteen he set off on a life of adventure on the high seas and in far lands. After trips to Mauritius, the Mediterranean, Holland and New Zealand he returned to England to attend a nautical school and pass a navigation examination. He then sailed in the *Thetis* for the Sandwich Islands. He returned to London but soon sailed again with the *Thetis* when, now aged between sixteen and seventeen, he was the youngest boat-steerer in the whaling fleet.

The *Thetis* arrived at the Bay of Islands in 1830 and here John and another lad named Tatham deserted ship by swimming ashore, pushing before them their clothes and worldly possessions packed in a tub. On landing they hid in the bush but soon found themselves in a bad plight from hunger and the millions of mosquitoes. In desperation they decided to return to the ship but it was too late—she was already sailing out of the bay.

They then risked lighting a fire, and this led to their being discovered by Maoris. When their legs and bodies were felt the boys were sure they were doomed to be killed and eaten. However, the Maoris were good to them and they soon learned that they were to be kept and traded for guns and ammunition with the first European vessel that came along.

The whare in which they were held captive was built on a very sandy place. One night they dug their way out with their hands and ran away, fortunately finding a

101

refuge with Gilbert Mair senior, an early settler and trader in the Bay of Islands, who took the boys to a mission station.

After a while young Tatham returned to England but John decided to stay on in New Zealand. He was soon again at sea, navigating in northern waters until he went down the East Coast to Mahia where he hoped to trade corn, pigs and flax to European vessels. This was not successful as the ships were few on account of fears of the Maoris, so from Mahia he went to Nelson.

He was present at the great fight at Cloudy Bay between Te Rauparaha and Te Rangihaeata and the two southern chiefs, Taiaroa and Tuhawaiki (otherwise known as Bloody Jack). It was on one of his trips to Kapiti that he married the lovely Te Aitu, and it is possible that Te Rauparaha traded her for goods.

Soon after the customary Maori marriage Te Aitu, John, and a mate named Dicky Prouse, sailed in a whaleboat from Kapiti to Palliser Bay. The bar of the Wairarapa lake was open, enabling them to sail through and up the Ruamahanga River to land eventually at Charles Robert Bidwill's residence near the banks of the river. Here the party was hospitably entertained.

The next morning the journey was continued with Te Aitu directing the whaleboat to an island of some fifty-five acres in extent in the Ruamahanga River. It was not far from her former home and she claimed ownership of the land. To prove her claim she directed John to a certain hollow tree where, she said, he would find the historical greenstone hoe which was an heirloom of her family and had been hidden there before her capture by Te Rauparaha.

The ancient hoe was found and is still in the possession of her descendants. It is of rough-hewn greenstone, measuring ten and a half inches across, and eleven inches from the base to the top of the shaped handle. This type of hoe was used only by chiefs of high rank to start off the new kumara cultivations.

The land became known as Jury's Island, but owing to the changed course of the river it is no longer an island; although it has now passed into the hands of other people it is still known as Jury's Island.

Here John built their first primitive home. Lacking timber, it was built of clay. Te Aitu's first baby was born there, a son whom they named John Albert, and her second, a daughter, was named Annie. For a time her husband settled down to establish himself, throwing his natural energy into his surroundings and planting bluegums that are now said to be among the largest in New Zealand.

However, his restlessness had not yet been tamed and in 1848 the sensational accounts of the Californian goldfields lured him away from Te Aitu. He joined a party with such men as S. Revens, R. Kemble, Sam White and others from the Hutt and Wellington, hired a vessel and sailed across the Pacific. The venture ended in a dead loss. After various adventures while working in the diggings, during which time he was once close to being murdered, he returned to New Zealand and to Te Aitu in 1851.

This time he really settled down to farming and about 1854 purchased from the Government the 800 acres which were to become the Glendower property. The land, at that time mainly flax and fern, was purchased for 10s an acre, but when the survey was complete it was found to be 100 acres short. After heated correspondence that

Bluegums planted by Te Aitu
Jury's husband at Jury's Island.
A modern photograph.

went on for nearly ten years, he was granted a further 100 acres on Kokotau flat in recompense, irrespective of the difference in value of the land.

John always held firmly to the belief that the Maoris should not part with their land and steadfastly refused to purchase any of their ground. He insisted that his family follow this practice and even preferred that they should not claim any of their mother's inherited property.

Te Aitu once pointed to a large area in Greytown, now very valuable and known as Kuratawhiti Street, telling John that it was all hers and begging him to take possession of it. He declared it to be useless—all swamp and flax—no good to him or anyone else. It is now a rich area of farms and fruit orchards, lovely homes and gardens.

After John returned from California Te Aitu, in due course, presented him with another son whom they named Charles Joseph. She died not long after his birth, and after her death John set forth for the last time on more travels.

Of her three children, John Albert grew to be a man of splendid physique and presence and was known as "Handsome Jack". At one time he was a ward of Sir George Grey and later became a Native Assessor at Wanganui.

Annie married Joseph Oates, a sheepfarmer of Parkvale and later of Taumata, an island formed by the division of the Ruamahanga River near Kokotau.

Charles Joseph, the youngest child, married Elizabeth Oates, the sister of his brother-in-law Joseph, and after her death he married Emily Burch. He eventually purchased Glendower from his father, and through him the descendants of Te Aitu are still on the land.

103

CHAPTER 23

Riperata Kahutia

Riperata Kahutia, born in 1839, was the daughter of Kahutia, a chief of Te Aitanga-a-Mahaki, and his wife, Uaia of Te Aitanga-a-Hauiti tribe of Uawa, Tolaga Bay. Descended from a long line of chiefs she developed into a tall handsome woman with dark wavy hair, straight brows and with the moko markings on her chin.

During the 1850s, while still in her teens, she married Mikaera Turangi, the son of Paratene Turangi, the chief who became the protector of John William Harris, the founder of Poverty Bay. Years later Harris described Paratene as being the most truthful and the most reliable Maori with whom he had ever dealt.

After leaving Tolaga Bay Riperata's early married life was spent at Makauri, seven miles west of Gisborne. She had two children—a son named Parekeiha and a daughter, Heni Materoa, who later became Lady Carroll (6).

A chieftainess in her own right, Riperata was the victor at the last Maori battle, which took place on the banks of the Taruheru River, where the Lytton Road bridge now stands. The battle was over a land dispute. In 1857, with her parents, brother and sister, her sister's husband and her own husband, she sold land to Mr H. S. Wardell who was the first resident magistrate in Poverty Bay. The land, bought on behalf of the Crown for £85, consisted of 57 acres backed by the Taruheru River and comprised the area subsequently used for the Makaraka cemetery and the Makaraka domain.

The deed, signed with a cross by Kahutia and his family, stated: *Now we have fully considered wept over and bidden farewell to and entirely given up the land bequeathed to us by our ancestors with its streams lakes waters timber minerals pasture plains and forests with its fertile spots and barren places and all above and all below the surface of the said land and everything thereunto pertaining we have entirely given up under the shining sun of this day as a lasting possession to Victoria the Queen of England and to the Kings or Queens who may succeed her for ever.*

In 1864, with the threatening advance of Hauhau rebels towards Poverty Bay, Riperata decided it would be wise to move to a more inhabited area of the district. The tribe therefore left Makauri and went to Turanganui, as Gisborne was then known, and established a pa at the mouth of the Waikanae Stream where they were joined by the people of Te Arai pa.

The men then went out to work on the surrounding properties during the day and returned to the pa each night. Across the river at Kaiti was the pa of Hirini te Kani, and at that time these were the only two large pas in the vicinity known to be loyal to the white people.

Riperata, whose word was law, had various pas in the district and spent her time moving between them. With other chiefs she eventually sold to the Crown what became officially known as Turanganui No. 2, the land extending up the right bank of the Turanganui as far as the junction of the Waimata and the Taruheru, and then up the Taruheru almost to Lytton Road, then striking towards the Waikanae Swamp, and east along the Waikanae or Mullet Stream. The purchase money for this land that became Gisborne City was £2,000.

At that time there were few white people in the district, while the outskirts of the settlement were a tangled mass of manuka and fern. The richness of the Poverty Bay flats was about to be appreciated and Riperata, who owned them, was considered a liberal landlady.

She was a wealthy woman whose knowledge of the English language was very limited. Her affairs were handled by a trustee. When she needed cash she went to this well-known early Gisborne resident and signed for him papers which she understood to be receipts for the cash received but which, in reality, were land transfers cunningly presented. In this disgraceful manner she was tricked into selling various areas of land to a Pakeha whose name is still well remembered by her descendants.

She also suffered through Te Kooti. In 1866 when this troublesome individual was shipped away to the Chatham Islands with other prisoners, Riperata's father-in-law Paratene Turangi was the man who ordered Te Kooti to go aboard the ship. The

Riperata Kahutia, 1839–87, wife of Mikaera Turangi and mother of Lady Carroll (6). In the late 1870s she journeyed to England to fight—and win—a land claim before the Privy Council.

rebel escaped from the Chathams in 1868 and, after the Matawhero massacre, turned for revenge on some of his own tribesmen.

He went to Oweta pa where Paratene Turangi and other chiefs were living at the time. As the old man approached him Te Kooti held out a hand in mock greeting while the other hand, held behind him, gripped a tomahawk. "Greetings, my father," Te Kooti is reputed to have said while he stroked Paratene's cheek as if in affection. "Greetings, my father, you who uttered the words—*go to the boat*." He then swung the sharp tomahawk with a terrible blow which almost decapitated Paratene as he fell lifeless to the ground.

As the years passed Riperata became a notable advocate in the Native Land Court where she gained much experience in arguing the cause of her people. During the late 1870s she became involved in a dispute concerning land and, despite her restricted knowledge of English, she personally took the case before the Privy Council. This meant leaving the warmth of Poverty Bay and voyaging to the coldness of England, but undaunted, she took her own interpreter with her, stood fearlessly in the Court to conduct her own case in Maori—and won it.

When she returned she built a large house at Waikanae and then imported a staff of fourteen from England to run it. White settlement had by then brought many new things to Gisborne and these fascinating amenities she proceeded to enjoy. But for only a short time as she died on 1 June 1887, at the age of forty-eight.

When Riperata died it was computed that she owned twice as much land as had been awarded to her by birthright. A possible reason for this is that she took her own lands out of the common pool but still retained her share in the tribal lands, and through this strategy her descendants now benefit.

On Maori land formerly occupied by the Awapuni pa, and where Lytton Road turns near the Poverty Bay golf course, an angel stands with outspread wings. It commemorates Riperata Kahutia, an outstanding woman of the Maori people.

Memorial at Gisborne to Riperata Kahutia, "a chieftainess in her own right."

CHAPTER 24

Sarah Lambert

Sarah Fenn, of Slough Farm in Essex, was born in 1823. A short, slim woman with blue eyes and a touch of bronze to her hair, for many years she had been courted by Alfred Lambert.

Alfred, born in 1820, was a tall, broadshouldered man who, from his photograph, appears to have gone grey at an early age. He came from Ardleigh, also in Essex, where he worked on farms and spent a great deal of his time handling sheep.

One day during the early 1850s his eye was caught by a newspaper advertisement which called for a man experienced with sheep to go to New Zealand. The advertiser was Henry St Hill, the resident magistrate of Wellington who, with his brothers Ashton and the Rev. Harry Woodford St Hill, had taken up the leasehold of the 40,000-acre Whangaehu property which lay on the east coast in the Porangahau district.

Alfred applied for the position and was accepted, the arrangements taking many months to complete on account of the time his application took to reach New Zealand and for the acceptance to reach England.

A few months before they were due to leave Sarah and Alfred were married. They sailed on the *Cornwallis*, and for Sarah the six-month voyage was not uneventful because, as the ship shuddered and rolled through the waves, her first baby was born. Later, as she held him in her arms and gazed at the vast expanse of blue, she decided to call him Alfred Ocean.

The vessel reached Tasmania at last and there they disembarked for a short period while Alfred arranged for the shipment of 500 in-lamb Merino ewes which had been ordered by the St Hills and were to be taken to Whangaehu. The voyage was then continued reaching Wellington about 1854, and no doubt at least one of the St Hill brothers was on the shore to greet their new employees and to look over the ewes.

The animals would then be rested for a short time to allow them to regain their land legs after the tossing on the Tasman, and then mustered again for the long trek to their new grazing land. The party to drive them consisted of Ashton, the younger brother of Henry St Hill, Alfred and Sarah Lambert, the latter carrying her baby, who had become known by his second name, Ocean. A packhorse carried flour and other provisions while a saddlehorse enabled Sarah to ride occasionally.

The slow journey began with the flock making its way from what is now the heart of Wellington City towards the Hutt Road, which at that time was little more than a wide, rough track winding through patches of rock at the foot of the hills. The tide allowed no resting on this stretch until the curve of Petone beach was reached, but here a short halt was possible and then they went on again, slowly round the harbour towards the high cliffs at Pencarrow.

Many obstacles now made a clear track round the shore impossible. The coast was lined in most places by sheer walls broken at places into steep gullies. Heavy forest covered the hills but at times the flat top of a bluff was accessible from either end which enabled the drovers to get the flock over, rather than round, a point which the sea made impassable at its base.

There were also deep streams and rivers to be crossed, and before reaching the mouth of the Mukamuka River a long detour had to be made on account of high cliffs; then, having worked back to the mouth of the river, the drovers encountered huge rocks forming a further series of obstacles to be negotiated.

After the difficulties at the Mukamuka River they turned their backs to the sea for a period to face many hill saddles. The usual route taken by the sheep of those early days then led into Wainuiomata, near Orongoronga, and then turned back to Lake Onoke which at that time was open to the sea, and where they were ferried across by Maoris. By this time the animals were so tired they were easily caught, tied and placed in the canoes.

After this they came to a dangerous tunnelled point which jutted into the sea. Known as Cole's Hole it had been named after the Rev. Mr Cole who had visited that part of the country some years earlier. Even when the tide was right out riders had to enter the sea, and if there was a swell nobody attempted to pass. The raising of the coast during the 1855 earthquake took away much of the danger from Cole's Hole.

Te Kopi harbour was later reached and then came a further slow inland trek over more hills, down more gullies, through swamps, over streams and along rivers with their numerous crossings until they finally came out on the coast some miles below Castlepoint. From there the journey was mainly along the coast.

Through all these difficulties Sarah cooked for the men over open fires or in the camp oven and cared for little Ocean. And although the saddlehorse was led along for her she found it necessary, because of the terrain, to walk most of the way. The weather was inclined to be cold and there were times when it was impossible to keep dry, particularly when the wind blew gusts of sleet from the south.

At some point along the route the journey was brought to a halt by the sight of a lamb, and when a second one appeared the drovers realised the whole flock was about to increase. This slowed the pace considerably and caused the journey from Wellington to Whangaehu to take as long as three months. Provisions carried with them began to dwindle but they were fortunate in being able to procure food from the numerous Maori settlements passed on the way. Such delicacies as crayfish, wild berries, tender heart of nikau palms, pigeons, eels, fernroot, kumara and bread made from raupo or fern-root helped to supplement their diminishing stores. There were also pipis, mussels, oysters, sea eggs and pauas, but coupled with all this assistance from the Maoris came the problem of guarding the ewes and lambs from Maori dogs.

Whangaehu was reached at last. The property, all leasehold with many Maori owners, was mainly high undulating land with ferncovered hills that swept down to the sea. A raupo-and-sod hut was built on the bank of the Kaitoki Stream, a tributary of the Porangahau, about one and a half miles south of the pa which also is south of the river. After seeing them settled in it Ashton St Hill returned to Wellington leaving Alfred in charge of the station.

Sarah was the only white woman living in that part of the district. With baby Ocean in her arms she probably stood gazing up at the hills but at that time she did not realise that Whangaehu had one hill with the longest name in the world. Its seventy-seven letters, Taumata-whaka-tangihangi-koauau-o-Tamatea-turi-pukaka-pikimaunga-pokai-whenua-kitana-kahu, mean "the hill on which Tamatea with the big knees, who roamed the country, played his lament on his flute to the memory of his brother".

Sarah may have found the isolation too hard to bear, because after a short time of living in the raupo whare they decided to move inland a little and, if possible, to the other side of the Porangahau where there was Maori settlement. But as this meant they would be living on land not included in the lease the Maoris tried to prevent them from crossing the river.

In the meantime it had come to the ears of Rawenia, a woman of high rank living in the pa, that there was a white baby across the river. Rawenia had never seen a white baby and she was intrigued by the thought of the small, pale infant. She went across the river and before long was holding the child in her arms, crooning over it as she talked to Sarah, who had already picked up a few Maori words. The result was that Rawenia, known in the Porangahau pa as Queen Rawenia, ordered the men to help the Lamberts over the river, thus making Sarah the first white woman to live at Porangahau.

Sarah and Rawenia became good friends, and when Sarah's next sons, Thomas Gersham and later Henry Arthur arrived, Rawenia was there to help her. The nearest doctor was at Napier, many miles away by Maori tracks, and Sarah learned to make her own medicines from native herbs. If she became ill Rawenia was there at once to nurse her. Her first daughter, Mary Ann Elizabeth, was born in 1859, and in 1860 Jemima Amelia arrived, followed by Eleanor Jane in 1862.

Conditions, for many years, were extremely primitive. Cooking was done outside over an open fire or in the three-legged camp oven, water had to be carried from a stream, lighting was provided by slush lamps made from a tin in which clay was placed and then filled with fat, the wick being a piece of old rag.

Sarah also learnt to expect mail and stores only once a year when they were left by the coastal vessel at either Whangaehu or Blackhead. The same ship took away the wool. A dozen boxes of matches cost 5s. Tea was 7s a pound. It was sweetened with wild honey and if tea ran short they made a sort of beverage from wheat browned in the camp oven and then crushed in a sack until it was powdered. Wheat when harvested was threshed and ground in a small handmill for flour. Wild turnips grew in the bush and vegetables were grown in a small garden plot. Clothing was scarce and expensive, but food from wild pigs, native birds and fish was plentiful.

Relations between Alfred Lambert and the Maoris were always very friendly and a good trade developed between them. For some years Alfred shipped supplies of Indian corn, potatoes, onions and pigs to Wellington by a small craft which managed to get into and up the Porangahau. But as time went on he became dissatisfied with these small gains and decided it would be an excellent speculation to load one of the craft with a full cargo which would return him a much larger sum. Unfortunately the vessel was wrecked and the whole cargo lost. Some time after this he gave up the charge of the Whangaehu sheep and settled on 150 acres of land he had bought in 1860 when Porangahau suburban sections had been offered for sale.

Sarah's next baby, Maria Charlotte, was born in 1866, and Unica Maud Doria in 1867. Then there were twins who died at an early age. Sarah's children were all born under primitive conditions but Rawenia was usually there to help her. By the late 1860s conditions had begun to improve a little thanks to the arrival of more settlers. A store had been opened at Porangahau by John White, who was also the postmaster, and mail was coming in every week.

During the early 1870s there were times when the local Maoris, as well as the settlers, feared the arrival of Hauhau rebels. On these occasions the white people collected what arms and ammunition they could, and gathered to spend the nights together in a whare while the local Maoris hid their wives and children in the flax along the river-bank. Fortunately real trouble never arrived.

Nevertheless the time came when Te Kooti paid a so-called friendly visit to the Porangahau pa. For five years after his pardon in 1883 the former rebel developed the habit of moving about the countryside preaching, prophesying and practising the laying-on of hands. With his bodyguard and numerous followers these unwelcome visits to the various pas were likened to the arrival of a horde of locusts which left the pa impoverished of food, and amounted to a crafty technique of living off other peoples' efforts.

At Porangahau the Maoris followed the safer policy of feasting rather than refusing hospitality and produced their dried fish, preserved pigeons, pipis, mutton, beef and pigs with much Pakeha food bought from the store. While the visitation lasted Alfred and Sarah, like the other white settlers, barred their windows and doors at night.

When Alfred died at the age of eighty in 1900 the strong and lasting esteem in which he had been held by the Maoris was evident from the handsome mats placed on his coffin by Maoris who came from far and near to pay their last respects.

Sarah died in 1910 at the age of eighty-seven and by that time she had lost her eyesight and had been bedridden for some time. She was laid to rest beside Alfred in the Porangahau Anglican Church cemetery. The land on which their first home was built is still occupied by their descendants.

CHAPTER 25

Frances Sarah Lysnar

Frances Sarah Brewer, known to her friends as Fanny, was the daughter of Henry Newson Brewer of HM Customs at the port of Onehunga. In 1862 she married William Dean Lysnar, a man of high principles and scholastic ability, and with him she was to face a life of constant change.

Born in London in 1822 he was educated at St Mark's College, Chelsea, London, which had been established for the training of church schoolmasters. In 1848 he left London for New York and taught in schools there. In 1857 he was teaching in Australia, and in 1859 he took a passage from Melbourne to New Zealand, landing at Onehunga. The fare was 7 guineas.

On 16 February 1859 William opened in Auckland what he called The Commercial School, but soon after getting it into good working order another man opened in Hobson Street what he too called The Commercial School. William immediately published a notice changing the name of his school to The Lyceum. The lease of his section in Alten Road was for twenty-one years at a yearly rental of £9 5s.

A passage in his reminiscences states: *While riding one afternoon with my brother, Charles, in an omnibus from Auckland to Onehunga, he nudged me with his elbow. I turned towards him when he said in a low whisper, "Look in front of you." I did so and saw a serious countenance under a bonnet and veil. I said to him "Well, what is it, Charles?" After a short pause he explained, "Don't you know who it is?" I looked again and observed a face twitching and the eyes sparkling, then, like a flash I recognised the personage to be Miss Frances Brewer, my engaged wife. She declared afterwards that it was her intention to sit quietly all the way, a distance of 9 miles, or until such time as I had left off stargazing and looked down on earthly things. My reply was, "It would ill accord with the scholastic dignity of the Principal of a large school to be peering under every lady's bonnet."*

When Fanny and William were married war was raging in the North Island and all available forces were being sent from Auckland to the front. The few police left did day duty only, while during the night the streets and outlying districts were patrolled by small bodies of armed men. From sunset to sunrise everybody was required to remain indoors.

Fanny's first child, George Henry, was born at The Lyceum in 1863. At that time William had an infection in his throat and found it necessary to retire from teaching for a while. He therefore gave up the school and let the larger portion to the Government for a printing office. The family moved to a house in Newton and their next child, Frances Brewer (Gypsy), was born there in 1864.

For a time William acted as a customhouse agent and then, his throat cured of its infection, they moved to New Plymouth where he took charge of a school under a private arrangement in Mr Shaw's house on Poverty Flat. This school was afterwards transferred by the Provincial Government to a building in Powderham Street, and of this he remained in charge. Fanny's third child, Ida Mary, was born there. William finished his private contract and the Province, "not being in present need of more education", they moved to Auckland where their next child, William Douglas, was born in 1867 at Onehunga.

In 1866 adverse conditions were brought about by the changing of the seat of Government from Auckland to Wellington, and in 1868 the mortgage on The Lyceum property was foreclosed. It was sold for less than £200, having cost William nearly £1,000, because the Government vacated the school building when they moved to Wellington. Fanny and William then moved to Whangarei with the intention of opening a school there, but within a few months they had returned to reopen The Lyceum in Alten Road. Fanny's next son, Frederick John, was born in 1869 in Summerside House on The Lyceum property.

At the end of that year they moved from The Lyceum to Wakefield Street, where William joined Mr McVeigh Baird of Wesley College. While they were living in Wakefield Street Edith Emma was born, in 1870, and Harold Godfrey in 1872. However, the position at Wesley was not a success and within a few months William had opened a school at the foot of Barrack Hill.

Then came the offer from Archdeacon L. W. Williams of the mastership of the Gisborne Public School, and in March 1872 they left Auckland in the schooner *Tawera* for Poverty Bay. The newly erected school stood at the corner of Lowe Street and Childers Road, with less than thirty children, including their own of school age, able to attend. William's annual salary was £150 while Fanny received £10 a year for teaching sewing.

A four-roomed house in Peel Street was bought from Captain Read for £100. This was enlarged and called the Cottage of Content, and Fanny's next child, Hilton Nesbit, was born there in 1873.

William and Fanny were soon held in high esteem by the people of Gisborne. At that time there was no resident clergyman in the entire district of Poverty Bay and by request William held divine service every Sunday, Archdeacon Williams giving him all instructions. Services were later moved from the Courthouse to the schoolroom, which had been enlarged to meet growing requirements. The school day also opened and closed with a prayer—but this, William was told by an inspector, was against the Education Act. He therefore compromised by introducing simple songs of an elevating tendency.

Fanny's sixth son, Wilfred Leonard, was born in the Cottage of Content in October 1874 but died in April 1875. About that time a favourable offer came to William from the committee of the Maori school at Omahu in Hawke's Bay and in June 1875 they moved from Gisborne to Napier. While driving in a coach with the whole family from Napier to Omahu the horses jibbed in the middle of the Tutaekuri River just beyond Taradale and they all had to be carried, one at a time, on horseback to the further bank.

When they drew near the schoolhouse they were welcomed by Maori children and

Renata Kawepo, who welcomed Frances
and William Lysnar at Omaho in 1875.
A portrait by Gottfried Lindauer.

adults of various ages who gathered round the coach. Fanny opened a large tin of
sweets and distributed them, much to the astonishment of her own children, who
never forgot the event. The Maori chief Renata Kawepo welcomed them at the house.
He had a large pig already killed and prepared which he sent to them from his own
house, also two live turkeys, a bag of potatoes, a large sack of flour and a pile of firewood which was already stacked in the yard at the back of the school.

Renata Kawepo, who had built the school, remained their good friend for the two
years they were at Omahu. The many interesting conversations they had with the chief
were interpreted by his relative, Airini Karauria, who spoke English well. When
Fanny's fourth daughter was born at Omahu in 1876 she was baptised Alice Olive
Airini.

To please the chief William opened evening classes for Maori adults but within a
short time an official protest against his system of adult Maori tuition came from the
Native Office. His reply that he was acting upon instructions from Renata Kawepa
brought no further complaint.

Although their relations with Renata Kawepo were so good it was thought better,
for various reasons, to move to Napier. They left Omahu in July, 1877 and William

opened a school in the Rechabite Hall. They lived at Chaucer House, where Fanny's fifth daughter (and eleventh child) was born in April 1878 but died three months later. About that time the new Free, Secular and Compulsory Education Act came into force with disastrous effects on private schools.

The following year, 1879, Fanny packed their belongings once more when William was appointed to take charge of a school at the old Whakato Maori mission station previously occupied by Bishop William Williams (51). The family sailed to Gisborne and on landing at the wharf were transferred with their furniture to a steam tug which took them up the Waipaoa to Whakato. On arrival they found a Maori family living in the orchard and had difficulty in getting into the school.

Trouble then arose when one day soon after their arrival a white man drove a cart into the school orchard and began loading it with the fruit. William ordered him off the place, but this annoyed some of the Maoris. That night a party of them surrounded the school buildings and tried to force an entry at the front door, where William stood waiting for them.

Fanny, who was very ill at the time, went into a fit of hysterics, uttering loud shrieks which rang through the schoolroom and caused the disturbers to imagine the devil was in the place. They left hastily, with the exception of one man who came forward with a blazing piece of wood to set fire to the building. William recognised him and the next day had an armed policeman out who arrested the man. The case came before the magistrate, the plea of the Maori's being their ownership of the land.

Soon after that the Lysnars moved to a section in Waerenga-o-kuri, where they built a comfortable whare on the flat part of the land near a running stream and close to bush for firewood. William took up private teaching in Gisborne but found the distance between the places too great so, in 1881, Fanny packed yet once more for a move to Gisborne.

For many years she had suffered ill health from a heart complaint for which the doctors could do very little but give her temporary relief. In 1889 she left for England accompanied by her eldest daughter, Gypsy, to consult several of the most eminent specialists on heart disease, but the London doctors were as puzzled with her strange sufferings as the doctors in New Zealand. One of them said, "Her heart was like a racehorse racing itself to death, and with her heart in such a condition she might die at any minute." They advised her to return to New Zealand as soon as possible, and this she did after a short visit to Brewer and Lysnar relatives.

In 1889 William bought a section on the Esplanade at Kaiti from Mr Mullooly. There he built Riverslea House, and Fanny returned from England to live in what was to be her last home. Her heart condition continued to puzzle the doctors and after a long and painful illness which extended over many years she was relieved of her sufferings when she died on 14 December 1898. She was long remembered by all who had known her.

Airini, the young Maori woman who had been so helpful to the Lysnars when they were at Omahu was the daughter of the chief, Karauria. She was a niece of Tareha and was closely allied by blood to other Ngati-Kahungunu chiefs including Tiakitai, Renata Kawepo, Te Moananui and others, which gave her a prestige and standing unique in Maori society. She was born about 1855 and during her early years lived at Omahu, near Hastings. In 1876 she met George Prior Donnelly who, at that time, was managing Gwavas station for A. S. G. Carlyon.

It is said that the meeting occurred one hot summer day when Airini, riding with a party of friends, breasted the brow of a hill to face a mob of sheep being driven from Gwavas to Omahu by Donnelly. George, who was a large handsome man, fell in love with her at first sight and they were married in 1877.

G. P. Donnelly was the son of Patrick Donnelly, a landed proprietor of Tipperary, Ireland. He was born at Brittus, an old family residence belonging to his mother's family, she being the daughter of John Prior of Waterford. George was educated in Limerick, and after the death of his father in 1862 he came to New Zealand with his mother, three brothers and three sisters. He farmed at Wairoa, leased property at Otahuhu, served in the New Zealand Cavalry during the Maori Wars and by 1866 had moved to Hawke's Bay. He was a man of immense energy, always awake and up before daylight.

Aftr her marriage Airini became known as Airini Tonore, the Maori version of Donnelly. A wealthy woman, she owned vast acres of land which enabled her husband to take up the leases of several properties. They took up residence at Crissoge on the Fernhill Road near Hastings, the place being named after a family property in Ireland.

Few white women lived in the style of Airini Tonore, and still fewer had her ability and beauty. She had maids to work in the house, gardeners to tend the grounds, the conservatory and glasshouse, grooms to care for the horses and carriage. She loved riding side-saddle and would take her horses to jump at the Canterbury A & P Shows. She was interested in racing, and she and her husband seldom missed a Wellington race meeting. Her only child, a daughter, also named Airini, was married from Crissoge when she became Mrs Perry.

The Donnellys also lived at Ngatarawa and from there moved to Ashbridge, a fine two-storeyed home on the hill at Taradale. This was bought from Henry Williams, a Napier businessman, and was surrounded by beautiful gardens which were cared for by two permanent gardeners, while on the flats below were the training stables. The name of the property was changed to, or perhaps reverted back to, the Maori name of Otatara.

Airini became well known for her lavish hospitality, and the Otatara home was the scene of most of their famous entertaining. The billiard room was fitted out as a lounge because she liked to keep her guests together, and while the billiard balls clicked the whiskey glasses were never empty. When George was away supervising their many properties she gave luncheon parties, dances and golfing parties. She loved golf and played a very good game.

She was also a prominent figure whenever illustrious European visitors were to be entertained, and in 1901 when the Duke and Duchess of York came to New Zealand the Donnellys went to Rotorua to meet them. They became friends and shortly afterwards, when the Donnellys toured Europe, the Duke and Duchess, with Their Majesties King Edward and Queen Alexandra, reciprocated their hospitality most royally. During that period, with her diamond tiara sparkling beneath the three ostrich plumes in her hair, Airini was presented at Court.

But far beyond her reputation as a social hostess was her celebrity as the champion of her people's cause. Her keen and able defence as she argued their rights in the Native Land Courts was acknowledged to be a revelation of advocacy and understanding of the law. It was also due to her influence with her people that ownership problems in the matter of the Heretaunga Plains were overcome.

Perhaps nothing showed her strength of character better than the way in which, despite her riches, she retained the esteem of both Maori and Pakeha people. At functions attended by the Governor she would farewell the royal representative and his suite, then ride across to her own people, squat on the ground with them and enjoy a good feed of pipis.

It is said that when she came to make her will Airini gave an airy wave of her hand and explained to her lawyer, C. P. Sherrett, "I leave my money to my people— George, he look after his own."

And so it was. She died in 1909 at the early age of fifty-four.

Airini Tonore, *circa* 1855–1909, wife of G. P. Donnelly of Otatara. "Her keen and able defence of her people's rights in the Native Land Courts was acknowledged to be a revelation of advocacy and understanding of the law."

CHAPTER 26

Douglas Mary McKain

In 1789 the wife of John Dunmore of Glasgow, Scotland, bestowed upon her infant daughter the rather masculine name of Douglas Mary. She herself may have been a Douglas or had Douglas connections. Apart from the fact that the child was brought up in the Protestant faith very little is known about her early years, but at the age of twenty-five she married a young Catholic named William McKain.

William was the son of Daniel McKain, who was of French origin and whose family had previously spelt their name Mequesne. The marriage took place on 26 April 1808, at the church of St Mary of the Castle, Guernsey, Channel Islands.

After their marriage William and Douglas Mary lived at Cheadle, Staffordshire, a village of coal pits and metal manufacturing. Here they raised a family of seven sons and five daughters, but three of the sons died, it is thought of tuberculosis which was so prevalent in those days. Then, at the age of fifty-one in 1837, William was killed in a hunting accident.

Perhaps it was the loss of husband and three sons which caused her to consider the New Zealand Company's glowing word-pictures and posters of the new colony where summer reigned for ever. Her remaining four sons were keen to answer the call of adventure and emigrate to the warmer climate, and by the end of 1840 she had decided to sail to New Zealand with them. Then, after the sad parting from her four married daughters—Julia, Mary, Douglas and Eliza—the new year of 1841 saw her on the *Olympus* with her sons, John Ward, James Buchanan, Frederick Dunmore, Isaac Septimus, and her youngest daughter, Robina (47). While at sea in January she wrote to those she had left at home, her letters now offering a distant view of early shipboard life:

My Beloved Children,
As there is a ship in sight I take the opportunity of writing a few lines to let you know we are all in good health and spirits. I wrote to you and to Mary, to Mrs Waugh, and to Nathan Loton on the 10th of Jan. by the ship Whitby, *of London, bound for Cork. We passed five vessels that day. The captain went on board the* Whitby *with six of the cabin passengers and then the* Whitby *came actually alongside of the* Olympus *to the great terror of most of us who could see the danger of two such ponderous machines coming so near each other. To add to the terror of the two commanders, the vessels refused to answer the helms and I fully expected the next move would crush them together. The seamen had to cut some of our ropes, and then to our great joy the space between the vessels widened. The* Whitby *dropped astern and soon after our captain and the other*

117

gentlemen came on board and brought a Cape sheep with them. The Whitby *soon after left us, and we gave them three cheers which her crew returned.*

We spoke to only one of the other vessels, the Jane, *of Glasgow, bound for New Zealand. She came near us at 6 o'clock in the evening, and our captain invited her captain to breakfast with him next morning, which invitation was accepted, and the* Jane *lay to for us all night. But we kept her at a respectful distance as we had been dreadfully alarmed by the too near approach of the* Whitby.

Next morning brought the captain and three gentlemen of the Jane, *bringing to our captain a present of fruit which they had brought from St Jagos where they had remained two or three days. I got one of the bananas which is a most delicious fruit. They stopped on board about two hours and then left us. They saluted us with one of their cannons, which our people returned by a discharge of small arms. She was soon out of sight as she was a much faster sailer than the* Olympus.

On the 15th Jan. we crossed the Line at 9 o'clock in the morning. Our superintendent, Dr Featherston, ordered a glass of rum to be served out to each adult. In the evening the sailors claimed the privilege of introducing Neptune and his wife on board. But there was no shaving or any ribaldry to extort money. Everyone who chose to give did it freely. I gave them 1/-, as much as I could afford. The sailor collected about £3 and they finished the evening's amusement with a song.

Your brothers and sister are well and happy. James works very hard helping the second mate getting the emigrants' stores out of the hold. If you were to see him sometimes you would think he was just come out of a coal pit.

I wrote you an account of the storm we encountered in the Bay of Biscay, but the danger from the Whitby's *proximity to us on the 10th was more apparent and the captain was more alarmed.*

We have plenty of good provisions. The water is getting very bad but we have it mixed for drinking with lime juice and sugar one day and next day half pint of grog.

On the 27th Jan. there was a fine boy born on board and he and the mother are doing well. On 29th we got out of the tropics so the most unhealthy part of our voyage is over. There have been three deaths on board, all children, which I think is not many in so long and perilous a voyage.

One of the emigrants has a violin and plays on it most evenings and many of the people dance on deck. We have singing and jokes of all sorts, and as a contrast, a man was put in irons one day for striking his wife. The assistant superintendent is not liked and has, this week, been suspended for striking one of the emigrants. So you see we have sport of all sorts.

Robina is teaching a class of children.

Kiss the dear children for me and tell them that one day the sea all around the ship was covered with great fish called porpoises. There seemed to be thousands of them. We have also seen a great number of what the sailors call black fish which are very large.

I have got into the way of making nice light bread. The steward gave me a small piece of yeast and showed me how to mix it and from time to time I save a piece and by that means have a constant supply of fresh bread. If we had double the quantity of flour and half the quantity of biscuits we should do well. Each adult has 2 lbs of flour a week, but I soak a little biscuit in water to a pulp and mix it with my flour either for bread or pudding. But I did not bring spices or carbonate of soda with me which was a great neglect. Oh! we do so long for a little cheese. The little we brought with us was much appreciated while it lasted.

There is some misunderstanding between the superintendent and the captain. They do not associate, nor do they dine at the same table. But I do not know but what it is in our favour, as the doctor insists on our rations being served out according to the scale in our rules. Our potatoes are all used and we have rice instead. Our tea is served out dry, and our coffee raw, and we roast it ourselves, which we much prefer to do.

Captain White says if this wind continues we shall be in New Zealand in another month.

The boys have lost five caps since we came on board. One of the cabin passengers lost two hats overboard in one day. I have lost several towels when drying them, a new flannel waistcoat of John's and an apron of Robina's. By-the-by she is a great favourite on board. John often wishes you were all with us. So do I if you could have come safely. I think Robina was never so happy in all her life.

April 20th, 1841. Here we are at last. We anchored about 10.30 this morning, but will not get on shore this day. A vessel sails for London tomorrow so I embrace the opportunity of sending this by her. I will write to you by the next opportunity.

God bless you, my dear children. Kiss your dear little boys for me. We are all well and in high spirits. The vessel I send this by is called the Lord Brougham. *Write to me every month. The place looks very mountainous, but the people who came on board give a good account of it. We have had an excellent doctor and captain.*

Your affectionate Mother, D. M. McKain, *Adieu, Adieu*

Douglas Mary's next letter to her daughters in England gives a glimpse of her early days in the colony:

My dear Children,

The Olympus *entered Cook's Straits at 8 o'clock at night, 17th April and we cleared them on the 18th at 10 p.m. The approach to New Zealand is most unpromising. On the morning of the 19th, when I went on deck I saw no appearance of vegetation on the land, but a bold, barren rocky or clay coast on every side. All the emigrants were very low-spirited. On that day Epuni's son, Henry, came on board to pilot the vessel into harbour.*

We anchored that night for the first time since we left the Downs. The next morning the anchor was weighed again and we soon entered Port Nicholson where a very different prospect met our view. The mountains are completely covered with timber, reaching within a quarter of a mile of the water's edge. Here are the most beautiful shrubs in full bloom, although I am told this is reckoned one of the worst months in the year, and it is indeed a season of storms.

We finally anchored on the 20th. On the 21st it began to blow hard, and towards night the gale increased to such a height that although we had both anchors out the vessel drifted dreadfully and we were every hour in expectation of being dashed on the rocks.

But, thank God, the wind abated and we all came safely on shore on the 23rd, and as fine a day as any I ever knew in England in summer. The fine weather continued for a few days and then it began to blow and rain, and the rain came pouring down through the roofs of the Depot houses until everything was wet and miserable. And what makes it more wretched there are no fireplaces in the houses. We make fires out of doors to cook by.

On the morning of the 25th we were ordered to attend at the camp stores for our rations. John and James brought home 35 lbs of beef and pork, with tea and sugar for Robina and myself, and on the following week we had the same rations served out by the Company's agent. Then we drew from the ship's stores that had been stopped over and above what we made use of on board—31 lbs of rice, 34 lbs split peas, 5 lbs of raisins, 350 lbs of biscuits and a quantity of pickled cabbage, mustard and salt, with 131 lbs of salt beef.

I have taken a piece of land as level as your house floor. The lease cost £4, the rent £12 a year for seven years. John and James are busy building a cottage on it. It is a most delightful situation. We have a full view of the harbour.

On the 20th May the Lord William Bentinck, *one of the Company ships, entered the harbour just that day month after the* Olympus *and on that day I received letters from my dear, dear children. It was your birthday and wedding day, dear Douglas; and it was Cheadle May Fair Day. Oh, I wept bitterly when reading your affectionate letters. Oh, may almighty God comfort you. My dear Mary, I shall never ask you to follow me.*

This is the winter here, yet some days it is most delightful and the sun quite hot. Then again it blows till we think the cottage will go over.

Things are very dear here. Skim milk 8d per quart. They do not sell the new milk— they make butter from the cream which they sell at 5/- per lb. Salt butter is 2/3 per lb, and 9d the 2 lb loaf. Soap is 7d and soda 8d per lb.

The cabin passengers are very dissatisfied with their situation as their sections of land lay a great way from the town. Some of them are selling their land for a third of what they paid for it, and some are going off to Sydney.

Captain White and Dr Featherston have given us a most excellent character to Colonel Wakefield and other gentlemen. The captain came to see me at the Depot and when he saw me so uncomfortable he told me that I must go on board and stay as long as the ship was in harbour. But I did not accept his kind invitation as I could not make myself content away from the family.

I have now been nearly two months in the colony. This is Whit Sunday and it is very cold. I think of you every hour of the day, and when I think of my dear native land, in a moment I seem to be there, but ah, recollections at hand soon hurry me back. No, not to despair, but to sorrow and love.

Oh, how I picture in my mind Julia busy with her dear little family, Mary always busy, Douglas at her domestic concerns and poor Eliza, what of her? Then I see you get together in deep lamentation over your poor old mother, your sister, Robina, and your four dear brothers. Your brothers never regret having come out here. Frederick and Isaac are delighted. John and James seem very happy but Robina and myself sigh after England. At least, I sigh for the loved ones I left there. God bless you my dear ones. Pray for the exiles in New Zealand.

D. M. McKain.

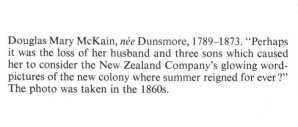

Te Aro Flat, Wellington, 1847. Here the widowed Douglas Mary McKain set up house in 1841, moving to the Esk Valley in 1860.

Douglas Mary McKain, *née* Dunsmore, 1789–1873. "Perhaps it was the loss of her husband and three sons which caused her to consider the New Zealand Company's glowing word-pictures of the new colony where summer reigned for ever?" The photo was taken in the 1860s.

Douglas Mary later acquired several cottages in Wellington but the severe earthquakes of 1848 and 1855 damaged them to the extent of costing her over £70 for repairs. Her joy was great when, during the 1840s, two of her daughters who had been left in England came to New Zealand with their husbands and children. They were Julia, who had married Joseph Torr (who was later the first member of the County Council for Petane in Hawke's Bay) and Mary, whose husband John McCarthy, was well to the fore in school and church building.

In 1850 Robina and James, who by then were both married, went with their families to live at The Spit at Ahuriri in Hawke's Bay. By 1855 other members of the family had joined them and had taken up sections of land at Petane in the Esk Valley.

In 1860 Douglas Mary too went to live in the Esk Valley. She spent her remaining years living with first one and then another of her children, sharing their anxieties during the troublesome times of Hauhau uprisings when the fight took place at Eskdale in 1866. She died in 1873 at the age of eighty-four and was buried in the Eskdale cemetery.

CHAPTER 27

Helen McKenzie

Helen Ross was born in Rosemarkie, Rossshire, Scotland, in 1811, and was thirty-three when she married John McKenzie; in those days she would have been considered almost an old maid. The banns were called by the Rev. Simon Fraser, minister of Fortrose.

John was two years older than Helen, having been born in 1809 at Contin in Rossshire. He was a well educated man who had held the position of schoolteacher or tutor, and it is understood that when he was a young man he travelled on the Continent engaged as a companion tutor. By 1848 he had made a change and was in business as a grocer and dealer in the town of Rosemarkie, close to Fortrose.

After three years Helen and John decided to emigrate to New Zealand, and with this serious undertaking in view she made preparation for the venture by training herself as a nurse. There were few nurses at that period and the knowledge she acquired was to prove invaluable in years to come.

Testimonials to the family's integrity were obtained by John from Inverness businessmen, the one written by Alexander Wood, Moderator, cautiously stating:—
that they conducted themselves while here in a suitable and becoming manner and that there is nothing known to us to hinder their Reception into any Christian Family of Society wherever Providence may be pleased to order their lot. By that time they had three children, Isabella, Donald, and young John, who was little more than a baby.

Their passages were booked on the fine new ship *Agra,* sailing on her maiden voyage from Plymouth at noon on 26 November, 1851. In those days passengers in the emigrant ships had to supply themselves with almost everything they might need on the voyage, although by that date the owners of new ships were providing mattresses, bolsters and a few cooking utensils. First-class passengers had food cooked for them but others had to do their own cooking at strictly regulated times, the firing being found at the ship's expense.

They set forth in a fair wind and after ten days at sea were near Madeira. December the 6th was a windy day that caused the ship to heave and rock as she breasted the white-crested waves. Helen, with five-year-old Bella, went down to the galley to prepare the family's lunch. Hearing a child crying, she told Bella to go back to the deck to find its mother.

Standing on the stove in the galley was a large square copper boiler filled with simmering soup enough for sixty people. The ship gave a violent lurch which sent Bella to the floor, and before she could rise to her feet the boiling soup had toppled from the stove and over her.

It is not difficult to imagine the agonising screams of the child as Helen flew to lift her from the scalding mess. Helen's feet, and hands were also badly burnt, but Bella's legs and feet were so bad that the skin came away with her stockings. After this accident both Helen and Bella were confined to their beds for six weeks, for four weeks of which they were unable to be moved, even to make their bunks.

Helen became ill with fever, and to complicate matters Johnny, the baby, would not stay a moment from her bed. Bella too was in such a high fever that her father wrote that it would not have hurt him so much to see her dead as to see her in the state in which she was after the accident. In fact she was so terribly injured that they did not expect her to live.

The days became hot as they neared the equator, the burning sun adding discomfort to the pain being endured in the stifling cabin. John and Donald slept in nothing but their nightshirts, and during one night Donald's restlessness caused him to fall out of his bunk which was about five feet above the floor. Fortunately he was not seriously hurt.

Little Bella's progress was slow but at last she recovered, which was more than could be said for two other children who were, as John wrote, "coffined" on the same day.

He also recorded that on 29 December he shaved, which rated in importance with the fact that on 19 February they were in sight of the hills of Van Diemen's Land. A week later they sighted New Zealand, anchoring in Wellington Harbour on 1 March 1852. Work and money were plentiful, they found. Wages for servant girls ranged from £14 to £20 a year, and on hearing of the ship's arrival people came in from the country hoping to hire domestic servants.

John and Helen began their life in the new country in Wellington. He advertised that he intended opening a store in Herbert Street while she advertised her services as a midwife. After a period in Wellington they moved to the Hutt Valley and opened a store in the vicinity of Taita. Their fourth child, a daughter whom they named Helen, was born there.

At that time the district was still mainly in forest, which began about half a mile from Petone beach and, apart from a few natural clearings, filled the entire valley. The trees were mainly totara, beech, rimu and kahikatea, with many of them being seventy-five to eighty feet in height to the first branches, and from six to seven feet in diameter. Crown grants of land were taken up by most of the settlers and the first electoral roll for 1854–55 records thirty-two householders living in the district. Christ Church, built of heart totara pitsawn in the local bush and hauled to the site by bullock dray, was erected to serve these people.

The valley was also inhabited by numerous Maoris with long memories that still harboured grievances caused by other white settlers. It was unwise to offend them in any way as one never knew how they would behave, and at that time they were doing their utmost to provide themselves with arms and ammunition. The maximum fine for selling a gun to a Maori was £200.

Helen always retained a vivid memory of the day when several large tattooed warriors paid her a visit when she was baking bread in the camp oven. They watched the process for some time but left quietly when she gave them some of the bread hot from the oven. This was not their only visit.

Her knowledge of nursing kept her in constant demand as there were few who could competently care for the sick or dress wounds. On one occasion, after giving assistance, she only just escaped being marooned by the flooded Hutt River by wading through the waters. John's services as an educated man and as a schoolteacher were also in demand by the settlers.

They were living at Taita at the time of the big earthquake in 1855. John was sitting in a chair near the fireplace when the river stones forming the chimney began to fall around him. Bella, Donald and Johnny, who had not yet gone to bed, scrambled under the table for shelter while Helen rushed to the next room to little Helen. Earthquakes were frequent in those days, and this one damaged most Wellington homes.

While living in the valley they paid £125 for twenty-six acres of land where the Silverstream railway station now stands, and they also owned at least one section at

Whangaehu homestead, built in 1874 for Helen McKenzie and her husband—a luxurious home compared with their earlier houses. A drawing by D. R. Neilson.

Upper Hutt. However, in 1862 they left the valley and moved to South Taratahi in the Wairarapa, where they took over a Crown grant of some 829 acres, two miles east of Carterton and known as Parkhill. The purchase involved dealings with Charles Rooking Carter, from whom John borrowed £200 for five years at 10½ per cent interest, his security being the land at Taratahi and Silverstream.

When they went to Parkhill the place was almost unfenced and the Maoris had formed the habit of helping themselves to the stock. Helen faced the problems common to all settlers' wives, isolation being only one of them, and life became a matter of constant hard toil to knock the place into shape and to make enough money to repay the loan and the interest.

In September 1867 Helen had to part with her elder daughter when Isabella was married to Henry James. He had been born at Treprisk Farm in Cardiganshire, Wales, and had run away from a stepmother when he was a boy. The wedding took place at the bride's home, the Rev. John Ross officiating.

John and Helen worked hard at Parkhill for eleven years before they sold in 1873 for £2,500 to Lewis Nix, the sale being witnessed by Henry James. By that time 550 chains of fences had been erected and the property had been divided into nine paddocks.

In the meantime John's agents had negotiated to buy a property for them at Whangaehu, a few miles out of Masterton, and they moved there in 1873. A new house was built for them the following year and John Jackson, the carpenter who worked on it, later married their younger daughter, Helen.

There was now much work to be done in the developing of the new property and in the building of the new home, and although John was now sixty-five and Helen sixty-three there was no thought of retirement. There was an unfortunate setback for John during 1874 when he had to have one of his feet amputated, the long-delayed after-effect of a boyhood incident when he had been knocked over a pile of stones by another lad. The leg had been injured and had always given sufficient trouble to prevent hard physical work. After the amputation he was restricted even more in the development of his new property, but he continued to do what he could until he died in 1884 at the age of seventy-five.

Helen lived until 1893 when, at the age of eighty-one, and having played her part in the early pioneering of the Wairarapa, she was buried beside John in the Masterton cemetery.

CHAPTER 28

Catherine Cochrane Maclaurin

Catherine Cochrane Macky, born at Otahuhu in 1866, was the daughter of William Macky who came from Coshquin, near Londonderry, Ireland. His two brothers, James and Thomas, had arrived in New Zealand in 1845 and 1849 respectively, and in 1853 William followed them in the *Cashmere*, arriving in Auckland where they were there to welcome him.

He entered the employ of a Mr Potter and was the first man to plough up Potter's Paddock which is now Alexander Park, Auckland. During that time he lived in a little stone house in Manukau Road almost opposite Greenlane junction. A short time later he was in charge of Baird's Wharf at Otahahu, from which much produce was taken down the Tamaki to Auckland.

In 1860 William married Anne Goodfellow, whose parents had come from Scotland in 1840 and whose father had walked from Wellington to Auckland to be in time for the first land sales. Their family eventually numbered ten children, Catherine, who was known as Kate, being their fourth daughter.

She was a small, dark girl with large brown eyes and a good sense of humour. She grew up in a home noted for its genuine hospitality where, despite the large family, there was always room for relatives from Auckland.

In 1873 her father purchased a property at Paterangi, about six miles from Te Awamutu, but employed a Mr Ryburn as manager until 1875, when he left Otahuhu to take over the place himself. The family then travelled in a springcart, their first stop being at Samuel Baird's farm at Ramarama and the next at Huntly. At Paterangi William Macky was the first man in the Waikato to grow turnips.

While her parents established a home for their growing family Kate spent much time with an aunt at Otahuhu for the sake of her education. She remained petite in build and at the age of twenty-one in 1887, she married William Gilbert Maclaurin.

William, born in the Shetland Islands about 1863, was the son of the Rev. Robert Maclaurin, and came to New Zealand with an aunt when about twelve years of age. When Kate met him he was in employment but had very little money and was living in a shack. Tall, slim, and of medium colouring, he was bearded and had a twinkle in his blue eyes. After their marriage Kate went with him to live in the shack and her first two children, Elizabeth and Robert, were born there.

They lived a very quiet life, saving all they could until 1892, when William rode off accompanied by a friend to look for some land of his own. They rode south through the Waikato to Taranaki, then down through Wanganui, over to Hawke's Bay and on to Poverty Bay, where William was able to purchase from the Crown 350 acres of

127

hilly bush country in the Matokitoki Valley. His first task was to fell timber to build a hut.

Later in 1892 Kate and the two small children went to Poverty Bay by sea. From Gisborne they drove out to the property in a cart, the chimney for the unfinished cottage balanced on top of their belongings as they bumped along the rough tracks.

In the loneliness of the bush and hills Kate began to make a home. Water had to be carried from a creek and all cooking was done in the camp oven. There was bread to be made, lamps to be trimmed, clothes to be mended and the vegetable garden to be planted and weeded. In 1893 she went into Gisborne to the home of Margaret Home Sievwright (40)—the friend of every woman in the district—for the birth of her next baby, James. And apart from that she did not leave the place for three years.

The property, difficult enough with its bush, was also precipitous in places. Once when two of the milking cows were missing they were eventually found dead by the two eldest children—led by the ghastly smell— to where they had fallen over a steep bank into a creek.

William worked hard on the property, spending the long hours of daylight cutting manuka. This was piled on to the horsedrawn wagon and taken into Gisborne to be sold as firewood, and on these trips he brought back the stores. As he cleared the land it was put into pasture, sheep were grazed, and when the wool went into Gisborne it was taken by bullock wagon. Kate also made a little extra during those hard days by raising fowls and selling the eggs.

By 1897 William had taken up another 1,000 acres of the adjoining Mangatuna land, and to reach this they went over the hills by tracks they made themselves. A small house was built there, with home-making and a garden to be started all over again.

A colonial oven was installed in the new house, this being a luxury when compared with the old camp oven. The water came from a strong spring in the limestone hills but unfortunately it was excessively hard and left a coating of lime in the kettles and a scum on the water used for washing. Its detrimental effect on the stove boiler made it necessary to replace the stove three times in twenty years.

Bill was born in this house. When she was expecting her next baby Kate went into town in the buggy with William. She held the reins while he went into a shop but somehow they got under the horse's tail. It thrashed out its legs in a frenzy of kicking, giving her a terrible fright, and that night she lost her baby. The next one to be born was Catherine Annie (Nancy), and with these additions to the family it was twice necessary to enlarge the house.

As the children grew the question of their schooling arose. The older ones, when they were able to do so, rode six miles along the muddy Matokitoki tracks to the Gisborne Central School, while the younger ones rode to Mangapapa, which was a little nearer. Elizabeth (Bessie) stayed with Mrs Sievwright when she was sitting school exams, and the two girls later went to Woodford House. Bessie eventually married Bertrand Coleman Watkins, a son of the well-known artist Kennett Watkins, and Nancy married John Dow Williams, a son of K. S. Williams of Matahiia.

Kate's father, William Macky, died in 1905, aged seventy-five, and was survived by his wife, Anne, and ten children. He had been night-blind before leaving Ireland but this had not hindered his activities. He was completely blind in his latter days but still managed to do jobs about the house such as attending to firewood and carrying in water—in fact this old blind man used to tell the small boys to keep clear of the well while he drew the water.

Anne Macky moved to live in a new home in Golf Road in Auckland, where she remained until she died in 1926 at the age of eighty-eight. Her life as the wife of a pioneer had been spent efficiently and cheerfully as one by one she overcame the hardships of those early days.

About 1909 William sold the Mangatuna property and bought 2000 acres at Hexton, five miles north-west of Gisborne. While the new home was being built there Kate spent a period of three months in Wellington, renting a house in Oriental Bay. Her sister, Dorcas, who had married William's brother, Dr James Maclaurin, also lived in Wellington.

The new house had a Shacklock coal range and a power plant until the electricity came during the 1920s, but Kate's real highlight was the purchase of a motorcar.

They remained in this house for the rest of their lives. William died in 1933 and Kate in 1949 at the age of eighty-three. They were both buried in the Taruheru cemetery.

Colonial oven and contemporary kitchen equipment, as used by Kate Maclaurin in the Matokitoki Valley in 1892—and by many other pioneer women. The display shown here is in the Norsewood Pioneer Museum.

CHAPTER 29

Sarah Bourton Masters

Sarah Bourton Masters was the elder daughter of Joseph Masters the founder of Masterton. Her father was born in Derbyshire and after learning the trade of a cooper joined the Life Guards, in which he served a period of five years. He married in 1826, and Sarah was born in 1827.

Five years later, after the birth of his second daughter, Mary Anne (who eventually became Mrs B. P. Perry, mother of Sir William Perry), Joseph secured an appointment with the London firm of John Gore & Co. which had interests in Tasmania. They sent him out to the new colony in 1832 and he intended sending for his wife and daughter as soon as he could see that conditions were favourable.

This, however, did not prove to be the case and ten years went by while his family waited for him at home. The girls therefore grew up having seen little of their father. Sarah shot up into a tall girl with dark wavy hair, developing later into a fairly large woman with a good sense of humour which has run strongly through her descendants.

Eventually Masters was able to write to his wife asking her to join him in New Zealand. Belongings were packed, farewells to friends and relatives were said and mother and daughters sailed on the *Maria Theresa,* arriving in Wellington in 1842.

In 1847 Sarah married Richard Iorns, who was born in Deddington, Oxfordshire, England, and who also had arrived in Wellington in 1842. The first of their four children, a daughter whom Sarah called Mary Anne, was born in 1848.

Richard and his father-in-law had previously formed a partnership as ginger-beer manufacturers but this was dissolved in 1847. By 1854 the two men were spending a great deal of their time in the new settlement of Masterton. In the September of that year James Smith, an auctioneer in Wellington, advertised that he would sell some Cuba Street property belonging to Richard Iorns "in consequence of the proprietor retiring into the interior".

The said proprietor was at that time in Masterton busily occupied with his father-in-law in building a shack to shelter the two men while they built a home for their families. The moment it was finished they turned to getting timber out of the bush.

Sarah's home was built of split slabs with a shingled roof, a clay chimney and calico windows. Her father, who was an expert with a draw-knife, soon had the edges fitting close. The cracks were covered with strips of totara bark tacked on to make them draught-proof, and Sarah was to find things very cosy in the little four-roomed cottage.

By 1855 good progress had been made with the house, and as another settler, Michael Dixon, was going to Wellington for stores, Richard asked him to convey a letter to

130

Sarah. In it he asked her to be ready the following week as he would be coming to Wellington to fetch her and the family.

The letter was handed to Sarah one evening in January 1855, while she was sitting at the supper table with her mother. As she was reading it there was a sudden tremor accompanied by a fearful rumbling beneath as the house rocked violently and lifted upwards. They staggered outside just in time to miss the toppling chimney, which crashed through the roof to flatten the chairs on which they had been sitting. Fortunately the three younger children were sleeping in a room well away from the chimney and they were lifted out into the dark night through the window.

After the tremors had subsided Sarah turned to the hasty packing of their clothes and any belongings which had remained unbroken. She knew that Richard would come rushing to see how they had fared in this 'quake, which had been severe enough to lift the seafront nine feet and make Wellington a scene of desolation.

Richard came over the Rimutakas, carefully examining the narrow, newly-cut track to see if it was passable for pack-bullocks, and deciding that it was. On arrival at Wellington one look at the devastation determined him to get his family out of the place at once.

They packed two bullock loads of necessary things into a cart, leaving the rest of their belongings stored in the two undamaged rooms. The next morning they set off for Masterton leading a two-year-old heifer in milk. Sarah had previously broken her in to carrying a pack on her back, so she not only shared the burden but had the duty of feeding the four children on the way.

For the children it was probably one splendid adventure. Mary Anne, who later became Mrs A. W. Cave, was seven years of age; William was five, Joseph was three and a half, and the baby girl who, years later became Mrs G. W. Cox of New Plymouth, was then nine months.

The journey began along the flat Hutt Road which ran between hills rising on their left and the sea pounding against the rocks on their right. All went well until the Hutt River had to be crossed by punt; the cart and luggage were put on but the bullock refused to put a hoof on the floating contraption, so he and the heifer were made to swim across. The first night was spent at the Hutt.

The next day Richard and Sarah took turns at riding as they made their way through bush and scrub towards Mangaroa, where there was an accommodation house. Here a couple of pack-bullocks awaited them. In the morning they were loaded, the quietest and most reliable one being chosen to carry William and Joseph. The two little boys were placed in cases which were lined with pillows for comfort, and these were balanced on either side of the bullock. Joseph's case had to be weighted to equalise the pack as he was lighter than his brother.

Sarah took the lead, carrying the baby in a shawl on her back and leading the heifer. Richard came next, leading the bullock which carried the boys, then came the second bullock tied to the first with a long rope. Mary Anne, with her parents, walked over the Rimutakas.

The ground now rose steadily towards the ranges. The rough narrow track, precipitous in parts, turned and twisted as it followed the winding contour of the bluffs and valleys. The stages were short but arduous between rests until at last they topped

The Rimutaka Range over which the Iorns family walked in 1855, Sarah Iorns carrying the baby in a shawl on her back and leading a heifer.

the last steep rise and began to make their way down to Burling's accommodation house, which was where Featherston now stands. Here they were thankful to spend the night.

The next was an easier day as they made their way to Greytown. The route was level and clear, the weather fine and the rivers low. They reached the home of Mr Kempton, an earlier settler, and spent the night beneath his roof. Next morning they made an early start for Masterton, going by Papawai then crossing the seven branches of the Waiohine River to come out at Parkvale.

Here they were met by Sarah's father with a cart he had made himself. Harnessed to it was Tiny, a huge Durham bullock with a horn spread of over six feet. When the cart was loaded and the occupants seated, Masters drove them across the Taratahi Plains. A mid-day break gave the animals a rest and time to graze, and just before dark they had crossed the Waingawa River. On the bank, in the perfect evening, they had tea while the full moon rose over the bush to the east. The last lap was then made past Donald's Manaia homestead. Donald's cattle now clustered about them with curious stares, escorting them for some distance, but at last the party crossed the Kuripuni Creek and came straight on to their own little cottage situated in what is now Queen Street. Despite the fact that it was then midnight they found the billy boiling and supper prepared for them by Edward Farmer Eaton(14) who lived nearby.

The next day was completely taken up by the welcome given them by the Maoris from the Ngaumutawa pa. Gifts of potatoes, pork, pigeons, and other foods were

132

brought, and for Sarah there was a special present of a flax kit containing two Maori rats, gift-wrapped in green leaves and picked clean ready for the oven. The feast was blessed by the Rev. William Ronaldson of the Church Missionary Society, who had arrived in the district.

After that they settled down to toil. Richard worked hard to enlarge the house as they intended opening a store and this, the first shop in Masterton, was opened later in 1855. During the winter Sarah made him new flannel underwear, but when the warmer days of spring came the coarse hairy material irritated his skin. One day while working hard he became overheated and pulled them off. The weather turned suddenly cooler and he caught a chill. He died of pneumonia in November 1855.

Before Richard's death word had been brought into Masterton that a man had been drowned in the river and that only his feet were sticking out of the mud. While a party went to bring in the body Richard dug a grave in the Cemetery Reserve. The drowning report proved to be false and the feet sticking out of the mud were merely a pair of discarded old boots. Shortly after this Richard died and was buried in the grave he himself had dug. E. F. Eaton made his coffin and read the burial service over him. He was the first person to be buried in the Masterton cemetery.

Sarah, left with the store and four young children, decided to carry on. The Maoris rallied round, giving her a great deal of assistance in the growing of wheat and the grinding of it into flour with the small handmill. They gathered puha, or sour thistle for her and taught her how to wash and dry grated potatoes to make a kind of arrowroot that could be browned with egg and milk in the oven.

In 1856, when she rode to Wellington to attend to Richard's affairs, the Post Office officials asked her if she would take on the duty of postmistress for Masterton at a salary of £5 a year. She agreed and rode home carrying the first mailbag for the new settlement. It contained one letter.

It was while riding to Wellington that she caught the eye and the interest of Henry Bannister, who was working on the Rimutaka road. His inquiries revealed her identity and when she was on her way back he invited her to lunch. During the next work-break most of the men went to Wellington but Henry went to Masterton.

He called on Sarah who, with her usual hospitality, invited him in for refreshments. Later, when they walked outside they discovered that her cows had made their way through the broken fence into her bachelor neighbour's section. Henry volunteered to bring them out and then mend the fence for her. As he approached the animals the neighbour, red in the face with anger, came stamping up to order him off the property.

Henry explained that he was about to mend the fence, which was something he, the neighbour, should have done. The neighbour lost his temper and let fly with a fist. Henry retaliated and the first round was his until the neighbour snatched at a titoki pole lying on the ground. It was nearly nine feet long and about as thick as a man's arm. He slashed at Henry's legs with it, breaking one of them and causing him to fall to the ground. As he lay on his back the man sat astride him, doing his best to gouge his eyes out with his thumbs.

Fortunately another person came along with a letter to post and went to Henry's assistance. With Sarah's help he got him into the house before hastening to fetch her father. When Masters arrived the draw-knife was brought into operation to fashion a

Bannister's Store, Masterton, 1860. It was founded by Sarah Masters' first husband, Richard Iorns, and its name was changed when his widow married Henry Bannister in 1857.

Sarah Bourton Masters, 1827–70, who married Richard Iorns and, after his death, Henry Bannister. She was the elder daughter of Joseph Masters, founder of Masterton.

pair of splints for the broken leg. Sarah nursed Henry until he could walk again, and married him on 2 May 1857. From then on the shop was run as "Bannister's Store" although it was wholly Sarah's under her first husband's will.

Henry Bannister was a kindly man who never hesitated to offer a helping hand. Born in 1815 at Sedgley, Dudleyside, in Staffordshire, he was a widower whose wife had died during the first year of their marriage. The sorrow of this loss had caused him to leave England, and after a period in Australia he came to New Zealand in 1842. In Masterton he took over the duties of postmaster, and with the cost of freight from Wellington dropping from £20 per ton to £10 10s, the store became a busy place.

Sarah also had her hands full. Apart from helping with the store and post office she had to contend with cramped living quarters, open-fire cooking in the clay chimney, the constant carrying of water from the well, to say nothing of coping with fleas, flies, mosquitoes, rats and mice. The house had neither bathroom nor laundry, and the toilet was at the bottom of the section. On top of this her life now became a succession of having more babies. The growing family had to be clothed, and while she was an expert needlewoman she also had the first little hand sewing machine in Masterton. She was instructed in its use by the Rev. William Ronaldson who had married her to Henry, and who also fixed watches and clocks for his parishioners during his travels around the district.

In 1870 the advent of the eighth Bannister baby brought the family number in the slab cottage to fourteen. After the birth Sarah, who had never had a doctor, suffered such bad toothache that a medical man had to be procured from Greytown. The doctor said she had erysipelas, but the family knew it was blood poisoning.

The end came fifteen days after the birth of the baby; by that time Mary Anne was twenty-two, and as she sat beside her dying mother she promised to take care of the new baby. This she did, and brought up the next little two-year-old sister as well.

Sarah was only forty-two when she died.

CHAPTER 30

Jane Caroline Meredith

Jane Caroline Chalmers was born in London on 11 Sept. 1832. She was the eldest daughter of Captain Frederick Edmund Chalmers, commander of the ship *Calcutta* which traded between Hobart and London. When she was only seven her mother died at the early age of thirty-nine. Her father took her from London to Hobart, placing her in the care of Mr and Mrs Butler of Stowell.

Janie, as she was known, grew to be an attractive girl with a sweet face. Despite lack of height she had a regal bearing, yet was acknowledged to be one of the most amiable and gentle girls in Tasmania. Her life was gay with social gatherings, balls and other entertainments of the day, nor did she lack for the home comforts of gracious living. She was certainly the belle of Hobart when she married Edwin Meredith on 14 December 1852. The stylish wedding took place in St David's Cathedral, Hobert, the ceremony being performed by Doctor Nixon, Bishop of Tasmania.

Janie had met Edwin through two of the young Butlers who were at school with him. Of Welsh descent and born in 1827 he was the youngest son of George Meredith and his wife Lucy, of Swanport, who were early settlers in Tasmania having emigrated there in 1821. Edwin was a well educated young man who had read and studied in Doctor Fry's private school.

In 1851 he had sailed to New Zealand, and after exploring the Otago district had applied at Dunedin for a Crown run of 80,000 acres. After much difficulty 1,400 sheep costing £1 per head were put on the run and a man named Alfred Hobbs was left in charge. Edwin then returned to marry Janie. Unfortunately this run, lying between what was then the Molyneaux River and the Kaihikui Range, was lost to him due to a misunderstanding between the English Government and the Otago Association which ended in an award to the Association of 200,000 acres which included almost the whole of Edwin's station.

Janie, in the meantime, had been preparing for life in New Zealand, and despite the loss of the run they sailed on 15 January 1853 on the *Munford* bound for Wellington. Their intention was to take up land in Canterbury and drive the sheep overland from Molyneaux. On board they had six valuable horses and sixty stud sheep.

It was near Tarawhite, nine days out from Hobert, that Janie saved the ship. The wind had died, it was a calm night and they were about three quarters of a mile from the shore. Everyone except Janie was at tea. She was up on deck and suddenly noticed that a very strong current was taking them towards a sunken rock. She rushed to give the alarm through the skylight to the captain, who immediately ran up on deck to let go the anchor which brought the brig up within twenty yards of the rock. Had the ship struck the rock the cargo, including the sheep and horses, would have been lost, although they considered there would have been no danger to life.

The next day they anchored in Wellington Harbour where, through lack of a wharf, the passengers were rowed ashore and the sheep and horses were landed by punt. Here the Merediths stayed at Baron's Hotel while awaiting the opportunity to go to Canterbury.

Janie found Wellington a small but gay place with unbounded hospitality showered upon them from all sides. The colonel and officers of the 65th Regiment gave them a ball at the barracks, which were decorated in military style for the occasion, and this was only a prelude to the round of balls and dinner parties given them by Sir George and Lady Grey, Colonel Gold, Colonel and Mrs McLeverty, Sir Charles and Lady Clifford, and others. Also, having their own horses, they were able to make up riding parties to see the surrounding country which at that time, with the forest growing right down to the water's edge, was very beautiful.

They left at last for Port Chalmers in the 40-ton schooner *Scotia*, a vessel built of heavy gum which, when in stormy seas, made her passengers realise her want of buoyancy. Her saloon was twelve feet long by about eight feet wide, most of which space was occupied by a table, there being only just enough room to walk between the table and the lockers which constituted the seats. Immediately behind the lockers were four bunks on each side of the saloon. There were no cabins, the only provision for privacy being a curtain that could be drawn to screen off the lockers and bunks. The feat of undressing was performed by standing on the locker and holding grimly to the bunk. Two tin bowls represented the whole provision for lavatory purposes. The voyage for several ladies and gentlemen on this vessel lasted eight days.

Edwin's efforts to take up land in Canterbury proved to be unsuccessful and he therefore turned to Hawke's Bay. At Waipukurau he purchased 2,000 acres and proceeded to build a homestead there, but on returning to Wellington he was informed at the Land Office that a mistake had been made and that H. R. Russell had a prior claim. Eventually, through determination and an incident of hard riding to forestall another interested party at the Land Office, he was able to take up land at Whareama. This was the 28,000 acre Orui property described as poor hilly country densely covered with fern. It had a six-mile coastline.

Janie, during his Hawke's Bay journeys, lived in a cottage on The Terrace in Wellington. Her baby son Edwin arrived in October 1853 and she now prepared to go to Orui. A small schooner, the *Seabird*, was chartered to precede them with timber for a small cottage, a horse-cart and all their belongings, together with twelve months' provisions in charge of a married couple who were to make the best preparations they could for the Merediths in the three-roomed cottage already standing on the place. About ten days later Edwin, Janie, the baby and a servant girl left by the *Shepherdess*, and about three days from Wellington were landed at Orui.

To their dismay they found that although the married couple had been landed, not one item of their goods had been put ashore but had been taken on and landed at Castlepoint, twelve miles away. Fortunately they had their clothes and bedding, but apart from this their household effects consisted of one kettle, two pannicans, one frying pan, a few biscuits, and a little tea and sugar which the married couple had with them. The whare in which they were expected to live was such a miserable affair that the married couple resented it and left.

With the help of his man Picket, Edwin put up another detached building of two bedrooms for themselves and the servant girl, the material being raupo thatched with totara and lined inside with toetoe canes. A small piece of ground was enclosed to grow vegetables while wheat purchased from the Maoris was ground into flour with a small handmill. When the flour ran out they ate potatoes.

Janie soon learnt that people passing between Hawke's Bay and Wellington expected to be given meals and a night's lodging, and this proved to be a real drain on her limited supply of food. But at least these people imparted fresh ideas and scraps of news from the outside world, from which they were almost severed as there were no mails except by the hands of those passing by who might carry letters to or from Wellington.

Edwin's time was fully occupied with his sheep, cattle and station work, but for Janie it was a different matter. She had been brought up with every comfort in the midst of a large circle of friends of her own age. Her social life had been full of amusements in a gay town where she had been such a favourite with all who knew her. But during the twelve months of this primitive life in the raupo whare at Orui, entirely cut off from all contact with members of her own sex, never once did she complain or wear other than a sweet and cheerful face.

She also found the many Maori owners of the large leasehold block to be disagreeable landlords. Apart from their habit of continually trying to forestall the rent, open house had to be kept for them. Very open indeed as they would go into every room, even the bedrooms, and expected to be constantly supplied with food. But, as Edwin said, they kept faith with their tenants and were honest, which was more than he could say for the Provincial landlords.

On the night of the 1855 earthquake Janie had gone to bed with a bad headache when, about 9.30 pm, the ground beneath the bed was struck with a tremendous violence, Edwin rushed into the bedroom as the walls, roof, rafters and everything else began to heave and toss up and down, turning their home into a ruin.

In 1855, not long after the earthquake, when they had been at Orui for thirteen months, a letter came from Edwin's brother-in-law Sir Richard Dry, informing them of his ill health and his intention to visit England for medical advice. He offered Edwin the management of Quamby, his property in Tasmania, for a term of five years. They accepted the offer and went there in May. However, early in 1858 Edwin suffered a serious knee injury, and a few months later met with still more serious internal injuries which forced him to seek the aid of doctors overseas.

Janie, during his absence of two years, remained in Tasmania with the children. Mary had been born in Hobart in 1855, Richard Reiby at Sayes Court, Bagdad (Tasmania), in 1857, and Clarence, at Quamby in 1858. By the time they returned to Orui it was early 1861, Rosina having been born in Wellington late in 1860.

At Orui they discovered that the cattle had deteriorated in quality and that scab had come into the sheep. The property had become involved in debt. Edwin was also now forced to buy the whole of Orui, which the Provincial Government had now put up for auction, and for which he had to borrow money at 10% interest to secure it against outsiders.

From 1861 to 1868 Janie shared seven years of almost unendurable anxiety with him when, due to his poor health and physically helpless state, managers involved the property deeper and deeper into debt until she realised at last that they were on the verge of insolvency. Then, just as things seemed to be at their very worst, the situation was saved by a legacy from Edwin's Uncle Charles.

Janie's sixth baby, John Montague, was born at Orui in 1862, and he was followed by Clara in 1865. In 1867 they moved from Orui to live a few miles away on the Riversdale part of the property, where Elsie Emmeline was born that year. Edith Dry was also born there in 1870.

In January 1872 the Riversdale house was burnt down and such was the demand for timber throughout New Zealand that it was not until June that a new one could be erected. During that interval neighbours took the younger children while Edwin, Janie and Mary lived in the woolshed where all domestic duties were performed under extreme inconveniences. Yet never once did Janie complain, despite the fact that she was pregnant with Janie Chalmers, who was born in the June of that year.

Four years later, in 1876, Gwendoline was born at Riversdale. In April 1879 they left Riversdale to live at Bellevue, in Masterton, and that year the twins, Melita Meredyth and Kathleen Meredyth, were born there.

The following year, 1880, they moved to a farm on the Upper Plain, Masterton, where their home, Llandaff, had been built. This was a fine two-storeyed home with orchard and gardens, and it was here in 1907 that Edwin died at the age of seventy-nine.

About 1912 Janie suffered from an infection in one eye which caused her to lose the sight of it. She wore a covering over it until she died in 1917, at the age of eighty-four.

CHAPTER 31

Mette Kirstine Nielsen

Mette Kirstine Bruun was born in 1873 at the city of Vejle, on Vejle Fjord, on the Danish peninsula of Jutland. Her father was a post office official and she was one of eleven children. She was blue-eyed with medium brown hair and grew to be a tall, capable girl of an always pleasant nature. Usually known as Kirstine, she went out to work as soon as she was old enough to do so.

About the year 1894 she married Hans Nielsen, who had been born in 1868. He was a brown-haired, tall slim man who had a cheerful hail-fellow-well-met disposition, who worked in a metal foundry. Within a few years they had three sons and a daughter, all of whom, strangely, bore the same initials to their names. They were Edvin Richard Bruun, who was usually known as Ted, Engelhardt Rudolph Bruun (Peter), Erna Rigmar Bruun (Nols), and Ernst Robert Bruun.

As the children grew up in Denmark Kirstine's husband, who had never been robust, began to suffer from indifferent health, and it was soon evident that unless something was done his condition was likely to become serious. In the meantime Kirstine's sister Jensine had married Morris Cohr and sailed with him to New Zealand.

The Cohrs had settled at Makaretu, and had later moved to Ngamoko on the eastern slopes of the Ruahines, a few miles from the headwaters of the Manawatu River. They were also a few miles from the Scandinavian settlement of Norsewood, and in this rugged country Morris Cohr operated a sawmilling plant. No doubt letters to home spoke of what must have been, to these Danish people, a much more agreeable climate, and eventually it was decided that Hans should join them.

In 1906 Kirstine and the children watched him leave to sail to a distant land. On arrival in New Zealand he worked for Morris Cohr for two years and then in 1908 Kirstine and the children followed him. They left Denmark at the end of the northern winter, crossing to London and spending a night there before embarking again on the Shaw Savill liner, S.S. *Arawa*. The voyage took seven weeks with calls at Teneriffe, Cape Town and Hobart.

There was a joyous reunion when Hans met them in Wellington. They then came up the Wairarapa by train as far as Ormondville, where they changed into Fred Smith's coach which took them to where they would live at Ngamoko.

During his period of sawmilling with Morris Cohr, Hans had kept an eye open for a suitable property so that by the time Kirstine and the children arrived he had bought a dairy farm of 74 acres. It was near the upper reaches of the Manawatu River which, in this area, was only a stream. There was a house on it and this was shared with the Cohrs while the Nielsens were building a house across the river.

Kirstine, who had always lived in a city, found difficulty in adjusting herself to New Zealand back-country life. The mountains were close and the air hazy with the smoke of a large bush fire which had raged only a short time before their arrival. The charred remains of trees lay about the farm and there was very little pasture. Hard work was the order of the day, the watch-word from morn till night being the continual urge to hurry up—hurry up—. There was bread for the household to be made, kerosene lamps to be tended, an endless supply of water to be drawn from the well, and the washing to be done in a tub erected on a stand in the backyard.

During those early days Kirstine spoke very little English, and as the grocer knew only a few words of Danish the ordering became complicated. However, the children soon learnt to speak English. They were able to attend the Ngamoko school which had been inaugurated in 1904 and was held in the dairy factory building at the corner of Ngamoko and Reserve Roads. It was attached to the main Norsewood school as a side school.

Hans began dairyfarming with thirty cows bought at Dave O'Hara's clearance sale at Maharahara. He had them tested, culled them out, and began breeding his own stock, and it was not long before he had twenty cows that were producing more than the original thirty. In summer, through lack of pasture, he grazed his cows on the roadside. Milking began at an early hour in the mornings, the milk being later taken to the Ngamoko creamery to be separated.

Despite the never-ending work of a dairy farm Kirstine's natural creative ability asserted itself. She became an expert in handcrafts of all types and a leading light in most women's organisations. Never were her fingers idle.

After about four years in New Zealand she took a trip home to Denmark, but this did not prove to be the joyful reunion she had looked forward to because everything at home had changed. The backyard of the old home she had known was now part of the railway yards, old friends had gone and nothing seemed the same. The period in New Zealand had left a gap that was impossible to bridge from either side, and she was glad to return to New Zealand.

Some years after her return Hans sold the farm because of health reasons and went to live in Norsewood, where he had acquired three and a half acres in Arthur's Road. The home, situated on a rise, faced north-east to look over a pleasant view of undulating country. Here she was usually to be found on the sunny front verandah, or on the lawn at a small table set in the shade of a large camellia tree, busily engaged at one of her handcrafts. Most of her friends knew that at three o'clock each afternoon they could rely on the aromatic odour of coffee made from the beans she roasted, and all knew they would be welcome to call.

Kirstine became friendly with Miss Jerome Spencer (41) of Country Women's Institute fame, and on 13 July 1922 she attended a public meeting held in the Norsewood Library to consider the formation of a Women's Institute in Norsewood. This was the second Institute to be formed in New Zealand and she was elected to the committee. Twelve months later, on the departure of the president, Mrs Hinds, Kirstine took her place as president.

She now threw herself into Institute work with enthusiasm, assisting and teaching all who were interested in handcrafts, and never reluctant in the generous imparting

Kirstine Nielsen, *née* Bruun, 1873–1938. Born and educated in Denmark, she was a founder-member of the Norsewood Country Women's Institute and was responsible for the introduction of Health Stamps in 1929.

of her knowledge. At Rakautatahi, about seven miles west of Takapau, she started an Institute for Maori women, and so sincerely did these women appreciate her efforts that they seldom passed her door without leaving a small gift of some sort.

As far as Norsewood was concerned she became an outstanding woman, organising many things which, without her efforts, would never have been started in that small community. She seemed to draw people to her, and as friends developed the habit of just arriving it was not unusual for nineteen or twenty to sit down to Sunday dinner.

And while she occupied herself with so many plans that would assist the people of Norsewood—such as persuading the Government to purchase the Lutheran Hall—there was one project that simmered in her mind above all others. It had been sparked off during her trip to Denmark when she had learnt about that country's excellent use of health seals which were sold to the public to be placed on letters, the money being put to hospitals and other health-promoting organisations. In fact she had returned home fired with the idea of a similar scheme being started in New Zealand.

In 1926 she explained the system to the Norsewood Institute. The value of such a plan was immediately recognised and it was agreed that she should approach the Government with a view to ascertaining the possibility of having a similar scheme introduced into New Zealand. She took a trip to Wellington and discussed the matter with Lady Fergusson, wife of the Governor-General.

Of course Kirstine could now write and speak English, but as she grew older more

Danish words seemed to creep back in. She therefore asked her son Peter to write to Sir George Hunter MP on the subject of the health seals and through him the proposal was submitted to the Postmaster General. It was favourably received by the Post and Telegraph Department, but it was decided that the issue of a stamp proper, having a postage as well as a charity value, would be preferable to the issue of a seal. This was the birth of the New Zealand Health Stamps, but it was 1929 before the first ones were issued.

Kirstine was president of the Norsewood Institute until 1932. During this time, in recognition of her work for the Institute, a fine chair with her name inscribed on it was obtained by the Institute for her use as president. She left Norsewood with Hans in 1937, their departure from the district being a real loss to the community. She died in 1938, aged sixty-five, and was buried in the Hastings cemetery.

There are now few people in New Zealand who realise that this country's Health Stamps originated from an idea brought from Denmark by Kirstine Nielsen. Nor must it be forgotten that it was her never-failing enthusiasm which launched the project on its way. It is to be hoped that these facts will be commemorated at some future date—perhaps in 1979, when the Health Stamps reach their fiftieth anniversary.

CHAPTER 32.

Neilsine Paget

Neilsine Nielson, born in Denmark in 1858, was one of the ten children of Lauritz and Meta Nielson. Her parents owned a small dairy farm on which the stock had to be housed and hand-fed in winter, and to supplement their income her father repaired boots. About 1871 they listened to the glowing reports circulated by New Zealand Government agents about the land of milk and honey where the sun shone every day and everyone had large herds and acres and acres of beautiful green grass. By 1872 they had decided to emigrate. There would be no more hand-feeding in the bitter cold and they would enter into a life of ease.

By this time Neilsine had grown to a short, sturdily built girl of fourteen years. Her straight hair with its golden lights was drawn back from a centre parting and at times her eyes flashed with sudden temper. Although the acknowledged spitfire of the family, of the ten children she was the closest to their mother.

As the ship left Copenhagen to plough through the North Sea towards England it became increasingly clear that Meta Nielson was ill. After ten pregnancies she was now on the way with her eleventh child and things were not going well. At Southampton she was so desperately ill that she had to be placed on a stretcher and carried from the ship to hospital.

Lauritz settled the family in a boardinghouse while he rushed between the emigration offices and the captain of the sailing ship which was to take them on to New Zealand. Lauritz could speak no English and the captain could speak only a little Danish, but it eventually became clear that the belongings of the twelve Nielsons had already been transferred and battened down in the hold of the sailing ship with the belongings of many other people on top. They could not easily be got at and by this time the ship was due to sail within a few hours.

Further, it was pointed out by the emigration authorities that it was against their regulations to send luggage without an owner, and that they could not be responsible for unaccompanied baggage. A member of the family must travel with it.

A plan was then formed which Lauritz did not like but accepted on the captain's advice. He returned to the boardinghouse and explained it to Ann, his eldest daughter, but not to Neilsine who, he knew, would never agree. Instead he told her that, despite the nearness of sailing time, the captain had kindly offered to show the two girls over the ship. Ann was subdued, but Neilsine was too excited to wonder why her mother wept a little as she kissed her goodbye and told her always to be a good girl.

The captain proved to be a jolly host, plying the girls with wine and biscuits in his cabin. Neilsine, unused to such worldly entertainment, emptied the glass he kept refilling and felt the wine go to her head. Soon it was difficult to keep her eyes open and before long she was asleep at the table. She woke several hours later to find herself on a bunk and Ann sitting beside it. The ship was well at sea on its way to New Zealand.

Neilsine's rage became uncontrolled. She refused to listen to Ann's explanation of the position. Nor would she take into consideration the fact that, being so close to her mother, they knew she would never leave her, and as Ann could not be sent alone with the luggage it had to be done this way. There was a mad rush up to the deck as Neilsine made for the rail and tried to scramble overboard with the intention of swimming back, but the captain grabbed her and locked her in her cabin where she lay for hours, weeping hysterically.

Eventually she became resigned to the situation. The many weeks of the voyage passed without incident except for occasions when Neilsine and Ann, who could not speak English, were blamed for the pranks of the other young people. This happened frequently, but the captain was always on the side of the Danish girls.

At last the ship reached Lyttelton where the girls were put into the cold immigrant barracks to await settlers who would come and look them over as prospective servants for house or farm. One woman from Akaroa looked Neilsine over several times before she finally decided to take her. Someone took Ann—and suddenly the sisters were parted.

At Akaroa Neilsine tried hard not to fret for Ann. It was difficult to learn the language and to know what was expected of her. Often she had to guess whether she was being asked for a glass of water or a cup of tea. A pile of dirty dishes or a filthy floor she understood at once, and with it all was the constant and desperate longing for Ann.

At last her mistress realised the cause of her unhappiness and made an effort to trace Ann through the barracks. She was successful and within a short time the girls were able to write to each other. This made all the difference.

Then came the day when Neilsine met Tom Paget. He called her a golden Venus, and she tossed her head. He went to see her, and she slammed the door in his face. He tried to speak to her in the street, and she ran away. She was sixteen and weighed only six stone when she married him in 1875.

Thomas Paget was born in England in 1850. He had run away from home while still only a lad and had worked his passage to New Zealand. At Akaroa he worked in the sawmills or on farms. He was a kindly man with a placid nature unless roused but then his ill-temper soon disappeared. Well built without being tall, he had blue eyes but went grey at an early age possibly because, from the age of twenty, he suffered badly from asthma.

Neilsine's first baby, Mary Elizabeth, was born in 1876, then came Jennie Sophia in 1878, William Louis in 1880, and Frederick Thomas in 1882. By this time the Pagets realised that the Akaroa climate was not the best for Tom's asthma so they moved to Hawke's Bay, where Ann and her Scottish husband, Frank Forward, were farming at South Makaretu.

In the meantime Lauritz and Meta Nielson had arrived in New Zealand with the rest of their family and had settled in Akaroa, where Lauritz did boot repairing. Later they also came to Hawke's Bay and had a small farm at Makotuku.

Tom leased land in the Seventy Mile Bush where the trees had to be felled before they could build a house, their first one being of pitsawn timber with a dirt floor. Neilsine's fifth child, Annie Adalina, was born here in 1884. When the baby was due Tom went for help but events started before he could return. Neilsine, realising this, locked the four little ones in the next room, heated some water, gave birth to Annie and herself tied the umbilical cord. Tom arrived with help in time to make the tea.

Neilsine's next baby, Maud Madeline, arrived in 1885, Georgina Florence in 1886, Amy Eleanor in 1888, and James Henry in 1889. Then came the twins, Arthur Ernest and Bertie Lauritz in 1891.

By this time Neilsine was one of the best loved and hardest working settlers in the district. With Tom she toiled on their bush property from daylight till dark, felling trees, burning scrub, raking and clearing the land to make a farm, digging post- holes, carrying battens, pitsawing timber for the house, making bread, candles, soap, and making furniture by covering boxes with chintz. She had knowledge and advice to give to all, and no matter how weary from her own long hours of toil she was never too tired to hold out a helping hand. She was doctor, midwife and general adviser to most of the back-country folk.

One of her boys once moved too near the slasher. She bound his arm with the dinner cloth, later stitching it with needle and cotton. There were nights when Tom's bad bouts of asthma kept her up all night, frustrated by her inability to relieve his choking and gasping for breath while he tore desperately at the neck of his shirt. During the Tarawera eruption in 1886 when everything was dark and every candle had to be lit although it was daylight, poor Tom suffered agonies.

Left: Neilsine Paget, *née* Neilson, 1858–1932, with her husband Thomas whom she married in 1875. "When her fifth baby was due Tom went for help but events started before he could return. Neilsine, realising this, heated some water, gave birth to Annie and herself tied the umbilical cord."

Top right: Makaretu Store, *circa* 1900.

Right: The Paget family, *circa* 1905. *Back row (left to right):* Clara, Bert, Henry, Mary, Fred, Florrie, Annie. *Middle row:* Willy (*sitting, left*) and Maude (*standing centre*). *Front row (left to right):* Nielsine, Arthur, Thomas Amy. *Sitting (front):* Francis, Roy, George. The photograph is of the second-eldest child, Jenny.

By this time they were in their second and larger home. Timber for it had been felled and then bullock-drayed to the creek where it had been put across on a wire rope. The children had then dragged it to the top of the hill whence horses had snigged it to the house site. The children were not continuously at home because whenever possible the older ones were sent away for schooling.

Neilsine was pregnant again during the ordeal of the 1892 bush fires that had been started by the carelessness of rabbiters. The flames roared and raced on gales of wind and, fearing that the smoke and heat would be the end of Tom, she lowered him and the youngest children down the well. Then, with the rest of the family she fought for hours to save their home from the surrounding furnace, beating the flames with sacks and running with buckets from the creek.

The ceiling under the high iron roof had never been completed. Sparks flew in and up to the attic roof to drop on the beds and burn holes in the blankets. If the children had cried they would have choked from the smoke, and if the house had burned they would have been unable to make their way through the blazing bush to safety. But at last there came a miraculous change in the roaring wind and their little home was saved. Some time later Tom was helped up from the well and surveyed his grimy, exhausted wife and family, and the blackened waste that lay about them on all sides.

As the years passed Neilsine acquired an amazing general knowledge through reading and self-education, passing on to the children all that she possibly could. At the same time more babies arrived, the next being Meta Clarisa, who was born in 1892 after the ordeal of the fire. Samuel Francis was born in 1894, George Edwin in 1896 and Roy Godfrey in 1897. Altogether there were fifteen children.

Neilsine and Tom knew much sadness when some of their children died at a comparatively young age. Jennie, Maude, Roy and Sam were still in their twenties when they died, the latter being killed in action in 1917. William was married and had a young family when he died in 1914 at the age of thirty-four.

During the First-War years, with Sam, Roy, George and Bert overseas, Neilsine became very busy with Red Cross work. By this time they had retired to live in Waipukurau, the farm having been handed over to a son. Roy died in 1924 as the result of war wounds, and the following year Tom's death came as a bitter blow.

So much had happened to Neilsine that at times she thought she should write a book, but after Tom's death her health failed, her eyesight became poor and the book was never written. This is a matter for lasting regret, because those who knew her declared her to be the most amazing person they had ever met.

But yet another death loomed before her own when Arthur died in the May of 1932, aged forty-one. And then Neilsine herself died two months later on 13 July 1932, aged seventy-four, and was buried in the Takapau cemetery.

At Takapau a signpost points to Pagets Road; it cannot tell you of the fine Danish woman who was the first to live there.

CHAPTER 33

Miriam Parker

Miriam Margoliouth who, as a child, migrated with her parents from Central Europe to England, was a bright, petite young woman. Born in 1835, she married William Parker of Cheshire, England, during the 1850s, and with their two children, William and Minnie, came to New Zealand in the sailing ship *Red Jacket*, arriving in Hawke's Bay in 1859. William's brother Henry also emigrated with them and shortly after their arrival the two brothers went into partnership with William Rich as stockdealers, shippers and butchers, their business employing many hands.

Miriam's third child, Frederick, was born in 1861 in New Zealand. In 1864 some of the Poverty Bay Maoris decided that far too much of their land was lying idle so three of them, representing most of the owners of Whakaupoko, came to Napier in search of Europeans to take up land in Poverty Bay. The three men were Henare Ruru, Otene Pitau, and a halfcaste named Tom Jones. Their meeting with William and Henry Parker resulted in the brothers taking up the Whataupoko property of about 20,000 acres on a twenty-one year lease at a rental of £200 per year with right of first refusal to purchase the freehold.

The land, covered with fern, scrub and swamp, lay between the Taruheru and Waimata Rivers and extended five or more miles up the Taruheru with all the land now known as the suburb of Whataupoko included in the block, which extended back almost as far as the Waimata settlement.

Henry took the sheep to the property by ship and was assisted by William Wilkinson Smith, but soon after landing the animals were attacked by Maori dogs, numbers of them being killed. Henry was so annoyed that he laid poison for the dogs, many of them taking the bait, and this in turn angered the Maoris, who threatened to take revenge on him. He left Poverty Bay and never returned.

In 1866 William and his cousin Robert Thelwall set out from Napier in the schooner *Ringleader* and were taken right up to the corner of the property, their landing place being the junction point of the two rivers. Robert had recently arrived in New Zealand and had received word of a £1,000 legacy which had enabled him to purchase an interest in Whataupoko.

In 1867 Miriam and her family left Napier in the *Cleopatra,* a small paddle steamer, for Poverty Bay. They passed between Portland Island and the mainland, and the following morning the little craft went up the Waipaoa River, pulling into the bank near where Captain (later Major) Charles Westrupp was living. From there, after disembarking, they made their way across the flats to Makaraka, carrying their belongings to the location of their new residence.

Instead of building a homestead they had decided to lease a large house belonging to Robert Espie, on the south side of the river. The house, previously occupied by Mr H. S. Wardell, the resident magistrate, was on the bank of the river not far from the Roseland Gardens and close to where the Roseland Hotel later stood. As the Whatau-poko property was across the river from the house access to the homestead was gained by means of a rope stretched over the water to enable the settlers, seated in a canoe, to pull themselves to and from side to side.

In those days the Taruheru was a wide, deep river with a shingly beach on either side. The beaches were favourite places with the Maoris as the layers of sand hid literally thousands of large pipis. At that time only about thirty people were living at what later became Gisborne.

It was a peaceful community where Miriam, in common with the wives of other settlers, cooked in a camp oven or an outside clay oven, carried water and sewed whatever she could procure to make clothes for the family. Robert Thelwall lived with them, and with the Parkers he put in strenuous work clearing the bush and scrub from the property. Mail and goods came once a week from Turanganui when young William went to fetch them. On one occasion he was chased up a tree by a wild pig and was kept there several hours before the animal went away.

On 8 November 1868 the household was happily contented to know that the first shearing of their 2,000 sheep had been completed. Hopes were high and prospects looked good. There was uneasiness over the fact that Te Kooti had escaped from the Chathams, but the redoubt being constructed at Turanganui (later Gisborne) was nearly completed. Settlers were advised to sleep in it at night and return to their homes during the day, but when Miriam suggested they should do this William reproved her for being an alarmist.

Sunday 9 November was a day of rest. The household consisted of Miriam and William, their two sons William and Frederick, Robert Thelwall, C. Smale, Daniel Munns and Bob Parkhouse. Minnie Parker and her baby brother John were staying with Mrs Bloomfield and her family, who lived on the banks of the Waipaoa River.

Miriam and William retired early that night, little expecting the horrors that began on the Monday morning between 3 and 4 am, when a rifle shot rang out to announce the beginning of the Poverty Bay massacre. Messrs Smale, Parkhouse, Munns and Thelwall, who were members of the Poverty Bay Mounted Rifles, immediately rushed for their guns.

Miriam, William and the children, clad only in their night attire, fled out into the scrub near their house, while Munns seized a nearby horse and raced down the road towards the other settlers. He met two Maoris who warned him that Te Kooti intended killing all the settlers, and as Munns turned his horse and galloped back the two Maoris, who were really Hauhaus, fired at him and wounded him in the back. He galloped into the scrub and eventually reached the stockade at Turanganui.

In the meantime Miriam, almost hysterical with fear, crouched in the manuka about two chains from the house. With William and the two frightened boys she counted twenty-eight Maoris standing near the door of the homestead. Some of them strode into the house and, seeing signs of hurried flight, thought the Parkers were well away. Intent upon more victims, they rode off into the semi-darkness.

After a while Miriam and William and the boys left the manuka and crept inside the house and quickly dressed themselves. They secured a few valuables, pulled themselves across the river and fled through the scrub on Whataupoko down to the stockade at Turanganui. Shortly after their departure the Hauhaus returned, looted the place and set the homestead and woolshed on fire.

In the meantime the Bloomfield household where Minnie Parker and her baby brother John were staying had been warned of the Hauhaus' approach. The women threw cloaks and shawls over their nightgowns and made off towards Awapuni and then along the beach to Turanganui.

Minnie, who was only a little girl, not only carried her brother over the greater part of the perilous journey, but had the presence of mind to fill his bottle before she left. Later the citizens of Napier subscribed freely towards a suitable gift in recognition of her bravery. Seven years later, on 29 April 1875, Minnie died from diphtheria.

Miriam lost another son, Frank, when he too died in his teens through diphtheria.

The Parker family worked hard on Whataupoko for years but unfortunately, through losses of stock and other setbacks, William lacked the finance for carrying on and developing the property and was obliged to relinquish it. The family eventually returned to Napier, where William became engaged in other work.

William junior joined the Lands and Survey Department, Frederick joined the staff of the Bank of New South Wales, being manager of the Gisborne branch from 1887 until 1915, and John engaged in secretarial work.

Miriam and William spent the rest of their lives in Napier, William dying there in 1894 at the age of seventy-one. After his death Miriam lived at 90 Milton Road until she too passed away in 1913, at seventy-eight years of age.

CHAPTER 34

Elizabeth Ramsden

Elizabeth Nairn was born in England on 15 June, 1819. Her grandfather was the only one of four Nairn brothers to escape the slaughter of the Battle of Culloden. He made his way to England where he later married a Miss Deans, daughter of a steward to the Earl of Coventry. They had a son, John, who was apprenticed at the age of ten to learn gardening from his grandfather, Mr Deans, and at the age of twelve his wages were one shilling a week.

By the time he was about twenty years of age John was working as under-gardener for Sir Joseph Paxton, and employed in the same place as a maid in the stillroom was Eliza Liston. John married her at St George's in Hanover Square, London, and by her he had one daughter and four sons, Elizabeth, Frank, Charles, John and Henry.

In 1839 Elizabeth was almost twenty, and her brother, Charles left home to go to sea. The following year her parents decided to emigrate to New Zealand, and at the end of 1840 they left in the *William Bryan,* the first of the ships sponsored by the Plymouth Company which was acting in cooperation with the New Zealand Company.

About 145 emigrants sailed on the *William Bryan,* most of them being from the south of England. The voyage was uneventful, the winds were favourable, and after about thirteen weeks the vessel anchored off the Sugar Loaf Islands on 31 March, 1841. Conditions were ideal, with the weather calm and the sea like a millpond. A whaleboat put off from the shore to greet the newcomers and the surprise and delight of the Nairns can be imagined when they saw Charles forming one of its crew. He had come to New Zealand in 1839 as a cabinboy on the *Tory* and was now assisting Frederic Carrington in the survey of the New Plymouth settlement.

Before despatching the first body of colonists the Plymouth Company had sent out a party of labourers equipped to prepare a place for the main body, so that by the time they arrived they would find houses built and crops already planted. However, due to initial difficulties, this had not worked out and the people on the *William Bryan,* having been promised that houses would be ready for them, arrived to find nothing. They had to improvise tents and shelter on Ngamotu beach, and through shortness of provisions and the bad weather which raged in from the Tasman Sea, they had a very miserable winter.

Nor was there any help to be expected from the Maori population who numbered only about twenty, and whose crops had been destroyed by hostile raiders. The Company's second ship, the *Amelia Thompson,* was overdue with another party of immigrants and extra food, and after four months there was still no sign of her. The food problem had became acute when Providence sent large shoals of fish ashore.

Men, women and children gathered up every one of them, and those that were not eaten were cleaned, cured and packed into barrels for future use. A whaling vessel called and sold the settlers barrels of ships biscuits, full of weevils, for £2 per barrel, while an American whaling vessel sold them flour that had been pressed into barrels and was so hard it had to be chopped out with a tomahawk and then rubbed through a sieve before it could be made into bread.

John Nairn senior, who had come out as a botanist to the Company, soon had crops planted on his sections. They lived first at Heinui and then at Taupiri on the Waiwa-kaiho River which rises on the northern slopes of Mt Egmont and enters the sea east of New Plymouth. The few Maoris in the district were living near the north head of the mouth of this river. Little better than their whares, or perhaps not even as good, were the homes of the new settlers, which were mainly small huts built of slabs roughly hewn from tree trunks with an axe or adze, the slabs being fitted as closely as possible with any cracks being filled in with clay.

It was five months before the *Amelia Thompson* arrived, and on board her was James Ramsden, who had been brought up to assist his father as a grain merchant in Halifax, Yorkshire. In New Plymouth he took a hand at anything that came his way, even to hotelkeeping, as he is recorded as having had the Ship Inn for a time.

Elizabeth married him in 1846, their first child, Emma Dora, being born on 18 June 1848. The following year James became ill with a fever which caused him to lose his voice. He took a sea trip in an effort to get it back, sailing between New Plymouth and Wanganui, but on the return trip the ship was blown off course and James landed in Wellington without a sixpence in his pocket.

In the meantime Elizabeth's three brothers, Frank, John and Henry, worked on their own sections and as money was scarce they found other employment where possible. They went in for road making and track cutting, making the first track round Egmont to Hawera, still known as Nairns Track.

Within a few years came trouble with the Maoris, who declared they had not been paid for the land. Those who had been paid were not the rightful owners, as many of these people were only now returning from the Waikato where they had been held as slaves.

To avoid conflict with the Maoris the Nairns went to live in the Wanganui district, and around 1851 and 1852 they took up a property known as The Grange. It consisted of 600 acres freehold and 400 acres leasehold, and lay about eight miles from Wanganui. James and Elizabeth decided to go with them. Elizabeth packed their belongings and, with her mother and four-year-old Dora, sailed in the *Shepherdess*, a small cutter which traded up and down the coast. James joined them at The Grange and although he was still frail from his illness and his voice had not fully returned, he did his best to assist with the work.

The first house at The Grange was a primitive building that stood at the edge of the bush. The walls were of raupo thatched with rushes, the floor was bare earth and the chimney was of clay. Elizabeth, James and Dora had been living in it with the family for just a year when, in May 1853, James decided to ride to New Plymouth to collect business papers and settle some affairs.

The weather was bad in New Plymouth but, being anxious to return to Elizabeth, he set out on the homeward journey. At Patea he met and had a meal with some men who were sheep-droving. They later watched him cross the river and ride up the hill but nothing was ever seen or heard of him again. His horse was found some distance down the river, the saddle bloodstained and pulled round beneath its belly, his papers intact in the saddlebag. It is possible he was attacked and murdered by Maoris, but nothing has ever come to light to prove this as a fact.

The shock of losing James sent Elizabeth quite deaf. She also lost her hair, which never grew again, and from then on she always wore a cap. She was pregnant at the time of his death and her son James Daniel Ramsden was born five months later on 12 October 1853.

Elizabeth continued to live with her parents and brothers. In 1856 the raupo cottage was burnt down and the boys built a larger house of wattle and daub walls, thatched roof and ironstone chimneys. It had a sittingroom, diningroom, hall, five bedrooms and a large kitchen, but only some of the floors were timbered.

In the meantime Elizabeth's brother Charles Nairn was establishing himself on the 50,000-acre Hawke's Bay coastal property, Pourerere. In 1857 he became very ill through overwork and the fumes from the materials used for fighting scab in the sheep. At this time John and Henry were also at Pourerere and they sent for Elizabeth to come and nurse Charles.

Taking young Dan with her she shipped to Wellington in the SS *Wonga Wonga* and from there in the SS *Queen* for Ahuriri where, she stayed at Munn's Royal Hotel at the foot of Hyderabad Road. The rivers were in flood and for more than a week she stared from the windows each day, watching across the expanse of water that is now Napier South, hoping to see someone coming to fetch her.

At last she was rewarded by the sight of her brother Henry and a Maori, Hoani Te Rangikanaiho, with two led horses splashing through the water towards the hotel. The men stayed in Napier for two days to rest the horses and allow the waters to recede, and then they set out for Pourerere on the coast.

Young Dan rode perched on top of the saddlebag of the led horse until they stopped for lunch at Paki Paki. Evening found them at the Tuki Tuki, which was a swiftly flowing yellow flood, and with Davis's accommodation house on its far bank. Hoani now took Dan in front of him and they crossed with the waters running over the back of Elizabeth's horse and drenching her to the waist. The next day they had lunch at Tamumu with Edward Collins, and by nightfall they had reached Pourerere.

Elizabeth looked after Charles and the men on the station until after shearing then returned to Wanganui by ship. During the next few years there were outbreaks of trouble with the Maoris. It was necessary to bar the doors and windows at night and there were times when the resident magistrate at Wanganui ordered all women and children into town as Hauhau rebels were threatening to kill all the settlers. Only four miles away Captain James Duff Hewitt of Toi Farm, near Kai Iwi, was murdered, his heart cut out and his head carried away on a pole.

Eventually the Nairn boys persuaded their parents to sell The Grange and move to Pourerere. The property went to Captain McGrath for £3,000 and Elizabeth, her parents and children went to Hawke's Bay, where, for comfort, extra rooms were added to the existing house of six rooms. She now found herself working hard for a

Pourere station, 1880. Elizabeth Ramsden's brother, Charles Nairn, took up 50,000 acres here in the 1850s, and the widowed Elizabeth joined him with her parents and her children.

household of nine adults and with the help of Dora she did all the cooking for the station. At times a Maori woman helped with the washing which, when the water was low, had to be taken to the creek.

And there was now the question of her son's schooling. At the age of seven Dan rode to boardingschool in Napier, and in 1867, aged fourteen, he rode with others to Wanganui Collegiate School.

Dora had no schooling. In 1872 she married Jerome Edward Knapp who had come from Lincolnshire in England to work as a cadet on the nearby Edenham station. He took Dora first to Te Whiti in the Wairarapa but they later settled at Tikokino in Central Hawke's Bay.

Elizabeth missed her daughter, and four years later she lost her mother when Mrs John Nairn senior died and was buried at Pourerere on a high mound of ground about half a mile from the sea. The following year, in 1877, a small church was erected on the hill but years later this was dismantled. A few Nairn graves are still to be seen there.

In 1887, when various members of the Nairn family were overseas, Pourerere was leased to William Busby for seven years. During this period Elizabeth boarded with the Hindmarsh family in Cobden Road, Napier, but eventually the Pourerere lease ended and when the Nairns returned she was able to use her own quarters in the homestead once more.

There were times when she visited Jerome and Dora Knapp and their large family at Tikokino, where Jerome had taken up land in 1874. At other times she stayed with Dan who had married Fanny Jerrard who, after being educated in France, had been a governess to Henry Nairn's children.

155

Elizabeth Ramsden, *née* Nairn, 1819–
1912. "The shock of losing her husband
sent her quite deaf. She also lost her
hair, which never grew again, and from
then on she always wore a cap."

Elizabeth ended her days in a Hastings private hospital run by her niece Flora, a
daughter of Henry Nairn. She died on 3 August 1912, aged ninety-three, and was
buried in the Havelock North cemetery.

CHAPTER 35

Margaret Reeves

Margaret Livingstone was born in 1843 at Gatehouse-on-Fleet, Scotland, and came to New Zealand with her parents when in her teens. The family settled at Petone. She was a tall, dark girl with a strong personality, and in 1868 she married Andrew Reeves, who was several years her senior.

Andrew, the son of a farmer, was born in 1832 at Moffat, Dumfriesshire, Scotland, and came to New Zealand in the *Southern Cross* in 1857. He bought a horse and rode to Hawke's Bay where he found employment on Purvis Russell's Woburn station at Waipukurau, and later became its manager. Woburn was eventually cut up to become the Hatuma district.

In 1863 Andrew Reeves took up the lease of a property on the south side of the Wairoa River and he was the first man to drive a mob of sheep from Hawke's Bay above Mohaka. Then, seeking a block of land that would suit him better, he bought Ihunui in the Uawa Valley from Captain Henry Glover, who had acquired it from Maori owners. This first block taken up consisted of about 2,500 acres, most of it swampy flat land covered in flax and raupo and with manuka scrub on the hills. The property, lying one mile inland from Tolaga Bay, was bounded by the Uawa River on one side and by seaward hills on the other.

When Margaret went to Tolaga Bay as a bride she was not the first white woman to live there but she was the first to settle permanently. Their first home was a Maori whare built of raupo and manuka, and they lived in it until a better cottage could be built. Cooking was done in the camp oven and water was carried from the stream until a windmill pump was installed near the cottage. Stores came twice a year from Auckland or Napier by schooner.

The European population consisted of about a dozen people, mainly missionaries and traders, the only transport from the place being by horse or ship. The cattle that Andrew brought to the property were the first in the district, the sight of them causing much consternation among the Maoris, who had never before seen such animals. The annual draft of wethers shipped to Auckland was loaded from the Tolaga beach. The sheep had their legs tied with flax and were lifted into the surf boat which plied back and forth with loads to the waiting vessel.

When Margaret's first baby was due she went by ship to Napier, where James Livingstone was born in 1867. When the child was six weeks old she set off again for home but bad weather and srong winds blew the cutter out to sea, causing it to take two weeks to reach Tolaga Bay.

She remained at home to have her second baby, and when he arrived in 1869 Andrew Ernest was the first white child to be born in the district.

Tolaga Bay, *circa* 1914. Margaret Reeves's second baby, born 1869, was the first white child born in the district.

A few months after the Poverty Bay massacre in November 1868 word came that Te Kooti and a band of his followers were in the vicinity of Tolaga Bay. The news forced the family, together with a few Europeans and a party of friendly Maoris, to spend several nights out in the bush until the scare was over. Baby Andrew was only a few months old at this time. Later, when the redoubt was built on the northern side of the Uawa River, they spent the nights within its shelter. The Tolaga Bay Maoris were always friendly towards the settlers and did their utmost to turn Te Kooti back.

The arrival of a daughter, Evelyn, gave Margaret three children, two born in Tolaga Bay, and by that time a few more white women were living in the district.

In 1873 Andrew purchased Waitaria, a flat 200-acre property at Patutahi, near Gisborne. This gave them suitable land on which to fatten cattle for sale to butchers as at that time there was no local market for cattle. Their next son, Charles Wellwood, was born at Tolaga Bay in 1874, and he was the first white child to be born on the west side of the Waipaoa River.

Margaret's next baby was another daughter, Matilda. After two years or more at Waitaria they returned to Tolaga Bay to resume life in the district still populated predominantly by Maoris. However, their relations with the Maoris were good, the only friction occurring when Maori dogs had to be shot for killing sheep. Margaret and Andrew always respected Maori customs and tapus and made a firm rule never to collect Maori artifacts or accept gifts unless presented in the manner according to custom.

Education for the children was provided by a governess, and by Margaret herself teaching them when necessary, and when the Tolaga Bay school opened Ernest was the only white pupil to attend. James and Ernest later went to Napier Boys' High School, while Wellwood was an early pupil at the Gisborne High School.

Terrible setbacks in the form of heavy legal expenses were incurred by Andrew when it was necessary to justify his land purchases and to establish his titles to the Wharekaka land he had taken up. His leasehold and freehold land amounted to about 6,000 acres and by 1877 he had 3,820 sheep on the property.

158

Left: Margaret Reeves, *née* Livingstone, 1843–1923. *Right:* Andrew Reeves, her husband.

After the crippling legal expenses he had to contend with the slump in sheep prices, the losses through sheep scab and the lack of market for them before the days of refrigeration. He was almost bankrupt three times but by sheer hard work managed to pull through.

Despite having so little money to spare Margaret was always ready to give. When the roads permitted and they possessed a buggy she went to the village several days each week taking Maori kits of food for the sick and needy. A lifetime of experience had taught her to be self-reliant and capable, and she was always willing to lend a hand in any emergency. She was hospitable and gladly welcomed friends who stayed overnight when passing through the district.

The roads, when they began to be formed, were poor for many years and almost impossible to negotiate in winter. Once when on her way home from Gisborne she was a passenger in a coach which overturned at a corner and rolled down a steep bank on the Tolaga hill. She spent a period in hospital after that experience.

Their financial struggle went on until 1902 when suddenly, for the first time, Andrew made a surplus of £2,000 which did not have to be put back into fences or

Margaret Reeves was a coach passenger on Tolaga hill when the vehicle overturned and rolled down a steep bank.

other expenses. But just as their farming venture became secure after the long years of hard work, he died on 5 December 1903.

After his death Margaret continued to live at Ihunui. The property was run by her sons, and in 1910 a new house was built to replace the old one, which had become infested by borer. Her daughter Evelyn had become Mrs H. Maude, while Matilda had married her cousin G. Livingstone.

Margaret, who remained a dominant personality respected by all, retained complete control of the land and household until she died on 28 January 1923.

CHAPTER 36

Meretene Ripeka

In December 1844 the brig *Nimrod* sailed southward from Auckland, beating its way round the coast towards Turanganui, Wairoa and Ahuriri on the East Coast. On board were the Colenso (9) and Hamlin (17) families who were to establish the first mission stations at Wairoa and Ahuriri, plus livestock, stores and a great deal of equipment. Also on board were two young Maoris a girl, Meretene Ripeka, and a man, Hamuera (Samuel) te Nehu, who were with William and Elizabeth Colenso.

Meretene Ripeka was usually known as Ripeka, which was the Maori for Rebecca. A pretty girl with dark curly hair, she had a happy, laughing nature. She was the daughter of an East Coast Kahungunu chief and a Ngapuhi mother and had been brought up in exile: her mother, born to a position of rank, had been taken captive in war when a child and carried away to the Bay of Islands. At Te Waimate Ripeka had been a public gift from her parents to William Colenso, and as a member of his household she had grown up and spent much time in the company of Hamuera.

Hamuera was Colenso's personal servant. In the Bay of Islands he had been a slave but, when a very little boy, had been saved by Archdeacon Henry Williams from being killed and eaten. Through scrofula, a tuberculous type of glandular disease, he had become an unpleasant sight as the disease had eaten large holes in his neck, armpits and breasts. Colenso took him in about 1835, bore with him patiently as recorded in his journal, and through God's blessing on the means Hamuera became perfectly cured.

As Colenso's servant he accompanied the missionary on his many journeys, suffering in some cases more hardships than his master. During the Rangitikei journey in 1848, while negotiating the difficult cliffs in pouring rain, he crippled himself by straining the sinews of his back, after which he spent a night in agony, and next day, while almost starving, still had to struggle along with the rest of the party.

While Hamuera attended to William Colenso, Ripeka assisted Elizabeth at the mission station. At times she does not appear to have had great resistance to illness, suffering a severe bout of influenza in the beginning of 1848, and becoming seriously ill again at the end of that year. During this latter illness she became delirious and for a time it was doubtful whether she would recover. In fact so great was Colenso's anxiety for Ripeka that he delayed the departure for his next journey, but by the time he returned she was convalescing.

It is not surprising that Colenso's eyes strayed towards Ripeka, who had developed into a beautiful young woman. Nor is it unlikely that Ripeka was unaware of the frigid marital relations existing between the Colensos. Elizabeth, though kindly

161

towards others and full of Christian principles, was cold and austere towards her husband. The marriage was anything but happy.

Nor is it surprising that, five years after the birth of their youngest child, the sex-starved William sought comfort with the warm and sympathetic Ripeka. During the winter of 1850 various reasons caused him to spend more time than usual at the mission. He also suffered bouts of sickness and constantly referred in his journal to his ill health. That year he wrote of her—*She was always kind and willing to do anything for me at all times by day or night, particularly when in pain and ever without a murmur or cross look; indeed she is a merry, laughing soul, the idol of the two children and the light in our house and so the connection between us took place.*

Their relationship does not appear to have been suspected, but the time came when Ripeka found herself to be pregnant. She had no intention that their liaison should leave her the unmarried partner of a Pakeha and she therefore turned to Hamuera.

With Hamuera she had grown up in the shelter of mission life. They had worked together, laughing or quarrelling as they had tended the garden or worked in the kitchen, and she had long since become used to the unsightliness of his appearance. With him she could find security for her baby and perhaps go away to live at Patangata where she would be a servant only to her husband. She found Hamuera only too willing to marry her, and the ceremony took place later in the year.

They were married before the altar of the Waitangi chapel. Who officiated has not been recorded, but Colenso made his disapproval of the marriage more than clear. A few months later, in the May of 1851, he had just returned from a trip to the Wairarapa when Ripeka called that it was time to fetch Riria, the midwife. A short time later she gave birth to a son.

After the birth Riria is reported to have noticed the baby's light skin and to have exclaimed, "Aue! He Pakeha!" but at the time this had merely amused them all. The

William Colenso, 1868. In 1850 he wrote in his diary that Meretene Ripeka " . . . is a merry, laughing soul, the idol of the two children and the light of our house."

child was christened Wiremu, the Maori name for William, and did very well despite the fact that he was weaned at an early age because of Ripeka's poor health. But at last it was Elizabeth's womanly curiosity and persistent questions which caused the bombshell to explode! Ripeka felt no shame and explained without hesitation that Colenso was the father of her child.

The shock this must have been to Elizabeth was no doubt tempered by the fact that there never had been any love between Colenso and herself. For years their marriage had been one in name only and she therefore continued her work with studied forbearance and hoped that Ripeka and Hamuera would take the child and go away to live at Patangata.

Ripeka now found herself between two fires. From one side came the barbed remarks of an injured wife which told her exactly what she thought of her, while from the other side came an extra rush of affection from Colenso. The situation became intolerable and she longed to leave the mission station, to escape the persecution of Elizabeth, to forget Colenso and to just be with Hamuera and her child.

But Colenso's love seemed to hold her in bondage; and, further, he would not part with the child. She became desperately unhappy, her days shadowed with gloom and her sleep disturbed by nightmares until she was in a state when she was seized by fits.

Writing as if addressing the baby, Colenso recorded in his autobiography: *Sometimes when out alone with you in her arms on the banks of the Waitangi creek, or on the sea shore, and finding her fit coming on, she would, not being able to return in time to the house, lay you down carefully on the ground and await it, and so you have been found.*

At the end of October 1851 Ripeka was again very ill with fever, and by December she decided, not without a struggle, to leave little Wiremu for a time with Elizabeth Colenso while she went with Hamuera to Patangata. At that place, which was more than a day's journey away up the Tuki Tuki, Hamuera was to look after the cows belonging to the chief, Wiremu Tipuna, and as he had been with Colenso for seventeen years he went to Patangata very much against the latter's wish.

During the time of their absence Bishop Selwyn visited the mission and, taking little Wiremu on his knee, declared him to be a fine child. Colenso then tried to summon courage to confess his lapse, but failed, and Elizabeth too remained silent.

After two months absence Ripeka and Hamuera returned to Waitangi and by this time it was February 1852. Ripeka was still most unhappy and after a month of discontent the couple hatched a plot to take the baby and run away in a small canoe. The plan was unsuccessful because although they themselves were able to get away, they were prevented from taking the little boy, who remained in the hands of Elizabeth.

Perhaps, with Colenso, Elizabeth was also fond of the child and feared to see him abandoned to the casual care of those in the pa. But Ripeka was in a state of fury at Colenso's fanatical determination to keep her baby. She was now carrying Hamuera's child but this did not mean she no longer cared for or wanted Wiremu. Angrily, she told her story to the people at Patangata, and while many questioned Colenso who replied in a guarded manner, others openly disbelieved her.

Coupled with this latter disturbing fact Ripeka found that many of the people at Patangata considered that she and Hamuera should not live there, and so they returned again to the mission in May. On 12 May her second baby was born but as it seemed unlikely to live Colenso was called to baptise it early in the morning. Some hours later it died, leaving Ripeka in an agony of grief. In the meantime Colenso had sent a letter of confession to Bishop Selwyn, admitting himself to be the father of Ripeka's son, Wiremu, whom the Bishop had considered such a fine boy.

Ripeka continued to work in the house and garden at the mission where she could at least be near her living child, who was just beginning to toddle and who was kept neat and clean by Elizabeth. She suspected that Elizabeth would leave the mission soon, but she also knew that this would not allow her to remain with Colenso because she was now the wife of Hamuera. Further, the elders at the pa had decided that both she and Hamuera must live at Patangata. After all, was she not the daughter of a Kahungunu?

During those days Hamuera was at Patangata forming a plan. On 17 November a well-manned canoe swung into the Ngaruroro below the station and after beaching the craft the paddlers went into the huts, where they were usually welcomed and offered food. Watching them, Colenso became suspicious and warned Elizabeth that she must not let little Wiremu out of her sight.

Elizabeth had been ill and was in no state to argue, but as the few remaining bundles were being stacked into the canoe she saw that Wiremu was being smuggled aboard. One of her little house girls raised a cry of alarm and Colenso rushed out from his study. Before the group on the bank could man the canoe into the river he had snatched the boy into his arms and had run back to the house.

The Patangata Maoris followed, and Colenso shouted for Karaitiana's people living across the river to come to his aid. He then stood guarding the door, deaf to the alternate pleadings and screams of rage from Ripeka. Blood would surely have been shed had help not come from across the river, but at last the Patangata people left while Ripeka and Hamuera remained sulking in an outhouse. A few days later they finally left for Patangata, still without Wiremu.

Bishop Selwyn now took a hand in the boy's fate. He suspended Colenso from missionary work and decided that Elizabeth should return to her own family and that she should take the child with her. However, as Wiremu was a "child of sin", her father refused him admittance into the Fairburn home and the boy was boarded out at £12 per year, first to a European home and then through Maoris to the Bay of Islands. There he attended mission schools when old enough to do so, but by 1861 was back in Hawke's Bay and at school in Napier. He grew into a handsome young man and entered the Navy. In 1876 he settled in England where he married Sarah Colenso, a cousin, but there were no children of the marriage. He lived until the age of forty-eight, dying in 1903.

Hamuera is known to have lived to a considerable age and is referred to in Colenso's diaries of the 1890s, but of Ripeka little is known.

Although there was a little correspondence between them, Colenso saw her only once and this was ten years after she had left the Waitangi mission station. And then in 1880, a distant relation of Colenso's who was leaving Napier reported (this was fifty years later) that while on the tugboat going out to the steamer she had sat opposite Ripeka—"a handsome woman with curly hair".

CHAPTER 38

Frances Ross

Frances Bee was born at Ocean Beach, near Waimarama, in 1855. She was a sister to Kate Bourke (5) and was therefore a daughter of Francis and Ann Bee who took up the 11,000 acre Waipuka block in 1852. Her early years were spent playing on the beach, but schooling came when the family moved to Havelock North. Like her sister she was an avid reader and did much to educate herself. The family called her Fanny.

In 1866 her father took over the 9,000 acre Mohaka station and the family moved north to live at the mouth of the Mohaka. It was here, during the troublesome days that led to the Mohaka massacre in 1869, that Fanny learned to live in fear of Te Kooti.

Francis Bee also leased the large Maungaharuru block lying about fourteen miles west of Lake Tutira. It was farmed by his son George, who lived in a small slab whare near a stream at the edge of the bush. At night the dogs were kept chained in front to give warning of prowling Hauhaus, while a trapdoor at the back afforded a hasty exit to the bush if necessary. George always slept with a gun beside his pillow.

At times Fanny and her younger sister Lizzie (who was later Mrs Chris Brandon of Putere station), spent sometime at Maungaharuru with George. On one occasion they ran out of food and George had to leave the two girls while he went home to Mohaka for stores. At this time they were aged about eleven and nine and, left alone in the hut all night, they were terrified. They shared the same bunk, clutching each other through the long hours of darkness and not sleeping a wink. The gurgling of the stream sounded like a howling war-cry, sending them with thudding hearts to peer through the small window and thinking every flaxbush a crouching Hauhau.

George in the meantime was seriously worried about leaving the two girls alone, and travelled all night to cover the twenty-five miles from Mohaka back to Maungaharuru. At daybreak he cooeed from the hilltop at the back of the shack and they crept out, thankful to see him. He carried not only stores but two cherry trees which he planted and named Fanny and Lizzie. Over the years these trees flourished and multiplied into the large, and once well-known, Maungaharuru grove of cherry trees, the site being where R. J. Heay's woolshed now stands.

Fanny grew to be a tall, graceful girl with wavy brown hair and hazel eyes that always held a twinkle. Her bright personality endeared her to everyone and caught the attention of David Ross. By this time her parents had retired to Gisborne, where Fanny and David were married.

David Melville Ross was born in Lyttelton in 1852. He ran away from school to join the cavalry of the Armed Constabulary and it is thought that they met at the

165

season's highlight, the Military Ball. After their marriage they lived at Napier and it was there that Fanny's first baby, Maude, was born and died in infancy.

Later they moved north when David managed the coastal Moeangiangi station. Almost a redhead, he was a small, wiry man for whom the day was never long enough. He was often to be found digging the vegetable garden by moonlight or cobbing corn by lamplight, and would continue blade shearing until long after the shearing day had finished.

At Moeangiangi Fanny knew real loneliness. The nearest road was about thirty miles away. There were only bridletracks to the small homestead which was set between high hills with the sea nearby and no other human habitation for miles.

They were there when the now pardoned Te Kooti came down the coast with some forty of his followers. Fanny was alone in the house when they appeared in the lonely valley. Afraid, she crept out to hide in the bush, but as they appeared to be moving about peacefully she ventured forth to offer them vegetables and milk. They remained talking to her for some time, interested in the fact that she could speak their language so fluently, and soon she was relieved to see them leave the valley.

Fanny and David later moved to Mohaka, where her ability to speak the language and her wise understanding of their problems, sent many Maoris to her for advice. She became their doctor, lawyer and mediator, and they called her Whani.

One day she was sent for to conciliate a husband and wife—the wife having almost chopped off her husband's ear with an axe because he had hit her. Whani told him it served him right; he must not hit his wife. Another time, when a Maori woman went mad and rushed about the pa flourishing an axe, Whani was sent for and soon had the demented woman weeping on her shoulder.

Another occasion arose when two Maoris became partners in a flock of ewes, the agreement being that each should pay half the cost of the necessary rams. One paid but the other did not. The man who had paid for the rams declared that all the lambs were his and the heated argument would have ended in bloodshed had not they appealed to Whani.

"No lambs if no rams," declared the one who had paid for the rams.

"No lambs if no mothers," Whani pointed out and then, after considerable discussion gave her decision. The lambs were to be divided provided each man paid his share of the rams.

By the time they had been at Mohaka for some years Fanny had five children. They were Phoebe, Jack, Frank, Daisy and Elsie. Throughout the years her husband David remained as restless as ever, always longing for a place of his own. In the latter part of the 1900s when Jack and Frank had only just left school he took them on a trip of exploration over the rugged, bushclad hill country about twelve miles north-west of Kotemaori in the Wairoa district.

They came to a little flat at the foot of a cliff overlooking the Mohaka River. Growing on it was a lonely willow tree which had possibly begun its life as a willow staff left stuck in the ground by a passing Maori. The view across the Mohaka from this clearing in the bush appealed to David Ross as a suitable place for a home, and in 1901 he took up a lease of 11,632 acres for a period of twenty-one years at an annual rental of £80. The land was part of the old Maungaharuru station, and they called it Willow Flat.

David moved there with the boys while Fanny and her three daughters remained at Mohaka for schooling. At first the men just lived in tents but later they built a two-roomed slab-sided whare with shingled roof and clay floor. Fanny and the girls visited them whenever possible and they were there during one period of school holidays when news was brought that the Mohaka house had been burnt down with a total loss of all their possessions.

She then had no option but to remain at Willow Flat, settling into the slab whare where the stars could be seen through the shingles and where mud pies had to be made to fill in the holes in the clay floor. The rough walls were covered with pictures ranging from racehorses to royalty, and each member of the family pasted up his or her own favourites.

Cooking was done over an open fire or in a camp oven. Water came from a waterfall about 100 yards away and was ingeniously piped to the whare through hollow cabbage-tree trunks raised up on forked branches. Food was kept cool in a wooden meatsafe placed in a fern-filled cave directly under the waterfall, which curved over it. Washing was done at the creek and stores came every six months.

It was also now necessary for the children to board away from home for the sake of their education, and this meant that, with the men away at the back of the run for days on end, Fanny was beset by loneliness. She slept with a gun beside her bed and at times she would climb a high hill just for the comfort of seeing a distant wisp of smoke which indicated there were other human beings in the district.

When David was on his way home he would light a fire when about two hours distant from home. Fanny would see this from her hilltop and would then hurry home to stoke up and prepare a meal which would be ready by the time he arrived.

Eventually a weatherboard house was built, but first the trees across the Mohaka had to be felled, pitsawn, and the timber slid across the river on a wire to the house site. Later this house too was burned down and again they had to live in tents with all the cooking being done outside.

When they rebuilt her great joy was a conservatory attached to the new home, and

Frances Ross, *née* Bee, 1855–1947. "Her ability to speak the Maori language and her wise understanding of their problems sent many Maoris to her for advice. She became their doctor, lawyer and mediator, and they called her 'Whani'."

her only extravagance during those hard-up days was to buy potted begonias and such for hanging in baskets. These came from John Anderson, the nurseryman at Napier, who packed them with special care for the sixty-mile coach journey which was followed by the horse ride back to Willow Flat.

A winter trip to Napier meant rising before daylight to ride the ten miles of rough track to catch the coach at the junction of the main road—and to be there in time to change into best clothes in the scrub before the coach arrived. If for some reason Fanny's own quiet mare was unavailable, a snorting kicking animal would have to be ridden round the yard a few times by David before she could mount.

On one occasion when returning from Napier by coach one of the leading reins broke and the horses bolted on the old coach road which went up and over the hills from Waikari. The men jumped clear but Fanny, inside the coach, was unable to do this. However, the parcels cushioned her fall as the coach rolled three or four

The Devil's Elbow on the Tutiroa-Napier-Wairoa road, 1905. Fanny Ross was in one of these coaches when it rolled downhill.

times down the hill and she suffered a couple of broken ribs, a damaged nose and bad bruises. In this state she walked several miles to a house where she was able to spend the night.

Willow Flat became a place that was loved and visited by many friends who enjoyed being taken to visit the site of the old Maori pa at the back of the property where there were palisading posts, an axe grinding stone and several skeletons that could be uncovered. They also enjoyed the Maungaharuru cherry grove which had become part of the Willow Flat property, and which was now a favourite rendezvous for most of the district's picnic parties.

Sorrow came to Fanny and David when they lost their two sons. Frank was killed in World War I; Jack died of illness when he was twenty-seven years of age and was buried at Willow Flat.

Before this time Fanny was fighting the Wairoa County Council for the formation of a road from Kotemaori to Willow Flat, but not until they had been there for thirty years was this road completed. She also fought for a suspension bridge to be put across the river opposite the homestead, and even went to Parliament to put this cause forward. The Mohaka, which is not a river to be trifled with, was forded on horseback for years until they were later able to cross it on the suspension bridge, but this eventually collapsed under a load of bullocks, most of which had then to be shot.

Throughout the years David retained his energy, but he had to admit defeat after his last muster of wild cattle at the age of eighty-four. The exhausting task over, he staggered to his room knowing he had performed it for the last time. Not long after that he became ill and bedridden until he had a stroke and died in 1938, aged eighty-six. He too, was buried at Willow Flat.

After David's death Fanny put a manager on the place until she sold to Donald Fraser. She then lived in turn with Daisy, who was Mrs Jago and lived at Frasertown, or with Elsie, whose husband Jack Borrie was managing Omarunui station. Her other daughter, Phoebe, who was Mrs Dewes and lived at Napier, predeceased her by about a couple of years. Fanny herself died in 1947, aged ninety-two; Her body was taken back to Willow Flat and after a service held on the verandah of her old home she was buried beside David and Jack.

A few years later a pilgrimage was made back to Willow Flat by Elsie Borrie and Daisy Jago. Accompanied by Elsie's husband Jack and Daisy's son David, they camped in the shearers' quarters on what was known as Run 38. From there, with the aid of a truck kindly lent by John Stovell (who by then with his father, H. V. Stovell, had bought Willow Flat from Donald Fraser) they carried stones and water to build a cairn over the resting places of Frances Ross, her husband and her son.

CHAPTER 38

Caroline Seymour

Caroline Levinge was a tall girl with brown eyes and an olive complexion. She was born in Ireland in 1846, her home, known as Newpark at Athlone, being a three-storeyed Georgian house standing within spacious grounds. She married Charles Seymour, a dark, bearded man of medium height born near Athlone in 1841. He was one of the five sons of Henry Seymour, a Dublin lawyer who emigrated with his family to Australia in 1841 and took up Mount Barker in the hills of Adelaide. They eventually took up Killanoola on the Bool Lagoon, sold Mount Barker and acquired yet another station, Mount Benson, near Robe. This comprised 162 square miles, 116 of them at 10s per square mile and 46 at 15s per square mile.

One day during the 1870s Charles's sister-in-law suggested that he should find himself a wife. He told her that the only girl he had ever loved was away over in Ireland and probably would refuse to have him in any case. His sister-in-law urged him to go to back to Ireland and make sure about it. So Charles obediently went back to Ireland and asked Caroline to marry him: she accepted him and they were married at Athlone.

They remained in Ireland for a time, possibly because Caroline's mother was in failing health, and their first child, Charles Henry, was born there. He was little more than a baby when they left Ireland and Caroline's second child, Evelyn Mary, was born in Australia. Caroline's mother died after she had arrived in Australia and her father eventually married again.

Henry Seymour died at Mount Benson in 1869. In 1875 his widow sent her son James to New Zealand and enabled him to purchase the lease of the Whangara run, consisting of 21,450 acres, from H. R. C. Wallace. The hilly bush country lay on the coast about twenty miles north of Gisborne, but unfortunately James did not do well with the property. Charles was then sent over to investigate, leaving Caroline and the children in Australia, and in 1881 James sold him the lease. He worked hard to put the land in order.

Later, Caroline decided to join Charles. She packed her belongings and with the two small children sailed for New Zealand, eventually arriving in Gisborne. There she was able to make arrangements with Maoris to row the family up the coast to Whangara in an open whaleboat.

The wind blew strongly, and as they left the shelter of Poverty Bay to nose slowly along the coast the sky darkened and the sea became rough. When they had covered about three quarters of the voyage the weather became worse and the Maoris refused to go any further. They pulled into the shore under the high bluff overlooking the beach at Pouawa, and there Caroline was put ashore to spend the night in the bush with the two little ones sleeping huddled beside her.

Next morning the Maoris came to them at daylight and said the weather had improved sufficiently for them to continue. The whaleboat was pushed into the sea and they were lifted into it once more. When they reached Whangara Caroline was astounded—and the children terrified—to be greeted by a wild haka of welcome from Maoris who had been squatting in the coastal scrub behind the sandhills awaiting their arrival. They were then carried ashore and their belongings taken to the small cottage, which was almost on the beach. Charles, who had no idea they were coming, was amazed to find his family waiting in the cottage when he returned at the end of the day. How the Maoris knew of it remained a mystery.

It was an odd little cottage with a verandah and a passage which divided the bedroom from the long narrow kitchen with its dirt floor, its colonial oven and big boiler. There was also a narrow livingroom, but all this was later improved by enlarging and adding a scullery. At the back of the house there was a hill, and half a mile along the beach was the Maori pa.

Caroline's life then became preoccupied with forming a home for Charles and the two little ones, making a garden and sewing for the family. Charles spent most of his time out on the property, burning off the bush on the hills and establishing pastures.

When her next baby, Ethel Eleanor (Nell) was born Caroline was alone except for

Caroline Seymour, *née* Levinge, 1846–1907. When she and her two small children reached Whangara she was "... astounded to be greeted by a wild haka of welcome from Maoris who had been squatting behind the sandhills."

a Maori girl in the kitchen and a man outside in the backyard, but between them they did what they could to help her. A week after the baby's birth Caroline was outside working in the garden, and by the time her next baby, Walter, arrived she had the assistance of a white woman named Louise who was living with them.

As the children grew up their education was attended to at home until they were old enough to go away to school. Trips to town for their clothing and other essentials were taken only once a year. Church services and baptisms could be held only when a clergyman happened to come up the coast, and this was usually the Rev W. L. Williams (5).

During the early years all transport up the coast was by horse-back or by the ship which brought the stores once a year and took away the wool. But unlike many of the pioneer women Caroline was seldom lonely, for the property lay on the main coast track and there was always someone riding past the homestead. It was situated between the Pakarae and Waimoko Rivers, which could be crossed only when the tide was right, and this meant there was always someone who was caught between the two rivers.

The Whangara homestead became a haven for people waiting to cross the rivers, going either one way or the other, and being of a most hospitable nature Caroline and Charles added a great long diningroom to the cottage so that there would always be plenty of room for these casual guests. In later years the wagons and drays came ploughing through the newly formed roads, and there was also the coach that might become stuck in the mud or caught in the rivers. By that time Caroline's trips to town were made once a year by coach.

At one period Charles had to return to Australia to put the Killanoola property in order, and after the Mount Benson land was sold he began to freehold the Whangara property for himself. Shortly after this a new Land Act made his title null and void. He took his case to court and lost it. Not satisfied, he took it before the Privy Council in England and lost it again. Then, as he considered that justice had not been done, and at enormous cost, he took it before the Privy Council for the second time. This time he was rewarded with a choice of 5,000 acres freehold from the 21,450 acres leased.

The extreme worry of these court cases made life miserable for them all and by 1901 Charles was in failing health. The doctor was sent for but did not come in time to help him, and he died on 5 March 1901 while lying on the verandah at Whangara.

After his death his eldest son Charles Henry took over the running of the station and before long a new bride came to live at Whangara. Caroline and her daughters moved to Gisborne and later took a trip to England. Evelyn married J. C. N. (Charles) Thomas, and Nell married W. R. B. (Rex) Willock. A couple of years after her return Caroline died at the age of sixty on 3 October 1907. The land was divided between her four children and is still being farmed by her descendants.

CHAPTER 39

Alice Georgina Sherratt, MBE

Alice Georgina Gary was born in Auckland in 1869. She was a slim girl of medium height with dark hair and brown eyes and she later went to Gisborne where, at the age of seventeen, in 1886, she married William Grice Sherratt.

William, born in Staffordshire in 1862, was tall, slim and bearded. He had fair hair and blue eyes, and though very active had a retiring nature until later in life. He came to New Zealand in 1879 to join his brother Richard, who was already in Gisborne. He worked for a while on a property in Hawke's Bay before going in 1881 to work for Charles Seymour on the Whangara property, where he gained more experience. Then, at the time of his marriage, he took over the management of the 9,000 acre Panikau station for Edward Murphy.

Alice was a town girl who had never ridden before her wedding, but after the ceremony she was placed on a horse to ride to Panikau. There were no roads and the tracks lay along the coastal route as far as Whangara, then turned inland for another twelve miles through hilly, bush country — a long and painful journey for one who has never before ridden a horse.

Her new home was a good cottage of pitsawn totara built from timber felled on the property. There were two bedrooms and in the kitchen was a colonial oven where the fire burned both below and on top where pots sat on a bar and kettles hung from hooks. Bathing was done in a tub carried into the kitchen. The house was surrounded by bush, intensely silent except when broken by the dawn and evening chorus of the birds fluttering in the many puriri trees. Stores were brought in by packhorse although eventually the tracks were wide enough for bullock drays.

Alice had to ride whenever she left the station, and in 1887 she rode side-saddle into Gisborne for the birth of Amy, her first child. Fifteen months later she rode in again when Muriel was due to be born, and on each of these rides she paused to rest for a time with Caroline Seymour (38) at Whangara.

In 1892 they left Panikau to manage Edward Murphy's 13,000-acre Waiau station, much further up the coast in the Waiapu district. The land was in heavy tawa bush and William was to break it in. Here they had a better house, though still pitsawn, but there was the added comfort of a verandah. They found the Maoris on the coast very friendly and always ready to give assistance, but the isolation was not so good for the children, who became very shy. They saw few people and, like frightened kittens, scurried away to hide under the house if a visitor appeared. Yolande, their third daughter, was born at Waiau, and while the children were young Alice herself attended to their early education.

Despite the distance from Gisborne Alice and William travelled there once a year for the Show and for balls. Friends wrote to them describing the new dance steps that were in fashion, and these they would learn and practise at home before leaving. In 1900 they left Waiau and moved to live in Gisborne, where they had a house in Sievwright's Lane. Mildred was born there in 1900, Margaret in 1902, and lastly, the twins, Olive and William, in 1906.

In Gisborne Alice's life changed completely. William, whose nature had previously been so retiring, now took an interest in public affairs. With C. D. Bennett he established the mercantile firm of Bennett & Sherratt, and not only was he chairman of the Cook County Council for five years, chairman of the Gisborne Harbour Board for four years, and chairman of the Cook Hospital Board for eight years, but he was also Mayor of Gisborne for five years 1914–19. He played polo, was Master of the hounds, president of the Poverty Bay Club and president of the A&P Association.

Alice took a keen interest in all his activities and as Mayoress of Gisborne attended many functions and entertained whenever necessary. She took a prominent part in all patriotic movements and in 1918 was awarded the MBE for her untiring work. By that time her life had become very far removed from the earlier years spent in the bush cottage at Panikau, and from the later solitude of Waiau.

William died in 1942 and Alice in 1945. Both were buried in the Taruheru cemetery.

It is appropriate, for reasons that will be seen later, to add a note on Edward Murphy, for whom William worked on the East Coast. Edward Murphy was born at Richmond, Victoria, in 1845. He was the son of John Robert Murphy (1806–91) who left Ireland for Australia in 1828 and experienced the terror of the ship in which he sailed being burned at sea. Fortunately most of the passengers and crew were rescued by a passing ship and taken to Hobart, but John Murphy lost his luggage and his letters of credit, and until the new letters arrived he had to work at jobs such as splitting timber, burning lime and distilling whiskey.

On 18 June 1835 he married Elizabeth Terry at New Norfolk in Tasmania. In 1838 he took an option on a farm in Warnambool, which he sold during the land boom of the 1840s at a considerable profit, and this he invested in real estate in the growing city of Melbourne and was able to send his five sons to Cheltenham in England to complete their education. A stained glass window in the Melbourne Anglican Church commemorates his name.

Edward, his son, was tall, bearded and erect, and so regular in his habits that it was said people set the clock by him. In 1873 he took up the lease of Paremata at Tolaga Bay and then went home to marry Edith Read Moore.

Edith was the daughter of Dr A. Moore of Fingal, Tasmania. Fair-haired and blue-eyed, she was not tall but was very active and quick in her movements. She was one of a family of four sons and four daughters, and was a cousin to Gabriel Read, whose discovery of Gabriel's Gully in 1861 set off the unprecedented rush to the Tuapeka goldfields.

After her marriage at Fingal in 1873 Edith was brought to New Zealand for her honeymoon and to settle at Tolaga Bay. Her new home was at Taharangi on the Uawa River and there, in a strange land and many miles from her own people, she learned to ignore loneliness and to cope with primitive conditions in a district where there were neither roads nor bridges, and journeys had to be made either on horseback or on foot.

Edith was a very friendly person. She became a keen gardener and proved to be an excellent housekeeper. By 1884 she had six children, Edward Rowley, John Rowley, Michael Rowley, Elizabeth, Robert Keith and Ralph Christian. With the exception of Ralph, who was born in New Zealand, she returned to her husband's people in Melbourne for her confinements.

By that time Edward had taken up Panikau, Waiau, and other properties. He became noted for his good horses, importing stallions from America, and in Europe he was successful in purchasing a stallion from the Emperor of Austria's Royal Lippizaner stud. He also founded the Panikau Shorthorn stud herd.

In 1884 Edward and Edith made their home at Kaiariki, Manutuke, near Gisborne, and from there he supervised the various properties he had taken up, placing William Sherratt at Panikau and later at Waiau. It was at Manutuke, in 1885, that he planted the first citrus fruit trees to be grown in Poverty Bay, and he was also the first man in New Zealand to add turnip seed to the mixture of cocksfoot, ryegrass and clovers sown for pastures. He died at Auckland in 1919, and among his benefactions was the Bethany (Edward Murphy Memorial) Hospital at Gisborne.

Edith lived until 1933. Her daughter Elizabeth married C. A. Sherriff, and her sons took over and ran the properties. Her youngest son, Ralph, married Muriel, the daughter of Alice and William Sherratt—and so two pioneer families were united.

CHAPTER 40

Margaret Home Sievwright

Margaret Home Sievwright was born in Scotland in 1844. She was tall and slender with a fair skin, and those who remembered her in youth declared her to have been quite beautiful. (Curiously, they left no record of her maiden name.) From an early age her thoughts were for other people, particularly the poor and the suffering. Her education fitted her for schoolteaching, but rather than take her place in the classroom in an Academy for Young Ladies she turned her energies towards the more unfortunate children of the poor, teaching in what was known as a "ragged school" in Edinburgh.

It is possible that the improving of their minds alone failed to satisfy her because she left schoolteaching to take up nursing and trained under Florence Nightingale. So many cases of misery among women came under her notice that she thenceforward dedicated her life to the emancipation of women.

She came to New Zealand in 1878, first to her brother-in-law in Dunedin, then to Wellington and finally, in 1883, to Gisborne where she lived with her husband, William Sievwright, a barrister who became a friend of the lawyer and statesman Sir Robert Stout.

They had several acres on the hill at Whataupoko and their home, situated in what became known as Sievwrights Lane, was approached by a long drive with roses planted along its length.

In Gisborne Margaret became a member of the Ladies' Benevolent Society, and in 1885 seven members of that Society and the Cook Hospital and the Charitable Aid Board helped to provide funds for the isolation wards of the local hospital. In 1891 the Old Men's Home in Roebuck Road was opened with help from the Benevolent Society.

Those were the years when women were fighting for their rights. Various groups were battling for alterations in the laws concerning marriage and divorce, the right for a woman to acquire an education, to earn her own living, to claim her own wages, and, if married, to own her own property. They even wanted the right to vote.

In Gisborne Margaret was the leader of the Women's Christian Temperance Union, which interested itself in all spheres of concern to women including feminist agitation for women's suffrage. It was not possible, the Union declared, for women to protect their homes and families from liquor and other vices unless they had a voice in public affairs.

It was not long before Margaret had won the respect and admiration of the people of Gisborne, and although she was a shy and sensitive women her love for humanity amounted to a passion which urged her to work untiringly when—to quote her own

176

Left: Margaret Home Sievwright, *née* ? , 1844–1905. "She left schoolteaching to take up nursing and trained under Florence Nightingale. So many cases of misery among women came under her notice that she thenceforward dedicated her life to the emancipation of women." *Right:* The Margaret Sievwright Memorial, Gisborne.

words: *United womanhood would stand for the extinction of poverty, ignorance, vice, crime, cruelty to man and beast, idleness, war, slavery, intemperance and selfishness.*

It has been stated that the Countess of Aberdeen, who was President of the International Council of Women, delegated to her the task of establishing the National Council of Women in New Zealand. If this is a fact records concerning it do not appear to exist.

The first meeting of the National Council of Women was held in Christchurch on 13 April 1896. It was convened by the Christchurch Women's Institute (not to be confused with today's Country Women's Institute which did not then exist). Margaret Sievwright attended this first meeting as a representative of the Gisborne Women's Political League and was elected as one of the four vice-presidents.

She had always been active on behalf of women and the fact that she now became even busier was reflected in an article published in the *Auckland Weekly News* of 10 April 1897. Unsigned, it attacked her activities in the fight for the economic independence of married women. Under the heading "Local Gossip" it states:

Those dreadful women of the Women's National Council have been in session again, displaying to the world their folly, and manifesting that they were unsexed creatures, neither male nor female, and yet presuming to speak in the name of the women of the colony. They have started now on papers adovcating land nationalisation. They want an old age pension, to which everybody is to be entitled, and the money is to be raised by additions to the income tax. Then we have Mrs Sievwright's resolutions, "That the marriage laws of New Zealand should be rendered remedial, not merely palliative, of the disabilities at present grievously affecting married women, and that to this end the whole law relating to marriage, founded on the old doctrine of possession, should be repealed." Then Mrs Sievwright goes on to move *"that every married woman should be held to share and share alike the earnings or income of her husband and that her share of the joint income should be paid to the wife's separate account, or that her name should be included with that of her husband in their common bank account.*

The irate correspondent than goes on to state: *These resolutions were agreed to unanimously. When I have said that, I feel as if I could add nothing more completely condemnatory of the Women's National Council. Do these women, if they are women, not consider etc. etc.*

An article written by E. N. Sampson and published in *Women Today* 1 September 1937, gives a further glimpse of Margaret Sievwright, and an extract from it tells of a meeting the author attended in 1902. Writing of it she states:

Most of the suffrage leaders were at the meeting. Looking back I know that I stumbled unawares into a group of exceptionally brave and gifted women, but I was then too young to appreciate the privilege, though I enjoyed the meeting immensely and carried away some vivid impressions of the ladies round the big table.

The President and Chairwoman was Mrs Sievwright. Physically, Mrs Sievwright was very beautiful. She was very tall and slender with big "maternal hands". It is difficult to convey the beauty of her face. It was not only that the big brown eyes and features were so lovely, but the expression of sweet sadness was haunting. It lives with me still. She was a woman of fine insight and great brain capacity and her unique personality made her the most outstanding woman there. She was loved by everyone and regarded as a being of a higher kind. She did not realise how she was revered, just never thought of herself at all, and lived entirely for the "cause". She made a lovely picture sitting at the head of the table.

Margaret Sievwright became president of the National Council of Women in 1901 and continued through 1902–1903 and 1904. In 1905 she became ill and died at Gisborne on 9 March.

The Executive, meeting in September that year passed the following motion:

We, the Executive officers of the National Council of Women of New Zealand, at our first meeting since the passing of our President, the late Margaret Sievwright, desire to place on record our appreciation of her noble character and far-reaching imperishable work. Her refined and gentle, yet strenuous nature, her love of truth and fidelity to principle, her courage and catholicity of sympathy as well as her highly cultured intellect, combined to make her a rare and beautiful example of true womanhood.

In Gisborne a drinking fountain was erected by her fellow-workers in grateful recognition of the self-sacrificing lifework of Margaret Home Sievwright. The inscription states that she was: *Ever a friend to the friendless, an uncompromising upholder of all that is merciful, temperate and just. Inasmuch as ye have done it unto one of the least of these my brethren ye have done it unto Me.*

The drinking fountain stands near the Peel Street bridge.

CHAPTER 41

Anna Elizabeth Jerome Spencer, OBE

In 1872 a child destined to brighten the lives of thousands of country women was born in Napier. Anna Elizabeth Jerome Spencer's father, Dr William Isaac Spencer, came to New Zealand with the 18th Irish Regiment during the Maori Wars. In 1868 he married Ann Heatley and settled in Tennyson Street, Napier, where he practised his profession. Bessie, as this daughter was affectionately called, was their third child.

Bessie grew to be a gay-hearted and alert child who not only enjoyed her lessons but took an interest in nature study. With her sister Emily and three brothers, she received her early education from governesses, and when nearly twelve she attended the newly-established Napier Girls' High School. Her lifelong and dearest friend, Amy Large, was also a first-year pupil, but while Amy entered the school on the opening day, Bessie and Emily began at the beginning of the third term.

Bessie started in Form 2 and passed the university matriculation examination in Form 5. While still a pupil she assisted with the teaching, at the same time beginning her studies for a university degree. She received coaching from some of the High School teachers and sat her examination in Napier as an extramural student of Canterbury College. In 1895 she took her BA, and three years later she was appointed first assistant at Napier Girls' High School.

She had now developed into a young woman of medium height; her mid-brown hair swept back from a high intellectual forehead, her brown eyes gazed steadily from a serious face which, when she smiled, lit as though the sun had suddenly broken through. In some intangible way she was different from other people. Her pupils loved her, and as she had a distance to travel to school each day they all subscribed towards a bicycle for her.

In 1901, at the age of twenty-eight, she was appointed principal of the High School. In the same year her friend Amy Large became matron of the school, remaining there for four years. At this time there were some sixty pupils including twelve boarders, and both Miss Jerome Spencer and Miss Large took a personal interest in each girl, stressing the value of study and encouraging additional interests and hobbies outside their schoolwork.

Natural history in all its aspects was a study that had always been close to Bessie Jerome Spencer's heart and she fostered a love of native birds and plants among her pupils. It is said that she widened the horizons of all pupils who came in contact with her, not only in the field of education, but in the world of culture. She also attended to their table manners.

Her intense interest in natural history and its pursuits caused her to yearn for the

179

outdoor life, and after eight years she resigned from her position at the High School, making it clear that she wished for no presentation on her retirement. She purchased a small fruit and honey farm about fifteen miles from Napier, but lived at Awataha with Mrs J. H. Absolom, formerly Geraldine Large, whom she helped. From here she was able to attend to her orchard and bees. By that time she was thirty-seven.

In the meantime Amy Large had married Francis Hutchinson and they were living at Omatua, not far from Awataha. Bessie spent much of her time at Omatua and two years later went there to live for nearly all the rest of her life.

Omatua is one of the oldest homesteads in Hawke's Bay. The house was built about 1861 when a military grant was made to Captain Anderson, who worked the land with Captain Carter. Roof curves, crooked walls and undulating floors show the strain it suffered during the 1863 earthquake. The land became part of Sir George Whitmore's 110,000-acre Rissington station, but eventually, after the cutting up of Rissington, Omatua was used as an outstation for the Apsley property.

When the Hutchinsons took over Omatua in 1907 the old home had fallen into disrepair. It was overgrown by trees and creepers and had stood unoccupied by anything but bees, their honey pouring down the stairs.

Bessie Jerome Spencer loved working in the garden at Omatua. At times she made the butter and fed the fowls, but most of the time she was kept busy with the hoeing of

Miss Jerome Spencer, OBE, 1872–1955. "Perhaps one of her attributes most vividly remembered was her utter un-selfishness coupled with a deep sympathy for others."

her own orchard garden, pruning the fruit trees, picking and packing the fruit. That her activities were widespread is proved by the interest she took in the local body affairs of Napier. At the same time her serious, ever-inquiring mind caused her to study the many religions of the world. She was, in fact, acknowledged to be an outstanding woman.

Perhaps one of her attributes most vividly remembered was her utter unselfishness coupled with a deep sympathy for others. When World War I broke out many of her women friends in England took up active service work. The knowledge of this roused her own patriotic zeal and suddenly she knew that her activities in the Red Cross, local body work, orchard-running, beekeeping, handcrafts, spinning, weaving and knitting for soldiers, teaching Bible classes (to name but a few of her interests) were not enough: she must do something on the Home Front. In 1916 she sailed in the *Turakina* for England.

For a time she worked at the hospital for New Zealand soldiers at Walton-on-Thames. She washed dishes, waited on tables and assisted in the wards. The following year she went to Lonsdale House, a hospital for shellshocked patients. After eighteen months there she joined the Women's International Street Patrol whose members patrolled the streets of London till late at night, protecting soldiers from undesirables, finding them comfortable lodgings and befriending them generally. New Zealand members of this force wore the familiar New Zealand peaked hats and so were easily recognised by the New Zealand servicemen.

Then, one afternoon in Westminster, she noticed a large placard on the Caxton Hall announcing a display of Women's Institute Handicrafts. She had never heard of the Women's Institute movement, but as handicrafts had always interested her she went in. Later a chance meeting with an ardent president of a County Federation, followed by a visit to the Headquarters in London, supplied her with the necessary literature and information. Her own natural enthusiasm did the rest.

The work of Women's Institutes, she learnt, had begun in Canada in 1897. The movement had spread rapidly throughout the country, the motto "For Home and Country" being adopted in 1902. In fact the Movement was considered of such value to Canadian rural life that the Agricultural Organisation Society, under the Ministry of Agriculture, had invited Mrs Alfred Watt, MA, MBE, of the Advisory Board, to travel to England to establish Women's Institutes there. The first Institute was established in Llanfair, a small village in Wales in 1915.

Bessie Jerome Spencer returned to New Zealand and Amy Hutchinson at the end of 1919. The days at Omatua were filled again with spinning, weaving and experimenting with native plants and lichens to produce dyes for woven yarns; but whatever the activity the conversation inevitably turned to the forming of Women's Institutes in New Zealand. Eventually, on a warm day in February 1921, several women of Rissington were invited to Omatua to discuss the beginning of such a movement.

Amy Hutchinson received the guests and led them to the gardenroom where the meeting was to be held. And there, in the peaceful surroundings of the old country homestead Bessie Jerome Spencer, standing erect as ever, outlined to the small audience the potential happiness and progress which lay within the Women's Institute Movement.

Omatua homestead, where the first Women's Institute meeting in New Zealand was held (1921). At Omatua Bessie Spencer and Amy Hutchinson's days were also filled " . . . with spinning, weaving, and experimenting with native plants and lichens to produce dyes for their woven yarns."

She defined her aims:

In the broadest terms a Woman's Institute is a gathering of country women who meet together at least once a month to discuss matters of interest to them all. Nothing could sound simpler, yet nothing has had such deep and far-reaching effects on country life in other countries. At these meetings all women of a district, rich and poor, learned and unlearned, of church or chapel, come together with the one idea of helping one another. All pay the same small subscription, have the same rights, the same responsibilities, the same privileges. "If you know a good thing pass it on is one of the principles of the Institute movement, and the result is a common bond of friendship which unites the women of the district and then through provincial and national and even international federations, the women of the country and the world.

The idea was received with enthusiasm. The Rissington Women's Institute was formed there and then. The news spread, and before long the Norsewood Women's Institute was formed.

From then on Bessie Spencer was impatient to see every village and back-country district blessed with the unity and good fellowship which sprang from the establishment of Women's Institutes and for the rest of her life she worked untiringly towards

Bessie Spencer "travelled the length and breadth of the country spending her own money on the Institute organisation . . . "

this end. She travelled the length and breadth of the country, spending her own money on the organisation and usually taking her own sheets to avoid extra work for the people with whom she stayed.

She was a welcome guest everywhere, being equally at home in conversation with all ages from the oldest to the youngest. She addressed hundreds of meetings and was self-controlled at all times, always doing the thing that needed to be done at that time. She asked nothing for herself.

The New Zealand Federation of Townswomen's Guilds also owes its existence to her. Conversant with Townswomen's Guilds overseas she considered that such an organisation in New Zealand would do much to bring the women of the towns together for mutual help and combined efforts. The first meeting was held in Napier in May 1932, and such was her enthusiasm that the Federation is now a very active and widespread organisation.

By 1954 more than 1,000 Women's Institutes had come into existence in New Zealand, joining in fellowship some 36,000 country women. At the end of that year 200 members of Northern, Central and Southern Hawke's Bay held a Christmas party in the Red Cross Hall, Napier, to honour their founder who, they sadly realised, was becoming very frail. Many tributes and gifts were sent by Institutes throughout the country, and her old friend Amy Hutchinson was beside her to take part in the function.

This useful life ended the following year. On 23 October 1955 Anna Elizabeth Jerome Spencer, OBE, died in Napier, aged 83 years. If you would seek her memorial, consider the unity and strength of New Zealand's Country Women's Institutes.

CHAPTER 42

Jessie Aitkenhead Stewart

Jessie Aitkenhead Wilson was the daughter of a sea captain and was born in 1865 at Bombay, India, during the days when the wives of senior officers were allowed to accompany their husbands. At that time her father, a Scotsman, was captain of a ship on the run between England and India.

She was the eldest of the family born to the Wilsons, but her father died at a comparatively early age. After his death her mother decided to emigrate with the family to New Zealand and eventually arrived at Havelock North, Hawke's Bay, where she invested in a small orchard. She worked it herself and brought up the children alone.

Jessie grew to be a petite girl whose height barely reached five feet. She had light brown eyes and was a bright, quick-witted person who could find an answer for everything. When she married Charles Edward Stewart at Havelock North about 1886 his six feet towered above her.

Charles, who was fair with blue eyes, came to New Zealand from Edinburgh when he was about nineteen years of age. He settled at Taradale where he later opened a store, and during the early 1880s he was a representative rugby player for Hawke's Bay. He was a good Scot who saved every penny, and although he ran the store at Taradale he really had his heart set on farming. His opportunity came in 1888 when he was able to take up 400 acres of Crown land at Nuhaka.

Jessie's first years of married life were spent at Taradale, her first baby, Fairley Charles, being born there. Then came the move to Nuhaka which took her even further away from her mother and friends and which, she knew, must place her in social isolation.

Nuhaka, lying just off the coast on the northern curve of Hawke's Bay, is twenty miles east of Wairoa, and at that time it consisted only of a substantial Maori population. The property taken up by Charles lay four miles up the Nuhaka River and was known as Whiorau, which means hundreds of whistles. The land was hilly and covered with bush.

Charles went to the property first and built a cottage for his family on the bank of the river near a place where four valleys meet. The birds also met there to render their dawn and evening chorus.

Jessie and fourteen-months-old Fairley went to their new home by ship to Waikokopu Bay, which lies about six miles from Nuhaka. From there they made their way to the Nuhaka River, carrying the bare essentials with them. At the mouth of the river their belongings were piled into a flat-bottomed boat and they were then poled four miles up the river to the property.

The Nuhaka home of Jessie Stewart. "Charles went to the property first and built a cottage near a place where four valleys met. The birds also met there to render their dawn and evening chorus."

The river was tidal, narrow and deep with steep bushclad sides. There were no roads in the district, the land between Nuhaka and both Gisborne and Wairoa being hilly, bush-covered and traversed only by Maori tracks.

The cottage was equipped with a tank to catch rainwater and a colonial oven, and when she carried her belongings from the boat to begin living in it Jessie found herself to be the first white settler's wife in the district. Their nearest neighbour was George Walker of the Wai station, who had a Maori wife. He was a kindly, bearded man who, when he saw the baby being fed on artificial food, declared they must have milk and promptly sent them a cow. It foraged for itself in the bush and had to wear a bell so that it could be found.

Little by little the comforts for their home arrived, first by ship to Waikokopu then by dray to the mouth of the river, where goods were put into the boat to finish the last four miles of their journey. Stores came twice a year by the same route, large boxes of prunes, sacks of flour, boxes of cornflour, etc., all had to come up the Nuhaka as it was some years before they could be shifted from the beach by horse and dray.

Jessie's next child was Mary Wilson, who was the first white child to be born in that part of the district. Then came Anne Douglas and, later, John Alexander. She had no doctor for any of her confinements but was usually assisted by a midwife who rode about the countryside on horseback, possibly coming from Wairoa.

John Alexander began to arrive before the midwife could get there and Charles hurriedly went to the pa to obtain the services of Old Sarah, who had probably lost count of the babies she had delivered. All went well and Jessie and Charles were grateful to her.

The next day most of the inhabitants of the pa arrived to see the new Pakeha baby, the elders deciding that he was to be called Tamakahu. However, it was pointed out that he was to be John Alexander. The elders were disappointed, declaring that the name *must* be Tamakahu. Relations with the Maori people had always been good so a compromise was made and although he was baptised in the name of his parents' choice he has always been known as Kahu Stewart.

Jessie left Whiorau for three weeks every year to visit her mother at Havelock North and to buy materials to be made up into clothing for the children. As the roads became formed in the district they were able to go by buggy, crossing the river at a place which, until the bridge was built, was known as Stewart's Ford.

185

Picnic at Nuhaka, 1897. Old Sarah, the Maori midwife, assisted at the birth of John Alexander Stewart.

The river was always treacherous because it would block at the mouth and become unexpectedly deep. More than one life was lost in it. On one occasion Charles and Fairley, then aged about thirteen, were crossing in the buggy when the horses became caught in the deep water and both animals were drowned.

Jessie was fond of gardening and her vegetable patch kept them in food. Fruit trees were planted and supplied them with whatever was in season. The children were healthy, never needing a doctor, who, if he had been wanted, would have had to be sent for to come from Wairoa.

The property was gradually added to until the original 400 acres had expanded to 2,000 acres, and in 1924 they had 5,171 sheep on Whiorau.

Education at Nuhaka began with Alfred Pinker and his wife, a Mormon couple who ran a school for Maori children. To attend this school the young Stewarts rode the four miles to Morere, the crossing of the river being hazardous and a constant worry in winter.

Charles and Jessie retired to live in Napier about 1919, and Charles died there in 1938, aged seventy-nine, Jessie never lost her brightness and was alert to the end of her days when, as a little white-haired old lady of ninety-one, she died in 1956. Husband and wife were buried in the Napier cemetery.

CHAPTER 43

Selina Sutherland

In 1839 a daughter was born to Baigrie and Janet Sutherland of Culgour in the parish of Loth, Sutherlandshire, Scotland. They named her after Janet's mother, who had formerly been Selina Murray.

The young Selina was a serious child and studiously inclined. As she grew older she read a great deal, her choice of literature usually veering towards anything which concerned bodily health. She was always conscious of the hardships of other people and perhaps it was the heartrending sight of the unfortunate crofters being evicted from their homes that made her long to help the poor and suffering.

Whatever the cause, as she grew up she made a study of medicine until at last she was capable of competent nursing and the rendering of first aid. By this time she had developed into a strong-minded young woman who stood erect and looked at the world through clear and steady eyes. She was also a law unto herself, as was demonstrated by the unorthodox sight she presented to her sister, Margaret Grant, when Selina arrived in New Zealand in 1862.

Margaret had not seen Selina for ten years. She had married the Scottish Robert Grant who had taken up 3,000 acres in the Gladstone district about twelve miles south of Masterton, and for the last two years had been assisting her husband to establish his Bannockburn station. Selina had not even written to say she was coming and at first Margaret did not recognise this woman with the straight figure who wore a most unfeminine type of coat and waistcoat, a man's glengarry on her unseemly short hair and—horror of horrors—a kilted skirt so short that it revealed *legs*. She refused at first to believe that this spectacle could be Selina, and almost turned her away.

To Margaret's humiliation, word soon spread round the district concerning the strange newcomer and her peculiar mode of dress, and while the women were shocked the men were amused. However, one and all they soon learnt to respect and appreciate her knowledge of medicine and her ability to nurse the sick, because at that time, in the whole of the large area, there was no doctor.

During those days the Wairarapa back-country roads were little better than tracks winding through the bush that covered the hills and gullies. In winter the unbridged rivers became raging torrents that were almost impossible to cross. But whatever the weather, whatever the hour, away Selina would ride—side-saddle, Margaret was thankful to see—to the aid of those who called for her help. Maori and Pakeha alike knew that neither flooded rivers nor stormy nights would keep Selina Sutherland from them in their hour of need.

She had little time for the house-proud settlers' wives with a display of silver on

Miss Selina Sutherland, 1839–1907. "Whatever the weather, whatever the hour, away Selina would ride—side-saddle, her sister was relieved to see—to the aid of those who called for her help."

the sideboard and new furniture in the drawingroom. Fixing them with her clear, steady gaze she would demand to see the state of their men's quarters. Stories praising her skill rang round the district. "If it hadn't been for Selina I'd have died," many people were heard to declare. Stories concerning her acts of kindness were also legion.

It was no hardship for her to ride as far as fifty miles to visit a patient. On one such long trek when rain had been falling for days, turning the countryside into a quagmire, she was forced to shelter for the night in an accommodation house. That night two drovers arrived in a state of exhaustion, completely drenched, their clothes and boots plastered with mud. They went straight to bed, handing their clothes through the door to the proprietor with the request that they be placed near the fire to dry.

Selina saw the sodden garments, and, knowing the men would need them in the morning, stayed up most of the night to keep the fire burning while she brushed and scraped at the mud and turned the wettest parts of the clothes towards the heat. Their boots she oiled with mutton fat as they dried. In the morning the drovers opened their door to find their clothes neatly folded and ready to wear, their boots dry and supple. Gratefully the men left at an early hour, but Selina's departure was only a short time later.

There is the story of how, singlehanded, she fought an outbreak of typhoid in the Alfredton district, turning somebody's woolshed into a makeshift hospital. Possibly it was this episode which brought home to her the dire need for a hospital in Masterton; right up to the late 1870s there was no such place for the sick people of the district and in the event of accident or sudden illness patients had to endure the lengthy and painful wagon or cart journey to the Greytown Hospital which had opened in 1875.

Once an idea took root in Selina's mind it was not to be shifted. The hospital became an obsession and she began working towards its establishment. Of course she knew it would cost money, but this would have to come from the community who would use it, so, nothing daunted, she organised a campaign to raise the funds. In this she was aided by many of the settlers while she herself rode all over the district begging for donations.

By 1 March 1877 it was reported that she had collected £40 and that Mr A. W. Renall—no doubt cajoled by Selina—had given half an acre on the Upper Plain for the site. During the rest of the year her energetic canvassing brought the project to a stage where it should be discussed at a public meeting and here, surprisingly, there was opposition from several who considered the whole idea to be premature. It was pointed out that a hospital already existed at Greytown, built at the cost of £400, which was costing over £300 per annum in upkeep. Also, it was very difficult to keep up the funds, towards which Masterton contributed very little.

It was asked whether the percentage of accidents would justify the outlay. Would it not be better to use part of the funds to secure a site for a future hospital and with the remainder form a benevolent fund to meet cases of accident? The meeting was then reminded that the funds had been subscribed for the erection of a hospital and for no other purpose. The hospital in Greytown was for accidents only, but the one proposed for Masterton would not be confined to accidents.

The meeting became noisy with unpleasant interjections and the chairman calling it to order. Selina then complained of the persistent objections of one or two present who had always endeavoured to thwart the movement but, she promised, the hospital would be built whether they assisted or not. This statement brought cheers.

A committee consisting of Selina and five others appointed to report on the best site, the probable cost of the building and the funds available, stated that the hospital would cost £500, of which £464 was promised or in hand. And although it was recommended that Mr Renall's offered half acre be accepted it was later seen that such an area would be too small. A committee consisting of Selina and Messrs R. G. Williams, M. Caselberg, W. Perry, A. R. Bunny, A. Bish and H. Jago, was appointed to proceed with the construction.

By the following May Selina had collected a further £60 from people on the East Coast. The donated section was sold for £150 and three acres were purchased from John Valentine Smith. A tender of £510 for erecting the building was accepted from Messrs Blinkhorne & Peacock and the hospital was opened in 1877 with Dr W. H. Hosking as medical superintendant. There is no official record of Selina as matron, but it is believed that she superintended an elderly couple who were put in charge of the place.

The Bannockburn homestead was burnt down in 1879. Selina then went to Wellington where—here again the official records are missing—it is believed she was called to be matron of the Wellington Hospital.

It was here that she had her first battle with a committee who had yet to be confronted by her determination. The issue arose over the question of allowing hard drinkers to have a limited amount of alcohol in hospital. Selina believed that too abrupt a change

The first public hospital, Masterton.

did them harm and made recovery slower. The committee did not agree with her and after two years in the position she resigned.

She then left New Zealand and went to Melbourne, where once more she threw herself into humanitarian work, doing much to assist the poor and suffering, particularly the human derelicts, of which there were many. A visit to Melbourne's slums appalled her. The sight of shivering children in ragged clothes, hunger written all over their faces and emaciated bodies was more than she could tolerate.

She knew that in some way they must be housed, clothed and fed, and she knew that she, Selina Sutherland, must do something about it. So once more she launched a campaign to raise money, this time for children's homes. The money was supplied by her friends and the many supporters who rallied to the call of this strong-minded woman. The homes were built and she managed them as matron. This was the beginning of the Sutherland Homes.

By this time the years were marching on and she was beginning to feel the weight of the load of work. A committee was formed to run the homes, but before long there was trouble because the committee expected Selina to do what they said and not what she thought best. They little knew this determined woman who was accustomed to run things in her own way.

The climax came when the committee ordered that the children should be made to wear uniforms to distinguish them from those who were more fortunate. Such an order infuriated Selina. She would resign rather than inflict upon the children the indignity of uniforms indicating that they came from a lower stratum of society. The committee was adamant: the inmates of the homes *must* be distinguished from other people's children.

Selina decided to depart. Her final day came but instead of leaving quietly and alone she strode out followed not only by the children but by the whole staff. The procession through the streets of Melbourne caused a sensation.

All Melbourne applauded the manner in which she had walked out with her orphans, leaving the committee gaping. It caught the imagination of the people and the money began to pour in for new and better Sutherland Homes.

Perhaps the highlight of her career came in 1897 when she was sent as a representative of Melbourne to be presented to Queen Victoria at the time of the Royal Diamond Jubilee. The Queen knew her story and with her congratulations presented Selina with a magnificent diamond. Much as Selina prized the gift she was not the diamond-wearing type, and there was only one thing to do with it; back in Melbourne she promptly sold it to raise more money for the homes.

Selina revisited New Zealand in 1905, but four years later, in 1909, she died at the age of seventy years. Thanks to the organising efforts of her old friends, Miss Isabelle Munro and Mr W. H. Beetham, a brass tablet to her memory was placed in the present Masterton Hospital in 1910. It reads:

In Memoriam

Selina Sutherland, who by her unswerving and self-sacrificing ministrations to the sick and afflicted and by her touching appeals on their behalf largely contributed to the establishment of the first hospital in the Wairarapa. In as much as ye have done it unto the least of these my brethren ye have done it unto Me.

It will be remembered that there was a hospital in Greytown before the Masterton Hospital was built, so the above wording is not strictly correct.

In Melbourne a granite memorial was placed over her grave. On it is written:

For 28 years an unwearied friend of Melbourne's poor, the truest helper of its fallen, and the devoted foster-mother of all destitute little ones, for whom she taught Victoria how to care, having herself rescued 3000 waifs from the streets and slums. She hath done what she could.

Those who remembered her first appearance at Gladstone no longer smiled with amusement; they were only proud to know she had lived among them.

CHAPTER 44

Elizabeth Tarr

Elizabeth Lane was born in 1812 in Kingsdon, Somerset. In 1834 she married John Tarr who had been born in the same village in 1808, and in 1841 they applied to come to New Zealand under the Wakefield scheme of assisted emigration, sailing on the *London* which arrived in Wellington on 1 May 1842. They were accompanied by their three children, William, aged seven years, Hannah, aged five, and Mary Anne, aged six months. The name Tarr is of Hungarian origin. In some publications John's christian name has been erroneously published as William, possibly because of his nickname, Billy.

Elizabeth was a tiny woman who often had to stand on a box to reach things, one usually being kept handy for the purpose. She had piercingly blue eyes and a sharp tongue which people quickly learned to respect. She always dressed in black and was never without a frilled lace cap on her head.

In 1845 the Tarrs were among the earliest settlers to go to Poverty Bay. They settled at Matawhero in a small slab hut near the banks of the Taruheru River and there, with the increases to their family, they had to live at first under cramped and primitive conditions. Cooking was done in a camp oven, or possibly in an outside clay oven in which a fire was made and the food put in after the hot embers had been raked out. Water would be carried from the river.

Food from native pigeons and wild pigs was plentiful and wheat was grown and ground into flour. In 1846 John Tarr grew the first large crop of wheat in the district for Robert Espie, the pioneer whaler. Clothing for the children, of whom there were

A camp oven—the iron god of the pioneer kitchen. The housewife was its slave and if she served it devotedly it would grant her succulent stews and excellent bread.

eventually twelve, was almost impossible to buy; and as the family increased the eldest ones assisted her during her confinements for the later arrivals.

Neither Elizabeth nor John could read or write and when the birth of their last child, Maria, was recorded, John "signed with his mark." In fact Maria was the only one of their children born in New Zealand whose birth was officially recorded.

Education for the children simply was not available, and when George Davis wanted to marry their fifteen-year-old Sarah they consented only on the condition that he would teach her to read and write.

George, as a lad, had come out to New Zealand on a ship with a captain who had promised his parents he would be returned to them in England. However, on reaching New Zealand George had run away, causing the captain to return emptyhanded, and had neglected to go back to England; he also neglected to teach Sarah to read and write.

Necessity forced Elizabeth to become an authority on curing the common ailments of the day. She knew which native plants to gather, what to do with them and exactly which troubles they would assist. As more people came to live in the district she walked miles to help at confinements or to nurse the sick, and the settlers automatically took their problems to her. To all and sundry she became known as Granny Tarr.

On 10 November 1868 Matawhero was the site of tragedy when Te Kooti and his Hauhaus struck murdering blows at the settlers. The Tarrs, warned in the early hours of the morning, had time only to throw coverings over their night attire and hasten along the banks of the Taruheru River. By that time many of the family were married and away from home, but nine-year-old Maria was with Elizabeth, crouching and hiding with her in the high reeds at the sight of Maoris or sound of voices until at last they reached the Kaiti redoubt five miles away.

One of Granny's daughters, Jane, was not so fortunate. Aged twenty-five, she was married to Trooper John McCulloch, and their child, Emily Jane, was two years old. Living with them in their cottage on the bank of the Waipaoa River was Jane's young brother, Sam Tarr (Granny's eleven-year old son), and there was also seven-year-old Mary McDonald who was a niece of either Jane or John McCulloch.

Redoubt at Gisborne, 1868. These primitive forts, with field gun and loopholed tower, were a safe haven when the Hauhaus were on the warpath.

That morning John had risen early and had gone out to milk his cows when suddenly he was surprised by armed Hauhaus. He turned to flee towards the house but they shot him as he clambered over the rails of his stockyard.

Jane had also risen early and from the house she saw him being chased by armed Maoris. She snatched up little Emily Jane, and with Mary and Sam tried to escape.

Sam rushed into the concealment of the scrub, begging the others to hurry, but shots rang out and he saw them fall. Then, while the Hauhaus looted the cottage he made his way silently through the scrub. As he drew near Turanganui (Gisborne) he was joined by Jane's nearest neighbour, Mrs James, who lived in a barn with her eight children and whose husband was away on a carpentering job.

She had been aroused by the shooting and had fled with her family towards the Waipaoa River. All were in their night attire. On the way they had passed the bodies of sixteen-year-old Maria Goldsmith and her small brother, who were also neighbours. For more than a mile Mrs James and her children crept along the riverbank until they reached the denser scrub. Later, with Sam, whom they found weeping bitterly, they entered the redoubt where they found Granny Tarr and gave her the sad news about Jane and her family.

Granny's son Henry also had a narrow escape on that fateful morning. He was living in a whare with a man named Jack Smith and at daylight had gone out to catch a horse. A rebel fired at him but missed. There had been no time to saddle up but Henry jumped on the horse, put it to a fence which it cleared, and he escaped through to Makaraka. His mate Smith did not come out of the whare and the rebels did not inspect it. He escaped by watching his chance and slipping into the scrub.

Granny's daughter Eliza Benson, with her husband and child, also made their way into the redoubt. With others they had received warning from a Maori girl, Meri Taiapu of nearby Patutahi, who, having heard the shots at Matawhero, swam the river to warn the settlers.

Eliza's husband William Benson was born at Leeds, Yorkshire, in 1840. During his years in New Zealand he fought in the Waikato with Major Jackson's Forest Rangers, and with Major von Tempsky in Wanganui. In 1865 he was on the East Coast, taking part in the expeditions against Te Kooti. He was reputed to be a man who was not to be trifled with, and this was proved when his wife was kidnapped by Maoris.

Eliza and William lived towards Patutahi near the bank of the Waipaoa River. A short time after the Matawhero massacre Eliza and another woman were taken away by rebels but later escaped or were released. By March 1869 a number of followers of Te Kooti who had taken part in the massacre had begun to filter back into Poverty Bay. Some of them had been rounded up in the back country and were being held overnight at the Patutahi pa, and among those people were Hemi te Ihoariki and Nikora, who had been accused of being the leaders in the kidnapping of the two women.

William Benson heard of their presence in the pa and with Captain Hardy and William Brown he went to the entrance and called the two men outside. As Ihoariki approached Benson raised his gun and shot him dead but Nikora, only slightly wounded, escaped into the scrub.

When the inquest was held Benson was accosted by a policeman who told him he was required to serve on the jury. It is said that he tried in vain to persuade the constable that he could not honestly act as a juryman because he was the man who had shot the ex-rebel. However, the explanation was brushed aside as a trifling excuse and Benson was hurried off to the jury-room.

On arrival he was perfectly frank with the coroner and jury-men, again trying to explain why he could not serve on the jury, but in turn they also refused to listen to him. The verdict brought in by this body of men stated that Ihoariki "had been shot by some person unknown and served him right". Nor was there a Pakeha in the district who disagreed with this verdict.

Granny Tarr's husband died in 1875. After his death she was cared for by Maria, Mrs Archie Gray. Despite the tragedies of the massacre and the later loss of loved ones, Granny lived to a good age, frequently walking the four miles each way to Gisborne and declaring anyone to be soft if they used a horse and gig in preference to their own legs.

She was in her ninety-sixth year when she died in 1908 and was buried in the Makaraka cemetery which, for a period, was known as Hauhauville cemetery.

CHAPTER 45

Jensine Thomsen

Jensine Nielsen was born in 1880 at Ashley Clinton, in the foothills of the Ruahine Ranges. She was the daughter of Niels Thyge Nielsen and his wife Christine, who had come to New Zealand from Denmark, arriving at Port Ahuriri in the mid 1870s. In Denmark Niels had been a bootmaker, while Christine had worked as a striker to a blacksmith in a cutlery factory, a special technique of light accurate blows being necessary for this work.

After landing they made their way to Ashley Clinton. The small settlement of those days lay in the dense Seventy Mile Bush, twenty miles from Waipawa, and was one of the areas first settled by Scandinavians who had been brought out to build roads and fell the bush.

At Ashley Clinton the Nielsens had to fell the trees before they could build a hut, and while engaged in this task Niels suffered a severe heart attack. Christine, though a slightly-built woman, continued with the work and erected the slab hut herself. She split the shingles for the roof and made the bricks to build her oven, toiling continuously from daylight till dark.

During the next few years eight children were born to Christine, who never ceased working. Her stores came from Waipawa, and she had no option but to walk there and fetch them herself. To walk the twenty miles there and back, crossing the unbridged Waipawa and Tuki Tuki Rivers, took her three days, but somehow she got her heavy load of purchases home.

As the children grew she made more bricks and built an even larger oven in which she made bread to sell to the roadworkers and bushmen. Niels' health continued to be delicate and Christine ran the small farm with her eldest son, burning the bush and sowing down pastures, eating sparingly herself and giving most of the food to her husband and children. During her many trips away for stores her daughter, Jensine, then aged about eight or nine, used to make the bread.

Of Christine's four sons and four daughters two of the girls died of diphtheria while a third died in the Cottage Hospital at Waipukurau. The Nielsen's friend, Johannes Thomsen, made the coffins for the two daughters and took them in his cart for burial at the Makaretu cemetery.

Jensine grew up in the slab hut and at the age of ten went to Dannevirke where she worked in a factory owned by a Jewish family, stitching buttons on men's vests and underpants and also checking garments before they left the factory.

One day a friend of her parents came with the sad news that her father had died. She returned with him to Ashley Clinton, riding on the back of his horse, and after

Christine Nielsen, Jensine Thomsen's mother, came to New Zealand in the mid-1870s. In Denmark she had worked as blacksmith's striker in a cutlery factory.

the funeral she went back to her work in Dannevirke. Ten days later the same man came riding to fetch her again; this time her mother had died.

When Christine Nielsen died Dr Godfray of Waipawa said that he could understand easily enough why this woman had died—what he could not understand was how such an overworked, emaciated body had lived for so long. Niels and Christine were both only forty-six when they died. Once again their friend Johannes Thomsen made the coffins, taking them in turn on his cart to the Makaretu cemetery.

Jensine Thomsen, *née* Nielsen, 1880–1952. A factory worker at the age of ten.

Jensine was wet through when she arrived home for her mother's funeral. In wet clothes she sat all night beside her mother's body, and a short time after this she became ill and was taken to the Waipukurau Cottage Hospital where she lay paralysed for some time. On several occasions the matron had to sit up with her all night.

At last she recovered and went to work for Mrs Dugald Grant of the Burnside property on the Takapau Plains. By that time she had developed into a fairly tall young woman, though of slight build. She had a round face with blue-green eyes and fine soft hair tending towards fairness.

Mrs Grant treated Jensine as her own daughter, clothing her well and taking her wherever she went. Although Jensine received no wages she had everything she wanted, and in fact more than she had ever before possessed. Her work consisted of looking after the Grants' small daughter, and she stayed at Burnside until she was sixteen. She then went to Mrs Carlyon at Gwavas station in the Tikokino district where her brother, Andrew Nielsen, was employed as the station engineer.

In this large home with its beautiful grounds Jensine took care of the two children, Rupert and Olga Carlyon. She waited at table and spent a very happy six years at Gwavas. Mrs Carlyon treated her extremely kindly and when Jensine left in 1901 to marry Marinus Thomsen Mrs Carlyon gave her a wedding dress, veil and trousseau which included a fine linen afternoon-tea cloth in drawn threadwork embroidered by herself.

Marinus Thomsen was the son of Johannes and Karen Marie Thomsen who had been such good friends to Jensine's parents. Born in 1871 at Skjarum-Sogn, Denmark, he was four years of age when he sailed in the *Terpsichore* with his parents and younger sister. It was a terrible trip of storms, the crew refusing to obey the captain's orders, most of the food being washed overboard and the passengers being forced to exist on bacon rinds, potato peelings and weevilly biscuits.

After working on the Wellington waterfront reclamation and the Rimutaka hill road, Johannes Thomsen took his family to Pukahu, near Hastings. From there they went to Makaretu and began bush-felling and farming.

Marinus also had farming in view. He spent his early years working on the properties of other people, and in 1901 when the Hatuma district was formed by the cutting up of Purvis Russell's Woburn property he drew the smallest section in the ballot. This area of 176 acres was bordered by the Waiou Stream, which flowed into the Maharakeke River, the cost of the L.I.P. tenure being 5s per acre.

Jensine and Marinus were married on 27 June 1901 by Pastor Ries at the Lutheran Church, Makaretu. The wedding was a pretty affair of four bridesmaids in white muslin and picture hats, and two flowergirls. Jensine's gown was of cream figured lustre. After the ceremony the couple left the church under heavy showers of rice.

The reception, held at the home of Johannes and Karen Thomsen, was a happy gathering of about 130 friends. During the sunny afternoon games were played on the lawn, and in the evening songs, recitations and speeches were given by the guests. And despite the fact that the bush was burning behind them, filling the air with haze and smoke, they drank horehound beer and danced all night in the gaily decorated woolshed.

The next day the couple left for their new home, both riding on Marinus's horse,

Jensine Nielsen and Marinus Thomsen were married at his parents' home in 1901. "Despite the fact that the bush was burning behind them, filling the air with haze and smoke, they drank horehound beer and danced all night in the gaily decorated woolshed."

Maida. They camped beside the little Waiou Stream under a cave-like rock. Jensine was the first white woman to settle in the new district.

Camping conditions lasted for quite some time as the land was completely lacking in timber for building purposes and it had to be brought from Johannes Thomsen's mill at Makaretu. Firewood too was non-existent and had to be carried from Makaretu on horseback, and Jensine also cut and dried flax roots for burning. These conditions lasted until a small house of one bedroom and kitchen was built on a rise above the swiftly flowing Maharakeke River. A tin chimney carried smoke from the fireplace where the camp oven, continually in use for all cooking, was placed. An added burden was the water, which had to be carried up a twenty-foot bank. Living in this state in the home they called Fairview, for two years Jensine did not see another woman.

On becoming settled her first task was to make Marinus a nightshirt from some of her own clothing, but having no machine she had to stitch it by hand, and as the babies arrived she was sewing continually.

The first child to arrive was Leslie Vincent, whose clothes were made from her own bridal gown. Then came Dulcie Alelia, Allen Rupert, Reginald Neal, Clarice Volna and Esther Unita. Winifred Joyce was the next but died the following year from pneumonia. This child was buried on the property and in later years when Jensine felt depressed she would sit beside the grave of this baby.

Her next son, was Sidney Merton, and then came Iris Alma who was followed by an unnamed baby girl who was still-born. Cecil Percival arrived next and then came her last child, Renold Vernon.

199

With six small children under the age of seven Jensine found herself making clothes at every spare moment and was also making all the clothes for their father. Eventually she acquired a small hand machine and at times she was working with this until two in the morning.

The house was enlarged as the family grew but at one stage there were six boys sleeping in one room. Times were hard for farmers and Marinus had often to leave her and seek work long distances from home. On one occasion when he was away shearing in Taihape she had nine of the children sick at the same time with measles. During this worrying time she sent a boy to bring the cow in, and when he did not return she sent another boy to find him. When he too failed to return she went herself and found both children asleep in some rushes, exhausted and sick with the measles. She carried them both home.

With her limited resources she worked hard to make a comfortable home, wasting nothing that could be put to use. Sugar bags made aprons and trousers for the boys. Wheat sacks dyed brown in Condy's crystals made good floor rugs.

Flour bags were most versatile, as two 100 lb flour bags could be turned into a single sheet while four bags made a double sheet; one 100 lb bag made a pillow slip, and half a bag made two tea-towels. One, folded into a square, became an embroidered afternoon-tea cloth, and all this linen was bleached white by being left out in the frost. Oilskins too were made from flour bags soaked in raw linseed oil.

Water, always a problem, had to be conserved. It was carried up the twenty feet from the river and stored in a barrel (where two-year-old Esther was once found head down, but Jensine was able to revive her). First the children were bathed in a galvanised tub, then the clothes were washed in the bath-water but rinsed in the river, and then the floor was washed with it. After that it watered the garden. The carrying of water went on for some years until a ram was installed, and eventually its place was taken by an electric pump.

A great deal of their food came from the garden which Jensine tended, and the main stores that came to the place were flour, salt, sugar and oatmeal. Salted bacon and

Makaretu *circa* 1900, standing in what was left of the Seventy Mile Bush.

porridge were also on the menu and while the family was growing up Jensine baked forty loaves of bread a week, while a milking-bucket of potatoes had be peeled each day.

Jensine and Marinus were both fond of music and he could play the violin and the accordian. When the children were young she taught them to dance the polka, the mazurka and the waltz to the strains of Marinus's lively music. She also had a deep appreciation of good literature and poetry.

Happy outings to visit relatives were always something to look forward to, although one nearly ended in disaster. This happened one evening as they returned from a visit to John Thomsen, Marinus's brother at Takapau. Marinus rode Maida while the buggy, filled with children, was driven by Jensine. When crossing the flooded Makaretu near Takapau the front wheel was blocked by a large boulder. Jensine whipped up the horse, the swingletree broke, and the horse departed leaving her with the six children in the buggy to float down the river. Marinus rode into the rushing waters on quiet old Maida and took the children off one by one until only Jensine remained. By that time the buggy, with its lightened load, was well down the river, but it was retrieved before it was too late.

During the 1920s Jensine's eyesight began to fail through cataracts forming over both eyes, and by the 1930s she was unable to read or sew. Nevertheless she could walk freely in her own home, cook a roast meal, bake scones and peel the vegetables, and until well into the 1940s she was still baking bread. She remained most particular about her appearance, usually dressing in navy or black, with a lace jabot held at her throat with a brooch.

A great occasion came in 1951 when Marinus and Jensine celebrated their golden wedding. Over one hundred relatives were at Fairview, including her former brides-maids. The following year, on 3 March 1952, Jensine died in Woburn Hospital at Waipukurau. She was seventy-two years of age and her six sons were her pallbearers. Three months later, on 30 June, Marinus died at the age of eighty-one, and the six sons again carried out the same sad duty.

Fairview is still in the hands of the descendants of this pioneer couple of the Hatuma district, and their son Sidney at present farms the property.

CHAPTER 46

Maria Tucker

Maria Harris, born in Taunton, Somerset, England, in 1860, was the daughter of John and Elizabeth Harris. She was a girl of medium height, with dark hair and blue eyes, and after the death of her father during the 1870s she came to New Zealand with her mother, three brothers and three sisters. Mrs Harris was a capable woman with auburn hair and a strong will, and the children, Samuel, Hiram, Raymond, Clara, Anne and Frances, had been brought up in the Quaker faith. They sailed in the ship *Hudson,* which landed them at Napier, and it was not long before Maria Harris had met Richard Tucker.

Richard was the son of Edward Tucker who had landed at New Plymouth from the first immigrant ship, *William Bryan,* in 1841. His parents had later moved to Auckland, where he had been born in 1854, and where their family had been educated. Richard was a slightly-built man of medium height with very blue eyes. He moved to Hawke's Bay and learnt the woolscouring business, eventually becoming an expert in anything pertaining to wool.

Maria was eighteen when they were married at Clive in 1878. Canon H. W. St Hill officiated in the Anglican service, and she wore dove-grey, her dark hair being tied back with a ribbon. Their home was a four-roomed cottage with a lean-to at the back situated in what became known as Tucker's Lane.

Their first child, William, was born at the end of 1879, then came Annie in 1881, Sarah Ellen in 1883, and by 1892 Emily, Joseph, Catherine and Raymond had been born. In 1893 Maria was pregnant with her eighth child.

That year the winter seemed endless. Day after day the rains pelted unceasingly through the spring months, drenching the countryside until well into December, and by that time Maria's pregnancy had advanced to the sixth month. When she went to bed on the night of 3 December the rain still hammered on the roof, but at two in the morning she awoke and lay listening in the darkness, conscious now of another sound. Alarmed, she realised it was the gentle lapping and swishing of water beside the bed.

She awakened Richard, who immediately leaped out of bed to find himself standing in more than a foot of water. Outside in the darkness the Ngaruroro and Tuki Tuki had both broken their banks to join forces and cover the land with floodwaters.

Richard moved swiftly. He placed a small table on the larger kitchen table and climbed up with the axe, which was fortunately kept indoors. A few hammering blows cut a hole in the ceiling large enough for him to climb through and hack out another opening in the roof. Then, one by one, the children were lifted up through the ceiling and out on to the roof.

Maria, in her sixth month, was in no state to be clambering through holes in the ceiling in the small hours of a wet morning, but with the help of Richard, William and Annie, she was eventually heaved up, shoved and pulled through the opening and out on to the roof. And there, through the hours of darkness, the family sat in misery enduring the pelting rain and listening to other voices calling for help.

Daylight brought a scene of desolation with submerged cottages standing in a vast sheet of water where branches of trees swept through windows and numbers of dead animals floated by. Clinging on the steep slant of their own shingled roof, and holding the little ones, Richard and Maria felt the cottage shift beneath them. They watched fearfully as the body of a draught horse bore towards the house, knowing that its weight would send the small building from its piles, but fortunately the current caused it to drift aside and it floated clear.

At last they heard voices shouting encouragement from the distance as sailors from a ship in port at Napier rowed to their rescue. The Tuckers were lifted into a boat and taken to the Clive Hotel, which at that time was a two-storeyed building. On the way the boat floated over their own high fence and across the top of an orchard. At the hotel it was moored to the upstairs balcony while Maria and the children were lifted out.

Other families were in the same predicament. The Haleys, who lived between the Ngaruroro and the Tuki Tuki, refused at first to leave their roof. At last they were

The flood at Clive, 1893.

persuaded to enter a boat but before they had reached the Clive Hotel their cottage had been swept out to sea.

Maria was put to bed for a week and during this time twelve-year-old Annie (who eventually married Archie Forbes from Scotland), took control of the five younger children. Many years later, as an elderly woman, Annie was still able to quote lines written after the flood by a local poet:

A tale of a night of terror, in December 'ninety-three,
Of a flood that struck the valley,
From the mountains to the sea.
Of a storm that desolated the Heretaunga Plains
With the overflow of rivers
And the long continued rains.

At last the waters receded and people went home to sweep out the mud and the silt that was many inches deep, cope with dead animals and the constant smell of dampness. The depth of the water can be imagined from the fact that for years later the bones of animals remained up in the trees where they had been caught. Birds picked them clean until the skeletons hung or perched like cages suspended among the leaves.

Nobody was drowned in the 1893 flood but in 1897 an even worse flood occurred and several lost their lives. However, by that time the Tuckers had moved to Havelock North. Lillian, known as the "flood baby", had arrived safely in 1894, and then came Gertrude in 1898 and Hilton in 1904.

At Havelock North Richard had eight acres of land lying half a mile from the bridge on the Hastings side. There he had a woolscouring works with a large area between the works and the homestead for drying the wool. Their home, a seven-roomed house, was later enlarged to ten rooms, and Maria's greatest delight was her garden of about quarter of an acre laid out in lawns, flowerbeds, shrubs, an orchard and a drive running towards the house. Each day she provided a hot meal for all the men working for Richard, and in this she was assisted by Annie, Sarah Ellen and Emily. They all attended the Presbyterian Church at Havelock North, where Richard became an elder.

During those days Maria was often called upon by Dr McDonnell of Hastings to assist him with confinements. She was not a trained nurse but midwives were necessary in those days and she loved this work. Dr McDonnell went to his patients in a gig driven by Richard's nephew George Tucker, and they would collect Maria and drive her to the patient's home.

She was also capable with the reins in her own hands. During school holidays her roan pony Jessie would be harnessed to the gig and, taking the three youngest children, she would drive to Taradale to visit her sister Anne (Mrs Frances Collinge), and her brother Samuel Harris. This was quite a journey from Havelock North, so a break for lunch and to rest the pony was made at Pakowhai where her brothers, Hiram and Raymond Harris, had orchards. In this way she had happy reunions with her family.

In 1910 Richard moved from Havelock North to Whakatu where he had founded a wool-scouring plant in 1895. A ten-roomed house with seven acres of land was

Wedding of Emily Tucker and Harry Kemp, 1913. Emily's parents are seated on the right.

purchased from Stephen Franklin and it was not long before Maria had the garden fragrant with her favourite roses and stocks.

Richard was now a recognised authority on wool, and men from all parts of New Zealand came to Whakatu to learn woolclassing. He also travelled about the district in a gig visiting farmers between Wairoa and Porangahau while canvassing for wool, and as they had many friends between Waikari and Elsthorpe Maria often went with him. At times they went to Gisborne by ship, or to Tokomaru Bay where William was farming at Lowden Hills, some miles inland. At Tokomaru they were lowered in strong baskets to the small lighter and then taken to the wharf whence they would ride to Lowden Hills.

However, sadness was at hand for them. Their son Raymond died in hospital and then, during World War I, Joseph was killed in action. Maria was extra-busy during the war years; as soon as war broke out she started knitting socks for soldiers, and organised a Red Cross sewing guild in the large room off the back verandah.

To do this she borrowed several sewing machines then recruited a dozen women to put them into action while she herself cut out pyjamas, hospital shirts and grey flannel shirts. She also supervised the neat finishing of each garment, and by the time the machines stopped humming at the end of the war more than 800 garments had left her home to be handed over to the Red Cross. Her war work was eventually recognised by a Certificate of Merit.

Maria suffered the sad blow of losing Richard when he died in 1923. She was his sole executrix and arranged with Samuel Jowett of Napier to take over the management of the works. She also arranged with her son William to take over the house, and she then built a house in Hastings on the corner of Cornwall Park and Tomoana Road where she lived with her unmarried daughter, Lilian.

By this time she was suffering from total deafness. She looked upon the isolation this caused her as just another challenge in life to be faced with courage and common sense and to be coped with in a practical manner. At least she could read, and she still had the pleasure of her garden, bright always with flowers in season. The room was full of her favourite stocks and roses when she died in 1930 in her seventieth year.

William Tucker eventually took over the woolscouring works and this well known business at Whakatu is still in the hands of the descendants of Richard and Maria.

CHAPTER 47

Robina Villers

Robina McKain was the youngest daughter of William and Douglas Mary McKain (26) of Cheadle, Staffordshire. In 1837, while still a young girl, Robina's father was killed in a hunting accident, and three years later her mother and four brothers made arrangements with the New Zealand Company to emigrate to the new colony.

They sailed on the *Olympus* at the end of 1840, and apart from missing her four sisters who had been left at home the voyage was a happy one for Robina. An attractive girl, she was a favourite on board, and much of her time was occupied by teaching a class of children.

They arrived in Wellington on 20 April 1841. Her mother leased a section of land and until her brothers, James and John, had built a cottage on it the family lived in one of the Depot houses belonging to the New Zealand Company.

Eventually they were in their own home with its full harbour view. Their neighbours were Mr and Mrs William Villers who had come from Sydney in 1840. Mrs Villers, who had been Mary Jean Lutton, married Villers, a carpenter by trade, on 10 March 1831. By 1847 she had six children and was failing rapidly.

Robina's instinctive kindness and thought for other people caused her to run in and out of the Villers' home, nursing Mrs Villers and caring for the children. Then, as Mary Jean Villers lay dying on 28th January 1847, she extracted a promise from Robina to the effect that, after her death, Robina would continue to look after her six children.

Robina found it impossible to refuse the dying woman's request and promised to do this. After her neighbour's death she proceeded to do her best for the children, cooking for them, attending to their clothes and doing her utmost to keep her promise to their mother.

It is not difficult to imagine Villers casting an eye of approval over the young Robina, nor is it surprising to learn that he pointed out that the best way of keeping her promise would be to marry him. Robina had no wish to marry this man who was years older than herself, but for the sake of the children and because of her promise to their mother, she agreed. The marriage took place on 18 February, 1847, a mere eighteen days after the death of Mary Jean.

No doubt Robina moved in and carried on where the previous Mrs Villers had left off. She soon learned that life with William Villers would not be the proverbial bed of roses. He was a hard, intolerant North of Ireland man, very narrow in his outlook. His children had to wear long sleeves and high necks even on the hottest days. Nor, despite any promises he might have made concerning the subject, would he allow Robina to continue to practise her Catholic faith.

Her first child, whom she named James McKain after her brother, was born in 1848. Her second child, a daughter named Douglas Mary after Robina's mother, was born in 1849, but that year her baby son died. Her next daughter, Lucinda, was born in 1850.

During 1850 William Villers and Robina's brother James McKain decided to move to Ahuriri in the Hawke's Bay district, their intention being to trade with the Maoris. James had married Sarah Barben who had arrived with her parents (2) on the *London* in December 1840, and they had two children.

The men went first to look over the prospects, returning from the East Coast on the *Lucy James* on 22 November and then leaving again with their families in the *Salopian* on 10 December.

With Robina were her own two children and the three youngest Villers. Her three remaining stepchildren were left at school in Wellington but followed later. Also in Wellington was their brother-in-law, Joseph Torr, who had married Julia McKain, and who was to act as their agent, supplying them with goods in return for the produce they expected to send to him. This was to include wheat and live pigs brought from Wairoa by Maoris in large canoes and whaleboats.

Robina and Sarah were the first white women to live at The Spit, or what was later to become known as Westshore. Napier did not then exist and Bluff Hill, known as Scinde Island, rose from a wide expanse of tidal mudflats and extensive lagoons. The Inner Harbour, covering approximately 7,500 acres, extended from the inner side of the shingle ridge stretching along the shore. What is now Napier South was practically under water and teeming with wild duck; a day's shooting which resulted in thirty or forty brace was considered a small bag. There was a large Maori pa on what later became the property of the Sailing Club, and another on the beach near the small bridge crossing the Esk River.

The Spit, Napier, in 1860—ten years after Robina Villers went to live there. She and her sister-in-law were the first two Pakeha women to live in this district.

On arrival the families were probably sheltered by tents, or perhaps the Maoris assisted them with huts of some kind. The place was lacking in timber but the beach was plentifully strewn with large pieces of pumice which were gathered in great quantities and squared off into blocks which were used to erect a four-roomed cottage which stood for many years on the Inner Harbour side of the present road a few chains from the entrance to the old bridge.

Later, when there was a sawmill at Big Bush, Mangateretere, they were able to obtain timber. This was brought on rafts down the Ngaruroro River, round the Bluff and landed at The Spit. Nor was there any fresh water at The Spit for Robina and Sarah and their young children. A considerable amount was necessary for all domestic purposes, and barrels were taken by boat for some miles up the Tutaekuri River, filled with fresh water, and brought down for use. All stores were brought from Wellington by the *Salopian,* and if their supply of flour ran short wheat had to be ground in a small handmill until fresh supplies arrived.

Their only recreation consisted of walking along the beach, where they sank ankle-deep in the shingle, or in going out in the boat with their husbands. On one occasion while the boat was crossing the channel, Sarah, who was nursing her baby, suddenly missed her little two-and-a-half year old Sarah. On frantically staring around she saw the child's white sun-bonnet bobbing about on the waves and being carried out to sea by the swiftly running current. A Maori boy named Heirere, who was in the boat with them, jumped overboard and swam to Sarah and brought her back safely.

Robina's next baby, a daughter named Mary Jane, arrived on 19 November 1851 and was the first white child to be born in the Napier district. Then came Selina, born in 1852, who died at the age of two years, and Julia, born in 1854, who also died at the age of two. Fanny, who was born in 1855, lived only until she was eighteen.

As more settlers passed through the district Sarah and James opened what became known as McKain's Accommodation House. Donald McLean, later Sir Donald, stayed there with other surveyors, being accommodated in the pumice cottage. An indication of the tariff was recorded when the Harding family, on their way to their sheep station, Mount Vernon, stayed there for ten days. The cost of their board was £14 10s (29s a day for six persons).

In 1855 the Villers and McKains left The Spit to take up sections of land at Petane. Each section was 100 acres at 5s per acre. Other members of the family left Wellington to join them in this venture. The sections taken up by William and Robina were on the Napier side of the Petane hills where the Bay View Hotel was later built, while those of James and Sarah McKain and others were on the Eskdale side.

There were no roads, and as the beach was so difficult to walk along the families with their household goods and furniture were taken by boat across the Inner Harbour, and then up the narrow Esk River as far as the boats could go. After that they went by bullock sledge to their new homes.

Sarah's home was a wooden hut built in the shape of a tent the interior being partitioned to form two rooms. Robina's house was probably similar at first but they no doubt enlarged it when they opened it as an accommodation house at the junction of the main roads to Taupo and Wairoa.

The sections of the Villers and McKains adjoined, and they all worked together.

In some of the paddocks enclosed by ditches or banks they grew wheat which, when ripe, was cut by sickles and reap hooks by the women and older girls. Later they acquired a threshing and winnowing machine which was worked by horses.

In 1857 Robina's daughter, little Robina, was born, and in 1859 Thomas arrived. Ada was born in 1860 and Clarence in 1862, the latter living only until he was sixteen. None of her children were baptised, as William retained his hard, narrow outlook on religion. However, he died in 1862, five months after the birth of Clarence, and Robina immediately took the family to Father Reignier for baptism and instruction.

After William's death his sons by his first marriage took over the running of the property and made trips to the growing settlement of Napier for stores. At times they were forced to walk along the shingle ridge between the Inner Harbour and the sea, carrying home such weights as 50 lb bags of flour. As horses were gradually acquired the women and girls rode on men's saddles but never astride, a rolled shawl usually strapped on to form a pommel, and any eggs and butter taken to be sold in Napier were strapped to the side of the saddle.

For Robina the work in the accommodation house was an endless routine of catering for travellers and caring for her family. During the 1860s there was the constant fear of Hauhau rebels when the Maoris at the nearby pa could be heard chanting as they danced about their flagstaff each evening, and during the Te Kooti trouble the women and children were taken to Napier.

Robina ended her days living among her children and she was probably buried in the Eskdale cemetery; unfortunately, a fire which swept through the cemetery years ago destroyed the old wooden headstones of the early Villers and McKain families, making it impossible to record dates. Official records, which could have verified the dates, were destroyed by fire during the Napier earthquake.

CHAPTER 48

Jane Evanson Wallis

Jane Evanson Beamish was the eldest child of Nathaniel Evanson Beamish and his wife Elizabeth. She was born in 1855 at Turakina in the Rangitikei district where her father was managing a property for his father-in-law, William Couper of Kahuranaki station in Hawke's Bay.

The homestead where she grew up was situated near the Turakina River, its small upstairs rooms being approached by a narrow stairway. The kitchen had a floor of hard clay which was whitewashed, as were the walls and also the path to the front gate. The children slept on beds made from wooden slats, their mattresses stuffed with straw and their pillows with the seedheads of raupo gathered from the swamp. Their mother attended to their education as there was no money to spare for a governess's salary.

Roads had not then been formed in that isolated district and the bridle tracks were through high scrub and swampy areas of raupo. Cattle roamed freely as there were few fences, and if Jane and her brothers came face to face with a bull on the narrow track their only hope of escape was to push into the swamp and trust that the animal would pass by.

Travellers and hawkers were frequent callers for a meal and a night's shelter, and were never refused. However, the rule was that they must grind their share of wheat into flour for the making of bread for breakfast. During those days the main source of income for Nathaniel Beamish was from cattle driven to the coast and then shipped to the goldfields on the west coast of the South Island.

Maori uprisings caused many fears among the family in its isolated position and on one occasion Jane's uncle decided it would be wise to bury their few valuables and silver. Nobody knew where he had hidden them and before he could pass on the information he was killed. The valuables are still in their hiding place.

In 1870, when Jane was fifteen years of age, Nathaniel Beamish took over the management of the Okawa property owned by his brother-in-law, Thomas Lowry. It meant leaving Turakina and at that time with the Manawatu Gorge Road not yet opened, travellers from the west coast wishing to reach Hawke's Bay had the option of going by ship or of using a track over the Ruahine Ranges near the gorge and then passing through some forty miles of the Seventy Mile Bush.

Jane's parents chose the latter route. The children's ages ranged from fifteen down to two years and they were mounted on eight riding hacks, the two youngest riding with their parents. One packhorse was led, heavily laden with the belongings and food for ten people on a six-day journey.

The first day's riding took them over Maori tracks as far as Palmerston North, where the first settlers had only just arrived to live in the clearing that was to become the site of the city. On the second day they went twelve miles through dense totara forest to the Pohangina River, near Ashhurst, where they spent the night on the riverbank.

The next morning, when they crawled from beneath their sleeping covers, the horses had gone. They had broken loose during the night and there was no sign of them. Jane and her brothers searched until they found the animals some distance away, rolling in the river sand to rid themselves of the mosquitoes that had driven them frantic all night. At last they were caught and saddled again, and after crossing the river the party followed the track that crossed the Ruahines which were covered by forest at that period. It followed, roughly, the line of the present Saddle Road running from Ashhurst to Woodville, climbing steeply through bush, turning and twisting in sharp elbow bends that were edged by steep drops. On this day the party rode fifteen miles to reach Ormond's clearing near Papatawa, about four miles north-east of present-day Woodville. This night too was spent out in the open.

The next day they rode only eight miles, following the track to Puketai, on the Manawatu River near Oringi, which was a junction where a track came from the Wairarapa. After Puketai the track continued through a very swampy area of bush to Tahoraiti, where Elmbranch had built a bush-licence accommodation house known as The Rest And Be Thankful. Here they stayed the night and were indeed thankful, as by then it was raining.

After Elmbranch's the track through the Seventy Mile Bush became narrow and tortuous because of the many giant trees standing in the way. In wet weather it was slippery and boggy, with the floodwaters of numerous creeks and rivers causing many hazards. It was like a long tunnel which seemed to have no end and, because of the trees meeting overhead, it was quite dark and the sky could rarely be seen. At last, after more than twenty miles, the tunnel ended and they came out of the bush at the Makaretu River somewhere near Takapau. The young ones, delighted to be out of the bush and to see the sky again, dug in their spurs and set off at a gallop.

They reached Waipukurau late that night, making a journey of forty miles for that day. The next day, being the Sabbath, they rested, and on the Monday they followed the road that had been made through Te Aute. Before reaching the Ngaruroro River this road turned right and wound towards Havelock North and their destination at Kahuranaki with the Coupers.

Within the next few years Jane, blue-eyed and auburn haired, had grown up into a slim young woman of five feet five inches in height, with an eighteen-inch waist and very small hands. She had a delightful Irish sense of humour. In 1877, when she was twenty-two, she married Arthur Henry Wallis.

A pioneer of boundless energy, Arthur was over six feet in height, slim, fair and bearded. He was born in 1851, the son of Dr Frederick Wallis of Bexhill, England. He began to study medicine but abandoned it in 1868 and sailed to New Zealand in the *Blue Jacket*. On arrival he went to his relative, William Nelson, and during his fifteen years in Hawke's Bay he also worked for J. N. Williams, having a hand in the breaking in of considerable tracts of country at Appley, Hakowhai and Edenham.

Jane Evanson Wallis, *née* Beamish
1855–1934. "She had a delightful
Irish sense of humour."

In 1883 he went up the East Coast to manage for J. N. Williams, choosing Waipiro as the location for his home as the bay was suitable for shipping.

What was generally spoken of as Waipiro included leases inland beyond Ihunga and southwards to Waipare and Pakarae, while later Arthur Wallis had the superintendence of the Turihaua property as well. During this period he built a house for his family, sought out the boundaries and devised means of getting from one point of the run to another. He spent Christmas Day 1883 with a few biscuits in his pocket as he forced his way through the fern and tutu to locate the line between the Waipiro and Matahiia blocks. The journey took him through Puketiti, where A. B. Williams now has his homestead.

Jane lived alone in Napier until Arthur had built a home for them and by that time she had four small daughters, Ella, Ethel, Maude and Edith. When they went to the property towards the end of 1884 he chartered Richardson's little steamer, the *Weka*, to convey them to their new home at Waipiro Bay, where they were landed by surf-boats. Jane discovered that he had chosen the northern slopes of the bay for their home as the Maoris were then living at Waikawa on the southern end.

Jane found herself to be the only white woman living in the district, and it was four months before she saw another. This was a person who had come to help her, who was landed on the beach, took one look at the outlandish place and got smartly back into the boat to return to Auckland and civilisation.

The district was completely without roads, the bridle paths following the old Maori tracks, and Arthur became personally responsible for laying out suitable tracks over the Waipiro area—tracks which in many cases have later been developed into the main motor roads. Most of the country was under fern, scrub and bush, and the magnitude of the task, which was the breaking-in of all the land later farmed by the Williams family, often made it necessary for him to stay out on the run for a week at a time, returning only at weekends.

Nor did Jane see much of her husband during the weekends, for he spent all Sunday attending to mail and doing what he could to doctor the Maoris who flocked to him

212

Loading wool at Waipiro Bay. Passengers, like the woolbales, were landed or embarked via surfboat.

with their ailments. There were also church services to be held in the church he had built.

In 1855 Jane had cause to be thankful for the confidence the Maoris had in Arthur. A grave quarrel arose over the Native Land Court's decision concerning the Waipiro Block. At the original hearing Pineamine and his people had been awarded the block, but at a rehearing of the case Tuta Nihoniho and his relatives were granted 10,000 acres; then, upon a further rehearing, the original decision was upheld, in favour of the triumphant Pineamine.

Tuta was furious. He sent Pineamine a letter threating that if he did not get his people off the 10,000 acres he would slay them. Pineamine refused to budge. Tuta then assembled his warriors at dusk on the hill overlooking Waipiro and prepared to attack at dawn next morning.

Some of the local Maoris then appealed to Arthur to intervene and Jane, terrified, watched him go out into the dark unarmed and alone to talk to the angry Tuta. However, Arthur's help and kindness to all Maoris on the Coast was well known to these people and because of it they listened to him and eventually abandoned their warlike intentions.

In the meantime soldiers had been hurriedly sent for from Auckland but by the time they arrived Tuta's men had already handed over their guns to Arthur for safe keeping. It is said that when the soldiers arrived the warriors greeted them with a lively rendering of *God Save The Queen*. Queen Victoria later sent Tuta a sword as a reward for keeping the peace, and this is still exhibited by the Jerusalem Maoris on all special occasions.

Jane's next two babies were Mildred and Nora, giving her six daughters. She lost Edith, who had fallen ill, because by the time a rider had reached Gisborne, taking a day to cover the ninety miles and another day to ride back with urgently needed medicine, the baby was dead. Mildred too died when young.

As the years passed other buildings were erected. There was a dumping shed on the beach from where wool was loaded on the wagons and then taken out to the schooner, and there was the smithy and the station store.

For years transport to Napier or Gisborne continued to be by coastal vessel which had to be boarded via the surfboat, and this also held its dangers. On one occasion Jane and the children were already on board a ship bound for Napier when they saw the surfboat, returning to the shore with Arthur and others, capsize in the rough

213

A bridle track to Gisborne enabled Arthur Wallis to pack his wool out on packhorses, twenty or so at a time. Small bales had to be used to allow the horses to sidle round narrow corners.

waves. They watched helplessly, knowing that he would be struggling to save others, but it was not until they reached Gisborne that they heard he was safe. They heard also that two had been drowned but that two had been saved because, being a strong swimmer, Arthur had rescued them.

For twenty years Jane made her home a centre for all who came up the coast, mothering many young cadets and keeping open house for them at weekends, but by then people were unable to form any impression of the desolation and the remoteness that had confronted her when she first arrived at Waipiro. Not until many years after the Wallises had settled there was there more than a bridle track to Gisborne, or bridges over the rivers. In 1900 came a wonderful step forward when a telephone line was put through to Gisborne.

In 1901 Jane and Arthur left Waipiro to live in Gisborne, building a home on their Maungaroa property at Kaiti, and from there he looked after his own interests at Horehore, Onetohunga and Pakarae. Their four remaining daughters married. Ella became Mrs A. R. Watson of Waimata; Maude became Mrs E. Shield of Waikonini, Hawke's Bay; Ethel became Mrs J. Biddle of Dargaville; and Nora became Mrs H. E. Williams, Ngamoe, Ruatoria.

Jane died in 1934 at the age of seventy-nine and Arthur died in 1938. Both were buried in Gisborne.

CHAPTER 49

Mary Anne White

Mary Anne White was born in 1832, the daughter of Mr Watkins, a barrister of Enniskillen, Northern Ireland, one of whose ancestors, though born in Wales in 1670, fought under William III in Ireland and was granted property there in 1690. Mary Anne's mother was Mary Anne Burke, a relative of the founder of *Burke's Peerage*.

Photographs indicate that Mary Anne grew to be a slim girl of medium height, with greyish eyes and straight fair hair tending towards auburn. Drawn softly back from a centre parting, it framed her face between two wings. Highly cultured, she was a talented musician who could transpose at sight. She had a good sense of humour and loved dancing. As a girl she attended dances at the Curragh—the Irish barracks built to accommodate 12,000 troops—with her cousin Katie Burke.

In 1850 she married Thomas White, son of James White of Walton House, Eastry, a small village in Kent not far from Sandwich. He was a tall, heavily-built man with fair curly hair crinkling back from a high forehead. She was then eighteen and did not realise that life with Thomas would be a restless existence incurring many moves between England, Ireland, India and finally New Zealand, and that she would be almost fifty before she could settle down in one place.

Thomas, who was born in 1816, and was therefore sixteen years her senior, became a civil engineer. He worked for a time under the celebrated engineer Brunel then spent three years in Australia and later returned to England.

In January 1855 Thomas and Mary Anne set out for India, leaving behind William, the eldest of their children, with Thomas's father, James White. Thomas went as a civil engineer to Bengal, then, as he believed there was more to be made out of contracting, he took up this form of work. He made a success of it to the extent of amassing a small fortune.

Then came the period of the Indian Mutiny. During this time, in 1857, Mary Anne was arrested. She was with Thomas at an up-country station when orders came that all white women and children were to go down to Calcutta by one of the river steamers or boats on the Ganges. Her quiet determination asserted itself when she said she would not go. The head government magistrate of the district, Mr Woods, who was a great friend (and who later settled with his family in the Waikato), told her she *must* leave. She still refused, declaring her place to be beside Thomas.

On the morning of the next boat's arrival a squad of trustworthy Indian troops arrived at the bungalow and marched her with her four children off to the boat, accompanied by some faithful retainers. During the day they had to endure the extreme heat and overpowering stenches while battened down under hatches; only at

215

dusk, when the boat was tied up for the night, were they allowed to emerge for fresh air and to stretch their cramped limbs by walking along the bank of the river. No doubt they could have been betrayed at any time, but loyalty to Thomas was very marked and showed itself on numerous occasions. Eventually, after much discomfort, they arrived at Calcutta.

Perhaps it was a relief to Mary Anne when, in 1860, they returned to England and bought a pleasant property in Sussex called Homebush at Ashington, near Brighton. Consisting of 600 acres or more it contained two tenant farms and was surrounded by parklike meadows.

The family started to increase. Frank was born here in 1861 and Hugh Watkins White in 1862. Meanwhile Mary Anne and Thomas lived the life of English country gentlefolk with plenty of domestic servants and their elder sons hunting with the county etc. However, English farming was not profitable enough to support a growing family so Thomas took a contract to build a railway in Southern Ireland. During this transit period and before moving his family to Ireland he took a house at Salt Hill, Slough, Buckinghamshire, near Windsor, where Charles Percy was born in 1864. The house faced Windsor Castle and had a large garden and stables where the coachman kept bantam fowls.

One day there was a meet of the staghounds to which they all drove out and presently the hunt passed across the road where the family coach was drawn up. Three-year-old Frank was on the box seat between the coachman and the footman. Suddenly a rider fell when jumping out of a field on to the road, his horse falling also. The footman jumped off the box seat and caught the rider's horse but was disappointed at not receiving a tip. He then found himself being roundly scolded by Mary Anne for having left her young son unattended high up on the box seat. The rider turned out to be the Duke of Edinburgh, brother of the Prince of Wales who later became King Edward VII.

Another move before going on to Ireland was for a short time to Hull, in Yorkshire. In Ireland at last they lived in a large country home called Ballynanty House in Ballynanty, Thurles, County Tipperary. The local hunt sometimes met here for the hunt breakfast, during which the whip was kept busy trying to keep the hounds off the flowerbeds.

The railway venture on which Thomas worked became absorbed later in the Southern Railway system of Ireland. Disaster came to him about the years 1867–68 when the company which had awarded him the contract failed.

He had spent over £12,000 of his own money on the work and the company owed him that amount plus the interest. Later the debt amounted to £21,000. He made several efforts to retrieve it and obtained a judgement, but his capital became finally and irretrievably lost to him when the company became bankrupt.

His position was then precarious enough, but was rendered even more acute by the pressure of an already large and ever increasing family. He and Mary Anne decided to return to India and, bringing the family back to London, they sold the carriage, the Irish jaunting car, the horses and the rest. Before they returned to Bombay an elder son, Jim, was apprenticed to the training ship *Worcester* for the Merchant Navy, Tom and Frank were sent to boardingschool at Hove near Brighton, Hugh and Effie were left at a small school in London, then Thomas and Mary Anne with Willie, Nellie, Ernest and Charles Percy, (known throughout his life as Dick) all went out to India.

When all hope of recovery of the capital from the railway company had to be abandoned, Thomas returned to England and collected his remaining children. He took up contracting work again, this time in Bombay, the construction of major railway bridges and similar projects now becoming his life's work. For this purpose he collected a great team of native workers, many of whom came from distant Bengal and Calcutta where they had last worked for him.

From Bombay Mary Anne and Thomas moved to Surat station, and here Nellie was married to Lieut Reilly, a gunner who had been attached to an elephant battery. Other moves were made to Breach Candy, near Bombay, to Kirkee, near Poona, where Thomas built a stone arch bridge over the Meeta Meela River, and to the Taptee River where he built the Hope bridge.

Then to Bandara and finally to Broach and the Nerbudda River. Here, the crowning work of his career was the building of the great Nerbudda bridge over the river, which is over a mile in width and situated about 200 miles from Bombay. Over 2,000 men were employed. His sons, Will and Tom, supervised the work which went on incessantly, except in times of flood, from 1876 until 1881, when the bridge was opened.

By this time Thomas's health had made retirement from the tropical heat and strenuous life an urgent necessity. With Mary Anne he had accomplished the difficult task of rebuilding a small fortune after the loss of the first in Ireland, and they had brought up a large family of sons and daughters. Three had died in India, also Jim,

Mary Anne White, *née* Watkins, 1832–1919. She was arrested for "insubordination" in India during the Mutiny.

who had been on the *Worcester* training ship. Florrie, a beautiful girl with auburn hair had died at Broach, aged ten, and two young children, Queenie and George, had died in babyhood.

Mary Anne bore up well, encountering all these difficulties and overcoming them, until in 1881 she sailed with Thomas, Effie, Hugh, Dick and Ernest for New Zealand. They landed at Napier. Frank and Tom stayed on in Broach to finish up a little extra work on the bridge.

From Napier the family went to Waipukurau, where they stayed for some months while looking round for land. They then heard of an empty hotel on the road between Takapau and Norsewood, which had been a coach stopping place until the railways reached Takapau in 1877. They moved to this place by bullock wagon and again looked around. It was here that Tom and Frank rejoined them, having arrived at Napier in the ship *Ringaruma*. William had meanwhile joined the Indian Civil Service and remained in India except for one subsequent visit to New Zealand; he rose very high in the Service and was awarded the Star of India decoration.

Thomas discovered that all the open land had already been taken up so he decided to investigate the possibility of settling on bush country, having rightly come to the conclusion that it was good land. A farm lying between Ashley Clinton and Makaretu came up for sale and he purchased it in 1882. Adjacent to part of the Ashcott estate, it was known as Sherwood. The house on the property was some miles up the valley at what is now known as Old Sherwood.

Thomas did not live long to enjoy his retirement. He died in 1883 and was buried at his own request in a grove of totara trees in front of the homestead. This house was

Old Sherwood homestead, 1883. Mary Anne White came here with her husband on his retirement.

A social gathering at Sherwood at the turn of the century. Mary Anne White had made numerous friends in the district by this time—"the days of buggies, wagonettes, dogcarts and high-stepping horses—for those who could afford them."

later burnt down and another built on the present site on the opposite side of the Makaretu road.

Mary Anne continued to live there while her sons farmed the property. She always wore a black gown and shawl and a white widow's cap. She made numerous friends about the district, among whom were the Herricks of Forest Gate, the A'Deanes of Ashcott, H. H. Bridge of Fairfield, the Lamberts of Lambertford (who were followed there by the Prices), the Johnstons of Orua Wharo, and others. With Sydney Johnston she loved to discuss world affairs and the Irish Home Rule question. She refused to vote, declaring it was not a woman's sphere, until Sydney Johnston, determined to make her vote and telling it was her duty to do so, carried her off to the polling booth.

During the evenings she tried to turn her sons into musicians, an uphill task with some of them, and never did she forget a birthday. Each New Year she sat up till midnight, then solemnly rose to open the door and let the New Year in.

Those were the days of buggies, wagonettes, dogcarts and high-stepping horses—for those who could afford them. There were country visits from one family to another, often over dreadful roads, flooded rivers and the still lingering fear of Hauhau rebels.

Servants were not difficult to find among the Scandinavians who had settled at Norsewood and Makaretu, although with most of them there was usually the language problem. One girl, Torina, whom Mary Anne found to be a good cook, could not bear to see the flaps of mutton thrown to the dogs. She stuffed, rolled and sewed them into sausages which, when boiled and pressed, made an appetising cold dish for lunch. The men called them "Torina's sausages", but she said they were called *pulsa*. After that they were known as "Torina's pulses".

When Torina's wedding day drew near she was unable to find the English words with which to give in her notice and it was only after much pointing to the ring on Mary Anne's own finger that it was understood that she was leaving to get married. The dress she had kept for special occasions while coming out to New Zealand was then shown, along with her best button-up boots, but as these were almost worn out Mary Anne found her a new pair. The boots, with a substantial addition to her wages, made Torina very happy.

The day before the wedding Mary Anne watched from the verandah as Torina's future husband accompanied her down the drive. At the gate she turned to wave. Mary Anne knew that Torina would walk most of the way to Norsewood, and that after the wedding in the morning, where there would be a cup of coffee and a gossip with a few Scandinavian friends, Torina would then have to walk to her home in the distant Seventy-Mile Bush.

During her long life Mary Anne remained a strict disciplinarian, with her grand-children having to toe the line. She attended church regularly and the visiting clergy usually stayed the night in the homestead. At times she would spend a fortnight at Kawau Island in the Hauraki Gulf, or in winter time at some other warm spot such as Kamo hot springs for her neuritis.

Devoted to her husband's memory to the end, she died on 10 September 1919 aged eighty-nine years, and was laid to rest in the grove of totara trees beside the grave of Thomas. Their descendants are still farming the land at Sherwood.

CHAPTER 50

Agnes Lydia Williams

Agnes Lydia Williams, the daughter of John and Sarah Williams, was born on 9 July 1855 at Pakaraka, which lay about twelve miles inland from the old Paihia mission station at the Bay of Islands. Her father was the fifth son of Archdeacon Henry Williams who entered the service of the Church Missionary Society and came to New Zealand in 1823. Her mother, the former Sarah Busby, was the daughter of James Busby of Waitangi who, in 1833, was appointed the first British Resident for New Zealand.

The eldest of the family, Agnes grew up on the property farmed by her father, her education coming from her mother and from schools conducted by the wives of missionaries. The community was mainly Maori and at an early age she learned to speak the Maori language. Her home during those early days was fairly isolated, and if sickness occurred a doctor had to be brought from Kororareka, now Russell.

During her childhood, hostilities among Maoris were still prevalent, with quarrels likely to break out at any time. In 1867 two tribes at Te Ahuahua, only a few miles away, were at war over a land dispute. Several chiefs had already been killed and a large general engagement was about to take place when news of the sudden death of Archdeacon Henry Williams was received. So deep was their love and respect for the pioneer missionary that the battle was immediately abandoned and never renewed.

In 1881 Agnes married her cousin, Thomas Sydney Williams. Born at Bay of Islands in 1847 he was the son of Judge Edward Marsh Williams of the Native Land Court who was also a son of Archdeacon Henry Williams. Edward Marsh Williams was also noted for his translation of the Maori Hymn book, which Maori scholars declared would remain as a monument to his memory.

Agnes spent the first few years of her married life home-making at Pakaraka, where Sydney farmed a Williams family property. Her first baby, a daughter named Eva Temple, was born in December 1882 and was followed by Rachel Millicent in 1886. A son, Oswald Temple, was born in 1889 and his brother Harold Edward arrived in 1892.

In 1894 the family moved to the east coat, where Sydney took over the management of the 20,000-acre Kaharau property lying two miles inland from Ruatoria. The land, a mass of scrub, fern, manuka and very little bush, was leased from Maori owners by Sir George Whitmore and then subleased by him to Sydney's uncle, Archdeacon Samuel Williams of Te Aute (53).

The family and their belongings went by sea to Gisborne where Agnes remained with the four children while Sydney went to Kaharau to prepare a home for them.

Archdeacon Henry Williams, 1782–1867, grandfather of Agnes Lydia Williams.

The kauri timber for the house was shipped from Auckland to Tuparoa Bay—an open roadstead—where it was tied into rafts, unloaded into the sea and towed to the breakers by surfboat. It was then cast loose to be tumbled ashore by the waves.

After that it was gathered up by Maori gangs employed by Sydney and carted by bullock wagon over seven miles of rough track through high manuka to the house site. Doors, windows, sashes and bricks were carried from the coastal vessel by surfboat to the landing and then placed in the bullock wagon. Already a large poplar tree was growing on the site; it had been a tall stake used by Maoris as a flagstaff to summon meetings, and it had remained to grow into a tree.

The day came at last when Agnes had to leave friends she had made in Gisborne, which was then a populated borough of some 3,800 people. By that time she was expecting her fifth child, Colin Sydney, who arrived in August 1894.

With the four children she boarded the coastal vessel which took them to Tuparoa, where they were put into the surfboats and rowed ashore. Then began the rough journey of bumping and jolting along the seven miles through the manuka to the house site on this large property where she would live without the benefit of any neighbours.

From that time forward her life consisted of forming a home for her husband and

"The Retreat", Archdeacon Henry Williams' home at Pakaraka. Agnes Lydia Williams was born at Pakaraka.

children. Stores for the household came every four months by ship, but if the sea was too rough the ship sailed past, taking the precious stores with it.

Life on this east coast station was a busy one. Her days began at five in the morning with washing to be done in water which came from the spring. There was bread to be made, sheets to be ironed, pillowshams and large tablecloths to be starched, and endless food to be prepared for the family and household. Cadets and shepherds always knew they would receive a warm welcome at the homestead. A certain amount of assistance was obtained from Maori girls, but they needed much supervision.

In 1897, after three years on the coast, Sydney took up on his own account a block of rough, heavy bush country at the head of the Tapuwaeroa Valley eighteen miles from the present township of Ruatoria. Under the gang system Maori labour was employed to cut manuka, burn off the fern and make fences. A woolshed was then built about four miles from the coast and the baled clip was carted by horse or bullock wagon to Tuparoa where it as dumped in sheds on the beach. When conditions permitted it went from wagons driven into the sea to the surf boats, and then out to the ship which took it to Napier for shipment to London. If the sea was rough the ship sailed on without taking the wool.

At the same time Sydney was developing Kaharau by stocking and fencing to overcome the tauhine scrub which had become a grave menace to the establishment of pasture on the papa faces. Later he took over the lease from his uncle and the whole area came under his management, being known as Tuparoa station.

In the meantime education for the children had to be considered. Despite the amount of work involved in running the household side of a large station, Agnes gave them as much tuition as she could until boardingschool became necessary. When the boys were old enough they went to Huntly School at Marton and then on to Wanganui Collegiate, while the girls went to Woodford House.

Packing trunks and attending to clothes for a whole term away from home was no small task. To get to the various schools the children took a long coach ride over the rough, hilly roads to Gisborne, which was about ninety-six miles from their home, and then went by ship to Napier. From there the boys went on by train to Marton or to Wanganui, their whole trip taking three days, while the girls went by coach to Havelock North.

For years Agnes was the only white woman for miles around. Experience taught her to cope with any crisis so that when the Maori people of Tuparoa or Ruatoria needed help they automatically went to her; nor was that help ever denied them. She did her utmost to tend to the sick, and when one man who was working on the station fell from his horse, ripping his ear until it hung only by a piece of skin, she patched it up to the best of her ability. He was B. C. Watkins, son of the artist, Kennett Watkins, and as soon as possible he took his injuries to a specialist in Auckland who told him that the job had been done so well he would not consider altering it in any way. Eventually there was a Doctor Davis living at Waipiro Bay, some twenty miles away. He was a Harley Street specialist who had come to New Zealand for his health and at Waipiro he lived mainly on goat's milk.

As the years passed the garden and orchard were developed. Citrus trees were easily grown and peaches flourished, the latter having sprung from peachstones taken to the

Agnes Lydia Williams, *née* Williams, 1855–1940. "Stores for the household came every four months by ship, but if the sea was too rough the ship sailed past, taking the precious stores with it."

east coast from trees grown by Archdeacon Henry Williams. The single-storeyed homestead, approached by a curving drive, was a place where large rooms with high ceilings opened from a central hall. The wide frontage and sides were flanked by verandahs that gave shelter from the hot east coast sun.

Agnes remained tall and slender, always holding herself very straight and with dignity. She was known for her gracious, old-world manners and was loved by everyone for her kindly and generous nature.

Sadness came to them in 1918 when their youngest son, Colin Sydney, was killed in action during World War I. Ten years later Agnes lost Sydney when he died in 1928 at the age of eighty-one, she herself living on until 1940, when she died aged eighty-five. Both are buried in a private cemetery in the orchard of their home, Kaharau, at Ruatoria.

Williams wool crossing the Waiapu at Ruatoria.

CHAPTER 51

Jane Williams

Jane, the daughter of James Nelson of Newark, Nottinghamshire, was born in 1801. A neat, slim girl, she was educated at a school for young ladies opened in Southwell by Mrs Williams, the widow of Thomas Williams, a lace manufacturer.

Deeply religious by nature, Mrs Williams strove earnestly to help her pupils in every way, and Jane proved such an apt and conscientious student that in 1817, at the age of sixteen, she was engaged as a pupil teacher. To take up her duties she walked the ten miles from Newark to Southwell, arriving at 9 am on a summer's morning looking cool and fresh. It was there that she met William Williams, the son of her employer.

William, a gentle and scholarly young man, was born in Nottinghamshire in 1800. It was at first proposed that he should take up the medical profession and with that object he was apprenticed to Mr Foster, a surgeon living in Southwell. During his study of medicine he heard that his brother Henry, who was over eight years his senior, had decided to abandon his naval career and enter the Church Missionary Society.

After much deliberation William decided to follow his brother's example, and offered himself for work in the missionary field so that he might join his brother in New Zealand. Mr Foster, however, would not allow him to leave before his period of apprenticeship had expired. In the meantime he found time to prepare himself for matriculation at Oxford and in due course he entered Magdalen Hall, now Hertford College, Oxford, where he spent two years.

William left college before taking his degree, but after a course of study at the Church Missionary Theological College at Islington he later received the BA degree. In September 1824 he was ordained deacon by the Bishop of London and received priest's orders at the same hands in December of the same year. Then, while awaiting an opportunity to sail to New Zealand, he spent most of his time gaining experience in the London hospitals.

There was no time for Jane to prepare for the type of wedding she would have liked. The order for William's sailing came suddenly, and because of the long period of residence required of the parties before marriage they were unable to have the ceremony at Jane's home in Newark. They were therefore married on 11 July 1825 in the home of the Rev John Blackburne, rector of Allercliff. Jane wore a simple white dress, the only one available at such short notice, and the only member of her family who could be present was her sister, Anna Maria Nelson.

The next day, after hurried visits of farewell to friends and relatives they boarded the 300-ton sailing ship *Sir George Osborne* at Lower Hope, six miles beyond Grave-

225

send. The voyage was fair though uneventful, and after 123 days they arrived at Sydney. They spent three months in Sydney waiting for a ship to take them on to New Zealand, but at last they arrived at Paihia, Bay of Islands, on the evening of 26 March 1826.

At Paihia the mission station had been established by Henry Williams when he arrived in 1823, and William and Jane at once entered fully into the life and routine work of teaching the Maoris. Apart from Henry and his wife Marianne there were nine other members of the Church Missionary staff, several with wives and children.

The first home occupied by William and Jane was a small cottage previously built and lived in by Henry and which he called his "Band Box". Within its limited space, seventeen days after landing, Jane's first baby arrived. This was Mary, born 12 April 1826.

Jane soon learned that the wives of the missionaries were expected to take an active part in mission work. There were thousands of Maoris waiting to be taught not only the Scriptures but also to read and write, and an endless number of Maori women and girls to be taught domestic duties. But first they themselves had to learn the Maori language; the task seemed tremendous.

Nor was the land as peaceful as the tranquillity and beauty of the Bay of Islands suggested. The tribes could be dangerous mobs of bloodthirsty cannibals whose only pleasure lay in the art of war. Further, the Maoris were now well armed. Hongi had recently arrived home from overseas laden with muskets and was clamouring for more guns.

As soon as Jane was well enough she began the duties of instructing in one way or another the Maori women clustering about the mission. Her second child, Jane Elizabeth, was born the following year in 1827 and Leonard William came in 1829.

In 1830 her husband built with his own hands a stone house of two storeys in which they lived for the next five years. Thomas Sydney was born in it in 1831. During those years William moved about the countryside teaching and establishing further mission sites.

For nine years they lived at Paihia near Henry and Marianne, their cottage becoming pretty with roses and woodbines growing through the trelliswork of the front verandah. In 1835 they moved to Waimate, where William was to take charge of a school for the sons of missionaries. The house they occupied there was unfinished for some time, causing Jane considerable inconvenience.

In 1836 the Rev Henry Bobart took charge of the school to allow William more time with his work among the Maoris, the revising of the translation of the New Testament and the correcting of proofs printed by William Colenso. In April Jane wrote concerning her son: *Leonard is a general favourite and is improving fast. His father has kept him back a little that he might not get before some of his seniors, but he is beginning Latin with Mr Bobart and amuses himself with learning the Greek Alphabet.* He was then six and a half years of age.

By this time Jane's two daughters were attending the English girls' school at Paihia which was under the control of their aunt, Marianne Williams. Her next son, James Nelson, was born in 1837. During that year they were visited by a Ngapuhi chief who had just returned from a prolonged visit to the east coast and who asked why it was that no missionary had been placed there. This was enough to send their thoughts in that direction, and before long William set off to investigate the possibilities of a mission in that district.

In February 1839 another daughter, Anna Maria, was born to Jane. Her husband returned from his visit to the east coast and it was not long before she found herself preparing to leave the company of her dear friends in the mission station for this isolated and unknown area. In October she went with the two youngest children to Paihia, where she was given time to prepare a supply of clothing for the family, some of whom they intended leaving at the Bay of Islands for the time being. A shipment of household requirements, books, and some cattle was then sent on ahead.

It was the middle of January 1840 when they reached Turanganui in Poverty Bay, Jane, of course, being the first white woman to live there. A great welcome was received from the Maoris, who swarmed into canoes and paddled out to surround the ship. When the party was ashore the captain became uneasy about the position of the ship and decided to move to the other side of the roadstead. The Maoris, thinking he was about to make off with the Williams's possessions immediately clambered aboard, overpowered the crew and brought all the cargo ashore in their canoes.

On his visit nine months earlier William had arranged for a raupo house to be built for them and this had been duly erected, but it was a mere shell of a building constructed Maori-fashion with walls of raupo attached to a wooden frame and a thatched roof of toetoe grass. There were no doors, no windows, no partitions or flooring, and it was swarming with fleas which could be expelled only with fire and boiling water. Nor could a house be completed until timber had been felled from the bush and then sawn and seasoned before being used.

For the first week the family had little peace; the Maoris continually surrounded the house in large numbers, shouting throughout the night sounds they imagined to be part of the missionaries' prayers. This first station at Poverty Bay was at Kaupapa about nine miles to the south-west of Turanganui (Gisborne), and not far from the mouth of the Waipaoa River. On the first Sunday at least 1,000 natives assembled for the open-air meeting.

A large amount of work fell on Jane's shoulders. Apart from the care of her own young family and the teaching of Maori girls, she had school lessons to give which included French to her eldest sons and two nephews, Henry and Thomas, who were also with them. These teenage boys were also reading Homer, Herodotus, Virgil and Cicero, on top of which there were lessons each day in Euclid, Latin, Hebrew and Greek.

By 1841 Jane's eldest daughter, fifteen-year-old Mary, who had been left at the Bay of Islands, came to what was now her home. She proved to be a great help with the new baby, Lydia Catherine, born 1841, who was the first white child to be born in Poverty Bay. The next baby to arrive was Marianne, born in 1843.

Mary was also a comfort to Jane when it was necessary for William to be away. By this time he had been appointed Archdeacon of East Cape including in his jurisdiction Opotiki, Rotorua, and Tauranga, which meant extensive travelling on foot and by sea down to Cape Palliser. During these periods Jane was beset by endless fears and worries until she saw his safe return.

William Williams, husband of Jane Williams. A drawing dated 1852, at which period they were visiting England on missionary and family business.

After a couple of winters, flooding of the Waipaoa River made a move from Kaupapa necessary. By February 1843 a new house at nearby Whakato was almost ready to move into when it was burnt down by the carelessness of a Maori who had made a fire too close to the building. It was not until 1846 that they were settled in the Whakato house and there, in February, Emma Caroline was born.

During the August of that year Jane and William and seven of their children paid a visit to Auckland, adverse weather causing the voyage to take twelve days. At the end of that month Mary and their nephew Samuel, the son of Archdeacon Henry Williams, were married. By mid-December Jane and William had returned to Poverty Bay, but as various assistants had left the mission during the year a heavy load of work now faced them.

In 1850 Jane and William went to England on both family and missionary business, returning in the April of 1853. In June 1853 their son William Leonard, who at this period was studying in England, married Sarah Wanklyn of Halecat, Westmoreland.

In 1855 land was acquired at Waerenga-a-hika for a Maori school. Referring to it Jane wrote in September 1855: *The Government will allow a certain sum of money for the establishment of native schools. We must go slowly to work and begin with raupo buildings, taking down our own wooden ones and having them rebuilt at the new place about six miles off.*

This was an arduous business that progressed by slow degrees. A large barge capable of carrying about twelve tons had first to be built, as this was needed to carry the timber and bricks from buildings and all the family goods and chattels about eight miles up the river, whence they would be carted about two miles to the site.

The piano suffered badly. Wrapped in blankets and packed in its own tin-lined case it was taken with twenty-four sacks of wheat and other packages to be placed on board the barge during the evening ready for a start at daylight. At first light it was discovered that the barge had sunk overnight in ten feet of water, the wheat sacks were at the bottom of the river and the piano case was floating in midstream. It was retrieved and dried out, but after eight hours or more in the water it was never the same instrument.

By 1854 the Rev. Leonard Williams, who had been admitted to deacon's orders by the Bishop of London, had returned with his wife to join the family at Waerenga-a-hika. They shared the load of toil, and in 1857 Jane wrote concerning a day's work:

The community was roused before sunrise by the ringing of the great Church bell at the pa about 100 yards from mission premises, and soon after sunrise it rang again for about five minutes as a call to prayers, which were taken by Archdeacon Williams or Leonard, after which there was an hour's school. Then breakfast and about an hour after Leonard Williams' school was held, immediately followed by the native dinner, spread on a long table formed of planks in the schoolroom. The afternoon was devoted to manual labour, some being employed ploughing, others at carpenter's work, fencing etc. which required constant superintendence. About an hour before sunset the bell rang for school again, which was followed by evening prayers at the native chapel.

The women take it in turns to cook for themselves, the men and boys, which includes breadmaking on a large scale. The girls belonging to the household have school in the afternoon in the men's schoolroom, conducted by Maria Williams and a Miss Jones who joined them in 1853. Kate Williams assisted Mrs Leonard Williams with her children and the household oversight, which she took charge of and helped in the school or supervised the women who preferred their own shiftless ways to systematic work. Much time was also required for arranging and supervising the making of clothing for the natives. Mr Baker assisted in Leonard's school.

One of Jane's occupations three mornings a week before breakfast was to stand over and direct two Maori men making bread in two large tubs sufficient to yield a daily supply of 100 lbs. This they afterwards baked, without needing further instruction, in a large brick oven. It fell to Maria's province to weigh out this bread twice daily, giving three quarters of a pound to each person for a meal. The oven, built by Leonard, was capable of baking 240 lb of bread while two iron pots boiled potatoes or other food. Some time later a "bread-making machine" proved a great acquisition.

In 1858 a letter came announcing William's appointment as first Bishop of Waiapu, and he was duly consecrated by the Rt Rev. Bishop Selwyn at St Peter's Church in Wellington on 3 April 1859.

As the years passed the mission grew and more buildings were erected. There was also much sickness to be fought with severe epidemics of influenza among the Maoris and in the family. Maria suffered an illness after which she never fully recovered normal health, and visits to Auckland for medical aid were necessary. Jane, too, was now having trouble with her eyes.

During the 1860s news of the wars in Taranaki began to filter through and they noticed a distinct unfriendliness from Maoris when they travelled. In 1865 news came that Patara and his Hauhaus were coming through to Poverty Bay with the express purpose of putting all clergymen to death and of driving the Pakehas out of the

The Williams home at Waerenga-a-hika, showing fire damage after the Hauhau raid of 1865.

country. The local Maoris assured them that Patara would not be allowed to harm them and would be sent away immediately,

But it was soon seen that a large number of Hauhaus were in the district and rapidly gaining the sympathy of local Maoris who joined them in great numbers, hypnotised in some peculiar way and completely under the power of the leaders.

Numbers of loyal Maoris went to Waerenga-a-hika to stand by the missionaries in their hour of need, but it was soon evident that the white people must leave for safety. The *St Kilda* was at anchor in the bay and the family hastily packed. The children and Maria were sent on a sledge drawn by bullocks and the adults rode to the coast on horseback. The *St Kilda* took them to Napier, where they received hospitality from the community and three days later they embarked on the SS *Ladybird* for Auckland.

At Waerenga-a-hika most of the missionary buildings were burned, the smoke being seen almost ten miles away. The nearby Waerenga-a-hika pa was also destroyed, with several being killed. Missionary work was at a halt. Jane and William, who had lost most of their possessions, then spent a period at Bay of Islands where the Bishop continued to conduct a school and worked on his book, *Christianity Among the New Zealanders*.

In 1867 it was decided that Hawke's Bay should be included in the Diocese of Waiapu, and by June of that year Jane and William had moved to live in Napier, where they rented a house at the top of Fitzroy Road. In 1868 their home, known as Hukarere, was built. There, on 26 March 1876, the fiftieth anniversary of his landing in New Zealand, Bishop William Williams suffered a stroke. He died two years later, aged seventy-six, and was buried at Napier. His memorials can be seen in his translation of the New Testament, his Maori dictionary, the founding of the Diocese of

The Williams home at Hukarere, *circa* 1876, where Bishop Williams died in 1878.

Jane Williams, *née* Nelson, 1801–1896. "A peaceful end to a beautiful life."

Waiapu, the Hukarere Maori Girls' College and the assistance he gave to the Te Aute Boys' School.

Jane continued to live at Hukarere. A description of her has been left in the diary of Mary Glover Bibby (4) who visited her in May 1891. She writes: *I climbed up the hill to Hukarere and visited the Williams's in their delightful house—a house with a view that reminds you of Mentone, the Bay of Naples or some such lovely place. The Williams's are delightful and were very glad to see any friend of Miss Butler and I was just delighted to see old Mrs Williams who is really a grand old lady.*

She is ninety years of age and is mother, grandmother and great-grandmother to a host of children, and it is now sixty-five years since she came to New Zealand. She is frail but as bright as a girl and with a bright wrinkled face—wrinkles, though, of peace and a well-spent, hard-working life. Her memory, hearing and faculties are perfect, and I never saw a more interesting old lady. Indeed, she is one who takes her place with Mrs Moffatt as one of the Heroines of the Mission Field.

In 1894 Sarah, the wife of Jane's son, Leonard, died while they were staying with her at Hukarere. Two years later, on 6 October 1896, she herself died, aged ninety-five, and was buried in Napier. Archdeacon Leonard Williams described her passing as "a peaceful end to a beautiful life".

CHAPTER 52

Lillian Mary Williams

Lillian Mary Ludbrook was the daughter of Samuel Blomfield Ludbrook and his wife Caroline Elizabeth, *née* Williams. She was born in 1870 at Onewaha, near Ohaewai, in the Bay of Islands district where her father was farming land he had bought from his father-in-law, Henry Williams. Of average height and with a good slim figure, she had brown hair, beautiful blue eyes and a keen sense of humour. In 1898 she married Kenneth Stuart Williams in the Pakaraka church, Canon Walsh officiating.

Kenneth, who was born at Pakaraka in 1870, was the son of John William Williams and his wife, the former Sarah Busby. Six feet in height, and with dark hair and blue eyes, he had been farming at Tuparoa on the East Coast since 1894 when he went there to assist his cousin Thomas Sydney Williams (50). The two men were breaking in land leased by their uncle, Archdeacon Samuel Williams of Te Aute (54). It was land previously administered by A. H. Wallis, and lack of capital, low wool prices, and access only over the open beaches at Waipiro Bay and Tuparoa made conditions difficult.

The Archdeacon promised the two men that if they could free his Waiapu properties of debt he would start them off farming on their own account on some of this land. After two years at Tuparoa Kenneth went to the Matahiia block of the property, six miles west of where Ruatoria is now situated.

After their marriage he took Lillian to the East Coast by steamer. The ship anchored off Tuparoa Bay where she was carried through the surf on the back of a hefty Maori. From there she went twelve miles by bullock dray to her new home at Matahiia where she lived in a two-storeyed cottage previously occupied by Mr Frank Kemp, a previous manager of Matahiia, and his family. The upper rooms were small and were approached by a narrow stairway. A wood range had been installed and lighting was by candles or kerosene lamps. Water was from a spring a quarter of a mile up the hill from the house. Lillian's nearest neighbour was Agnes Lydia, the wife of Thomas Sydney Williams, who lived six miles away on another part of the station.

Her first baby, Charles Kenneth, was born on the place. His was a difficult birth which kept her in labour for three days in an isolated district where very little help was available. Therefore, when her second child was due she returned by ship to her own people at the Bay of Islands. This was a daughter, Mona Caroline. The next two, John Dow and Peter, were born in Gisborne, giving her four babies in four years, and her days were then full sewing and mending for them. Peter, who was delicate from birth, died from measles at the age of eight years. His grave was made on the property where a private cemetery was established.

Matahiia homestead, home of Lillian and Kenneth Williams. "Those working on neighbouring stations were always welcome at weekends, and loved to come for tennis parties and singsongs round the piano in the evenings."

Lillian's only help during those early days came from untrained Maori girls whom she trained herself. Stores were brought in by wagon from Tuparoa while the wool was going out, and this had to be done before the rains made the unmetalled roads too boggy and impossible to negotiate. The order for all requirements was put in with the storekeeper at Tuparoa and he then telegraphed Auckland for them to be shipped. On one dreadful occasion Lillian forgot to put the order in and the ship arrived without stores for Matahiia. Kenneth never said a word, and Lillian never forgot again.

The Mata, unbridged until 1932, was inclined to flood, and in conjunction with the Aorangiwai and Makarika creeks kept them restricted to the property. If anyone became ill during flood times they either recovered or died. On one occasion Lillian nursed a member of the staff who had been badly kicked in the stomach by a horse, it being quite impossible to get the man out, or help into the station.

It was necessary too to send the children away to boardingschool for their education, the boys going to Huntly at Marton and then to Christ's College. On three occasions young Charles rode the many miles to Gisborne to catch the ship for Napier, and eighty-four times he went to Tokomaru Bay to be loaded by basket into the *Waima* launch piloted by Captain Plummer.

As the years passed the house was enlarged and the grounds developed into gardens and an orchard where Kentish cherries grew well. Once, when the neighbouring Williams family came and picked cherries the buggy was too full of people to take home the kerosene cases of cherries as well. They were left to be collected next day but the river came up and made this impossible so Lillian made the lot into jam and preserves. To let them waste would have been unthinkable, particularly as it was important to keep the station store-cupboards full.

Lillian took a great interest in all young people and she was loved by them all.

233

Left: Kenneth Stuart Williams, MP, 1870–1935. *Right:* Lillian Mary Williams, *née* Ludbrook, 1870–1963.

Those working on neighbouring stations were always welcome at weekends, and loved to come for tennis parties on the two courts that had been laid out, and for singsongs round the piano in the evenings. She had only to hear of a baby's pending arrival to begin knitting.

She lived at Matahiia from 1898 to 1920, when Kenneth became the Parliamentary Member for Bay of Plenty in the Reform Party. He was elected unopposed three times and they lived in Wellington while Parliament was in session. In the Coates Cabinet he was Minister for Public Works.

In 1935, after pneumonia had seriously weakened his heart, Kenneth decided to retire from his public activities. A large garden party was held in his honour in the attractive grounds of Charles Gordon's home at Opotiki, and after the host had given a speech which was followed by another from a member of the Upper House, it was Kenneth's turn to speak. He turned to where Lillian was sitting at an angle from him across the lawn, smiled at her, gave a small cough—and died.

Kenneth was sixty-five when he died. He was taken home to the private cemetery on the property. Strangely enough, he was buried on election day.

After his death Lillian returned to live at Matahiia where her eldest son Charles Kenneth, had been managing the property since 1924. In 1938 the old homestead was burned down while the family was away during Easter. A new cottage was built in the garden for Lillian and a new home erected for Charles and his family.

Lillian spent the remainder of her years at Matahiia but died in the Te Puia Hospital in 1963 at the age of ninety-three. She was buried beside Kenneth at Matahiia.

CHAPTER 53

Mary Williams

Mary Williams was the eldest child of the Rev. William Williams and his wife, who had formerly been Jane Nelson (51). She was born at Paihia, Bay of Islands, on 21 April 1826, only nine days after her parents had stepped ashore from the ship *Sir George Osborne*. Her father, a doctor who had joined the Church Missionary Society, had come to work with his brother, the Rev. Henry Williams, who had arrived three years earlier.

As a little girl Mary was looked after by Maori nurses and played with Maori children, so she learned to speak Maori fluently. Her education was attended to by her mother and her aunt, Mrs Henry Williams, who between them taught the children at the mission settlement. When she was nine her father was ordered to Waimate to take charge of the boardingschool established there for the sons of missionaries and Mary then attended the boardingschool for the daughters of missionaries run by her aunt.

As she grew she developed into a capable and kindly girl with a placid nature. Her colouring tended towards fairness and she was short with a nicely rounded figure. In 1840, when she was fourteen, her parents moved to Turanganui (Gisborne) where her father, who by then had been appointed Archdeacon, had taken charge of the mission work on the East Coast. In a letter dated 24 August 1841 he wrote: *The presence at home of our eldest daughter, Mary, now fifteen years of age, has been a source of great comfort to her mother. She is industrious in her habits and takes an equal share with her mother in all household duties: indeed without her I know not how she would get through the difficulties of her present situation, the eldest of our three youngest children being only four years of age.*

At the end of 1844 Mary's cousin Samuel Williams, who was attending St John's College in Auckland, came to stay with them during his vacation. Two years later he and Mary were married.

Samuel, born at Cheltenham on 17 January 1822, was the son of the Rev. (later Archdeacon) Henry Williams. His father had been a lieutenant in the Royal Navy and had taken part in several engagements, including the bombardment of Copenhagen. Thankfulness for his safe deliverence from the perils of this voyage awakened him to serious reflections and finally led to his changing his career, and he therefore decided to retire from the Navy and enter the Church Missionary Society.

Samuel was only eight months old when, on 17 September 1822, he sailed with his parents, brother and sister, on the *Lord Sidmouth,* a ship carrying women convicts to Australia. They arrived in New Zealand on 3 August 1823, landing at Paihia, where they settled and established a mission station.

Samuel was not educated with the Maori boys but at Waimate under his uncle, William Williams, where the boys were taught to turn their hands to almost anything. Spoken of as being the flower of the family, he was hampered by weak eyesight, and at the age of fourteen began to outgrow what poor strength he possessed. At the age of fifteen, after three years at the mission school, he began farming at Pakaraka with his brother Edward, but this he later gave up to enter St John's College and become a theological student. He was ordained on 20 September 1846.

Ten days later, at 11 am on 30 September, Mary and Samuel were married by Bishop Selwyn at the Tamaki Church (St Thomas's) near St John's College. After the ceremony about fifty guests "partook of a sumptious collation" in the College Hall and the bride and groom later took their departure to the house which the Rev. G. A. Kissling had lent to them. This was at Kohimarama.

The following week Samuel moved with his wife to a comfortable house at Purewa near the College, where he continued his work for several months until, in the February of 1848, they left Auckland for the mission stations at Otaki and Waikanae.

These two stations had been established in 1839 by the Rev. Octavius Hadfield. It was a district where quarrels continually simmered between the Waikanae Maoris and Te Rauparaha's people, and to avoid clashes through jealousy he had established houses at both places and divided his time between them. Unfortunately his health was poor, and Samuel went to Otaki as his co-adjutor.

A description of Otaki at that time has been left by Charlotte Godley in her *Letters From Early New Zealand*. She visited the Rev. Octavius Hadfield in 1850 and later wrote that Otaki was a place of low sandhills where, unless one knew the track, one was apt to become bogged. The village was flat and lay not far from the river. It was scattered, with no two houses standing close together, and each with a quarter acre for garden and potatoes. A brook or small river ran through it, and the bush, with very fine trees coming close to the cultivations, had been left in patches of wood that ornamented the countryside which had a beautiful background of well-wooded hills.

Tamihana (known as Thompson), the son of Te Rauparaha, had a weatherboard house with a deep verandah and French windows opening to the ground. It was painted white with green trelliswork, and decorated inside with much red-and-white Maori painting and handwork. His large, well-kept garden was full of English plants. His wife, when she attended the Government House ball for the Queen's birthday, wore a frock of pink-and-white silky gauze with badly made flounces and a black silk scarf.

The home of Octavius Hadfield was a little low cottage built of reeds and thatched with toetoe. It had a door in the middle with his bedroom on one side and his sitting-room on the other.

Mary and Samuel lived in a raupo whare which Samuel nearly burnt down one night when he fixed his candle in a cleftstick on the side of the whare and then fell asleep. The candle burnt down to its socket and the whare was almost on fire when Mary awoke him with cries of alarm.

At Otaki their routine began at 5 am. The bell rang each morning at 6 am for prayers, after which both men and women attended school until 8 am. At this stage the famous church, Rangiatea, with its three lofty pillars, each a single tree rising to support the eighty-six feet long ridgepole formed from another single tree, was being built.

Mary devoted a great deal of time to teaching Maori women and girls the art of cooking and household management. She had Maori girls as servants, one being the daughter of a young chief, who received no wages but was there to learn all she could. Maori boys worked in the garden, learning agriculture in the same way. In the meantime Samuel made frequent visits to places several miles away where the Maoris assembled in hundreds to listen to him.

Two events occurred in 1852, one bringing joy to Mary when the Rev. Octavius Hadfield married Samuel's sister Kate Williams, but the other bringing sorrow when her first baby, Marianne Jane, was born in September but died a week later.

The following year came an urgent request from the Governor, Sir George Grey, for Samuel to open a Maori school in the central Hawke's Bay district. He agreed reluctantly, and in 1854 the move was made to Te Aute.

On 6 July 1854 Mary's second baby, Anna Lydia, was born, and in October, with the baby only three months old, Mary began the journey to Te Aute.

The party consisted of twelve Maori boys who were to be the first pupils at the school, and members of the Ngati Raukawa tribe who carried their household goods and chattels and attended to the leading of a cow. The first stage took them to the Manawatu River, where they embarked in canoes. The heavily laden craft were paddled up river against the strongly flowing current while the cow was led along the bank. Progress during the daytime was slow and the nights were spent camping on the riverbanks which at that time were covered with bush.

In the Gorge the bush also clothed the high steep hills from summit to water, with bold masses of rock peeping out at intervals. In one place the rapids forced them to unload the canoes, carry the contents along the bank for a distance, and then reload. In the meantime the cow was urged along a narrow Maori track running above water level.

Canoe travel was possible only as far as Puehutai, near Oringi, and from here they still had sixty miles to travel overland. From this place, because of previous quarrels, the Ngati Raukawa decided to return home, and there were now not enough bearers to carry all the goods. Many things had to be left behind to be collected later, and it was several months before these goods eventually reached Te Aute. In fact Mary's treasured wood range and large sofa never left Oringi as it was impossible to find any means of transport for them.

So, laden like packhorses, they began the sixty-mile trek to Te Aute. The track led through the gloom and damp slipperiness of boggy patches in the Seventy Mile Bush, down steep gullies to cross streams and the upper reaches of the Manawatu, and then out at last to face the Ruataniwha Plains, which stretched as far as their eyes could see. Beyond this the Tuki Tuki and then the Waipawa Rivers had to be crossed.

At last they came to the lake, Roto-a-Tara, the scene of much earlier fighting among the tribes, and a short distance beyond its shores was the land decided upon for the college. This comprised 7,799 acres of impenetrable fern and scrub with portions of forest and a great swamp. It had no natural boundaries. The wearisome journey to reach it had taken from two to three weeks.

Mary Williams, *née* Williams, 1826–1900, with one of her daughters. Her hospitality to travellers earned the Williams house the nickname of "The Wayfarer's Rest."

When they arrived, the only place to shelter Mary and her baby was a Maori *pataka,* a storehouse built up on high piles to guard against rats; it could be entered only by climbing a ladder. It was fourteen feet long by eight feet wide and the walls were three feet six inches in height, and under these horribly cramped conditions she lived and nursed baby Lydia until Samuel was able to build a two-roomed raupo whare with thatched roof. This had a detached kitchen with fireplace and chimney built of mud, supported by a wooden frame. The earth floors were covered with matting. About a year later a third room was added and in this raupo whare they lived for six years.

However, they were not unhappy years and their son William Temple was born there in March 1856. The whare stood on the main north-south track and as there were no hotels their tiny house was used constantly as an overnight stopping place for the many travellers who had begun passing up and down the newly opened district. And as hospitality was never denied it was not long before the place became known as the "Wayfarers' Rest".

The first horses about the place were a problem. There were no fences to keep them enclosed and they were often to be found nibbling the raupo walls of the Wayfarers' Rest. When this occurred at night Samuel's head appeared at the window and a well-aimed fowling-piece loaded with coarse salt soon sent them galloping towards safer pastures.

Mary's next baby, Thomas Leonard, was born in 1858, and Francis Henry arrived in 1859, his birth giving her four children under the age of five years. Apart from

238

A Maori *pataka*. "Under these horribly cramped conditions" Mary Williams and Samuel lived until he built a two-roomed whare.

caring for her own little ones her days were filled by giving elementary education and training in household duties to Maori girls. She ran the mission Sunday school and was responsible for all mails, keeping what became virtually a post office. She also had parish duties and taught her own children as they grew old enough to learn.

By 1860 the raupo whare had been replaced by a wooden house in which, under Samuel's supervision, a huge brick oven had been built on the spot. A fire was lit inside and when thoroughly heated the embers were removed and the bread baked in the heat retained by the bricks. The family lived a spartan life with few comforts, and furniture was kept only to bare necessities. Morning prayers at 5 am began a long working day which lasted well into the night.

From her supply of medicines, which could not be easily replaced, Mary treated the ailments of the Maori residents and Pakeha runholders who called almost daily for medical aid. The uninvited guests who arrived so frequently for a meal and bed often ate what had been intended for the family's breakfast, which meant that after their retirement to bed Mary would then have to turn to baking more bread for the morning, usually adding a tasty something for the travellers to take with them.

Her supply of linen, another commodity difficult to replace, was also fairly limited, and if she knew a person would be returning soon she usually put his sheets away with his name pinned to them. Her washing soap also had to be made by herself with a substance known as lye, made from wood ashes and taking the place of soda.

"The Wayfarer's Rest" at Te Aute, *circa* 1860/70. Here Mary Williams was caring for her four children, all under five years, educating and training Maori girls, running the Sunday school and acting as a postmistress.

After five years of hard toil to establish the College Samuel was forced to close it down through lack of finance. He had trusted in the terms of Sir George Grey's agreement wherein Grey had promised not less than £300 per annum for developing the school. This was paid till after his term of office ended, but the Government then saw fit to cancel that promise and give a capitation allowance of £8 instead. This was quite inadequate as Samuel was only able to lease the property for £4 odd, and it cost him around £20 per pupil. He was confronted, also, by the heavy loss suffered in a fire which completely destroyed the barns and woolshed and a large quantity of grain, stores and implements.

He realised that it was imperative for the College to become self-supporting, and with this in view he himself took out an unregistered lease of the land and began farming it to provide some revenue. This was the beginning of Te Aute station, but any money he made was poured back into the College, which already owed him well over £1000. At the same time his parish duties were not neglected.

In 1868 Mary's next child, Lucy Frances, was born, but in 1870 her next baby, Mary, lived only two days. With the assistance of money borrowed from England her husband leased land from the Government, eventually increasing his leasehold, over the years, to 20,000 acres which stretched from the range of hills behind Te Aute to Drumpeel Road and the Tuki Tuki River. In the busy season, the bell used as the cookhouse dinner gong regularly called from thirty to forty hands to meals. A flourmill and a butcher's shop were also established on the property.

Life in the homestead was still being lived on frugal lines and the first armchair Mary and Samuel possessed was presented to them by the station hands. In 1872 they had the satisfaction of seeing the school reopen with John Reynolds as headmaster.

Three years later, in 1875, the railway reached Te Aute, bringing with it a severe outbreak of typhoid fever. The outbreak was caused through insanitary conditions in the men's camps at Opapa and Te Aute, and was soon raging through the district. Both Mary and Samuel had acquired an extensive experience in medical treatment and together they worked day and night in an unceasing struggle to care for the stricken

Samuel Williams, 1822–1907. His farming work, undertaken to finance Te Aute College, brought him "years of worry and much hostile criticism."

Te Aute College. "As the years passed it made good progress."

and to get the epidemic under control. Their medicine chest was a small but beautifully made walnut box equipped with what medical supplies were available at that time.

When conditions returned to normal their patients showed their appreciation by sending to England for a chest containing a handsome silver salver, tea and coffee service. This was engraved with the names of the donors and *Presented to Rev. Samuel Williams and Lady by the Inhabitants of Te Aute and Kaikora as a token of gratitude for their unceasing attention to the sick of the district during the most trying season of 1875.*

By that time Mary had become known over the whole district as the one to whom people turned when help was necessary. When the Campbell children at neighbouring Poukawa were left motherless, Catherine, the eldest daughter, took charge of her delicate little brother, Hugh McLean Campbell, later of Horonui. She always declared that she could never have reared him but for the advice and help she received from Mary Williams at Te Aute.

Mary would always find a meal and an odd job for anyone who wanted work. Monetary aid was always given to those in need, but to enable this to be done, economy was still practised in the home. Each week after the washing was done everything was carefully examined by Mary to see what mending was necessary, and each year the carpets were unpicked, turned round and resewn by hand to give more wear.

As the years passed the College made good progress. Hawke's Bay became more settled and work became more arduous in Samuel's parish, which stretched over a large district. During the 1880s he decided to lease and take up land on the east coast, but this caused him years of worry, brought him much hostile criticism, and at times it was so precarious that it appeared that he was almost facing ruin.

Another of his projects was the colossal task of draining the Te Aute swamp lands and Lake Roto-a-Tara. He achieved this only after many years of hard work, but it resulted in approximately 3,000 extra acres of rich pasture land.

Throughout the years when difficult situations were endemic Mary remained placid, encouraging her husband against all adversaries and backing him to the full in everything he did. In 1888 she saw him appointed Archdeacon of Hawke's Bay.

Twelve years later in 1900, after forty-six years of witnessing the district being transformed from a wilderness, Mary Williams died at Te Aute and was buried in its small private cemetery. Samuel died in 1907 and was buried beside her.

241

CHAPTER 54

Alice Sweetnam Wilson

Alice Sweetnam Beamish, the daughter of George and Jane Beamish, was born in 1836 at Kilkern, County Cork, Ireland. In 1849 her elder brother Nathaniel sailed for New Zealand in the *Lady Nugent*. In Wellington he met William Couper, who held land at Turakina in the Rangitikei district, and who offered him the management of this property.

In 1850 George and Jane Beamish left Ireland with their remaining son and four unmarried daughters, and in the October of that year they arrived at New Plymouth in the barque *Eden*. They joined Nathaniel at Turakina, living with him in what was then known as Plains House.

At this time Alice was fourteen years of age. She had grown to be a fairly tall slim girl whose auburn hair, parted in the centre, held the slightest hint of a wave. The family lived in an isolated area, but many happy days were spent in summer swimming in the Turakina River.

A few years later she met Lieutenant James Wilson of the New Zealand Militia. Born in 1836 at Belevedere, Kent, he was a tall, dark handsome man with mutton-chop side-whiskers. They were married in 1859 at Turakina. In 1860 their son, James George, was born, and in 1862 their daughter Alice arrived. She was followed by little Edwin John in 1864.

During this time the Wilsons appear to have been living in Hawke's Bay where, because of the Hauhau uprisings, Alice soon learnt to live with the anxiety common to all soldiers' wives.

In September 1865 James was detailed to take twenty-six military settlers from Hawke's Bay to Poverty Bay, where they built a stockade on Kaiti some 200 yards east of the present War Memorial. It became known as Wilson's Redoubt and was ninety-three feet square with towers at the angles. In the enclosure there was a wooden building, sixty feet by sixteen feet, and also a powder magazine.

In November James took part in the siege of Waerenga-a-hika and with a party of twenty military settlers was sent into the scrub on the right of the pa to a point that would command the rebels' water supply. The party was soon discovered and came under fire, five of his men being killed before the bugle call brought reinforcements.

The following year he took part in the Omarunui engagement a few miles from Napier, and it was after this fight that Te Kooti was shipped to the Chatham Islands with other Hauhau rebels.

By this time Alice's sister Maria had married Thomas Lowry of Okawa in Hawke's Bay, and in 1866 James Wilson and Thomas Lowry went into partnership in the

Captain James Wilson and his son Jimmie.

Rikirangi Te Turuki Te Kooti, who terrorised Maori and Pakeha alike. He would never agree to be drawn or photographed, and this sketch is thought to be the best likeness of him.

Poverty Bay property, Maraetaha. James saw to the running of it from their home at Matawhero.

In 1867 Alice's next baby was born, a girl whom she called Jessie Gertrude. Their home was two-storeyed where she slept downstairs with her husband and the baby, while Jimmy, Alice and Edwin slept in the small upstairs rooms. Working for them, but living in an outside whare about fifty yards from the house, was Private John Moran, aged sixty, of the New Zealand Militia, who went by the nickname of Jacky Pumpkin.

In the July of 1868 Te Kooti escaped from the Chathams, returning to Poverty Bay thirsting for revenge. The settlement at Matawhero was small, with less than a dozen homesteads in the district, the nearest neighbours to the Wilsons being Major Reginald Newton Biggs and his nineteen-year-old wife, formerly Emily Maria Dudley of Broom, Canterbury. Living with them was twenty-six-year-old Jane Farrell, who was employed as a nurse to care for their baby son George.

Emily, whose husband was twice her age, was a noted horsewoman, and despite the assistance she received from Jane Farrell she was no doubt glad to have the advice of the more experienced Alice so close at hand. Their husbands had fought together in many campaigns and by that time James had been promoted to the rank of captain.

Nor had their campaigning against Te Kooti been forgotten by the rebel.

During November 1868 Major Biggs was told by friendly Maoris that an attack from Te Kooti was due to take place. They had also mentioned the route his warriors would take, but Biggs had paid little or no heed to the warnings, declaring that his scouts would bring news in plenty of time to raise the alarm.

In the meantime Te Kooti, with a large body of followers, was advancing over the bushclad ranges towards Hangaroa via an overgrown track that had not been used for years. The route took them to Patutahi where, on the night of 9 November, he paused to address his leaders. Much blood would flow at Matawhero that night, from the weapons in their right hands, he is reputed to have told them, and much plunder would be taken in their left hands. He was leading them by the upper ford instead of by the shortest way so that they would not be seen. They would divide into small bands and he himself would strike the chief of the Pakehas (Major Biggs), while Nama would lead others to the lesser chief (Captain Wilson). Smaller bands would each go into the other Pakeha houses and surprise the people thereof, but they must use only the silent weapons rather than the guns. His word had gone forth and blood must be spilled. None were to be spared.

The main body of men then crossed the Waipaoa and advanced towards Matawhero where, halting in the scrub beside Major Biggs's home, Te Kooti sent about twenty men to surprise Captain Wilson.

That night Major Biggs had sat up late to write letters. It was later reported by a lad, Charlie James, who worked for Biggs, that the Major had been awakened at 3 am by a noise outside the house. Under the impression that some of his scouts had returned, he went out to investigate. A shot was fired at him and as he rushed back into the house he shouted to the others to run for the scrub.

The rebels then forced their way into the house, dragged Biggs outside and laid him on the ground, where his head was beaten in with the butt of a gun. Emily, in her nightdress, struggled to go to him, and Jane Farrell, holding the baby, declared she

Alice Sweetnam Wilson, *née* Beamish, 1836–1868, with Alice and Edwin. Some two years after this photograph was taken, both children and their 18-month-old sister Jessie were brutally murdered by Hauhau raiders; shortly afterwards Alice died of wounds.

would stay by her side and live or die with her. Emily, Jane and the baby were then attacked, their bodies falling close to where Biggs's body was lying. Charlie James, who had been able to slip beneath a grating which led from the back door to an outbuilding, was able to escape. He rushed to warn neighbours, and as he passed the Wilson's home he heard the door being battered in and the noise of shooting. Flames later shot out of the windows.

Captain Wilson too had gone to bed late after attending to mail, but at some time during the early hours of the morning he had heard the dogs barking. There was a gentle knock at the back door and he got up to ask who was there. A Maori voice replied that he had an important message for him from Hirini te Kani, a friendly chief. James told him to push it under the door, but the Maori replied that he wished to speak to him. James pulled the blind aside and in the dim light saw that the house was surrounded.

He called to John Moran who, if he had wished, could have escaped into the scrub, but the old man made his way into the house to stand beside the family. As he entered the house he was grasped by a Maori who released him only when fired upon by James.

Alice threw a shawl over her nightdress and crept upstairs to reassure the frightened children. Jimmy was then eight years of age, Alice was six and Edwin had turned four. Baby Jessie, who slept downstairs, was just eighteen months. In the meantime Moran had taken his stand at the front door with a rifle while James stood near the back door with a revolver.

The rebels broke down the back door but, not daring to enter, fired several volleys into the house from a safe distance. Some of them then crept under the house and set fire to it at both ends. James went upstairs and brought all the children down, but soon all were being scorched from the heat of the roaring flames. James then had no option but to take them out on to the verandah. A Maori who had received many gifts of food from Alice assured them that no harm would be done, and they were led away into the darkness.

Alice carried baby Jessie while little Alice clung to her nightdress. Moran carried Edwin and James took off his coat, put it on Jimmy and lifted him on to his back. They had gone only a short distance when Moran was suddenly bayoneted.

James set Jimmy down and rushed to Alice's side while the children cried in terror. In a soft voice she entreated Jimmy to escape, and she hardly saw him slip into the bush and disappear before the rest of the party were attacked. She became aware of her husband's dying moans and then, numb with horror, she knew that Alice and Edwin had been killed.

Her baby was then snatched from her, its brains dashed out and its head hammered to a pulp before it was thrust back into her arms.

They then set about Alice herself with bayonets. She was wounded twice in the arm, one sword-cut pinning her to the ground while another on the wrist transfixed her and the baby which lay dead beneath her. Still conscious enough to be aware of James's dying gasps she tried to turn towards her attackers and immediately received a bayonet stab in the abdomen; then, after beating her breasts with the butts of their rifles, they left her for dead, one of them snatching away the shawl as she lay unconscious. Later she opened her eyes and looked at the bodies lying around her, then found the strength to crawl away to a small nearby shed.

Jimmy in the meantime had escaped to a neighbour's house, which he found deserted. Hiding beneath a bush he spent some hours in sleep, and the next day called on a Maori who gave him food. He also went to the site of his old home and tethered his pony, then, still wandering about, he found some food in another deserted whare. It wasn't exactly stealing, he told himself, because the owner had gone away and left it. He then returned to the bush where he had previously slept.

The next day when he again went to his pony he thought he heard a movement in the shed, and at that moment Alice, who was still alive, called to him. She told him to find some eggs and under her guidance he boiled them in a kettle. After that she told him to return to his hiding place for the night.

Next morning he took her some potatoes obtained from the Maori who had previously given him food. He was still wearing his father's coat, and, searching in the pockets, Alice found a card case and a small piece of pencil. With great difficulty and after several vain attempts she managed to write the following message:

Could some kind friend come to our help, for God's sake? I am very much wounded, lying in a little house on our place. My poor son James is with me. Come quick, ALICE WILSON, We have little or no clothing and are in dreadful suffering.

During the next two days eight-year-old Jimmy tried to find his way to Turanganui some five miles distant, but each time he became confused by the various tracks and had to return to his mother. He was now accompanied by his little dog. On Monday, six days after the massacre, he set forth again and was near the present hotel at Makaraka when he heard people approaching. Terrified that they would be Hauhaus

Jimmie Wilson, only member of the family to survive the Hauhau attack. He became a surveyor and represented New Zealand at Bisley in 1902.

he crept into the scrub to hide, but as they drew near the dog ran out of the scrub and barked.

The men, following the dog, soon found Jimmy crouching in the scrub. Fortunately they were a scouting party and help was sent for with Dr Gibbs starting off at once with a relief party. A spring cart was loaded with mattresses to bring Alice out, but she was in such agony from the terrible wounds that she was unable to bear the jolting. She was then put on a stretcher and taken to the cottage of Archdeacon W. L. Williams, where she was nursed by Mrs Jennings, the wife of a military settler.

When news of the tragedy was received by Alice's sister, Maria Lowry of Okawa in Hawke's Bay, she left at once on horseback, and accompanied only by one Maori boy rode from Okawa through the Hauhau-infested country to her sister in Gisborne.

On 14 December a vessel was chartered to remove Alice to Napier, but despite the care and skill of Dr Spencer she died on 17 December and was buried at Napier.

In Poverty Bay Captain James Wilson, his three children, and John Moran, were buried in one grave. Major and Mrs Biggs and their baby son George were buried together, while a separate grave was made for Jane Farrell.

Jimmy remained at Okawa, where he was brought up and cared for by his aunt. He was later awarded the Victoria Medal for bravery. For a time he went to his grandparents in London where he was partly educated at the North London Collegiate School, and on his return to New Zealand he attended the Napier Grammar School and Wellington College. He became a surveyor, later living at Woodville, and he was also recognised as one of the best shots in the colony, representing New Zealand at Bisley in 1902. Some of his later years were also spent back in Poverty Bay.

Some Pioneer Recipes

Back-country cookery in the early days was done with the most primitive equipment. Imported ingredients bought from the store were hard on a small housekeeping budget, and frugality had to be the order of the day.

The following recipes give some indication of what was set before the family.

Perhaps the most impressive is Emily Eaton's recipe for bread: many of the households mentioned in the book amounted to twelve or more persons in the family with additional demands being made on the bread supply by wayfarers and visiting Maoris. This would involve a weekly baking of seventy or more pounds of flour by the laborious method detailed below—and the housewife had also to make the fire and prepare the yeast,

RECIPES FROM THE RECIPE BOOK OF EMILY GATES EATON (14)

Potted Head

Take half a bullock's head and clean it and soak it in warm water with a cow heel 2 or 3 hours, then boil it with the heel till tender. When done cut them in small pieces and lay them aside, after which strain the liquor in which they have been boiled and let it stand till cold and take off the fat. Put the whole into a saucepan, boil half an-hour, season with pepper and salt according to taste, put into tin or earthenware shapes or basins and when quite cold it forms a jelly and is ready for use. If it does not come out easily dip the shape in hot water. Garnish with sprigs of parsley.

To Dress Lamb's Head and Pluck

Take the head with neck attached, split up the forehead and take out the brains and lay aside. Wash the head, take out the eyes, clean out the nose with salt, put it on with the lungs or lights and heart to boil for an hour and a quarter. Take them out and dry the head and neck with a cloth. Rub it over with an egg well beaten, strew crumbs of bread, pepper and salt over it, stick small pieces of butter over it and lay it on a dish before a clear fire to be browned lightly.

Mince the lungs and heart with part of the liver and with onion, parsley, pepper and salt, a little flour, grated nutmeg, tablespoon of ketchup. Add some of the liquor in which the head was boiled to form gravy and simmer half an hour. Take the brains, beat them well with 2 eggs, 2 tablespoonfuls of flour, a sprig of parsley finely chopped, pepper, salt, 2 or 3 tablespoons milk, the whole forming a batter.

Have a frypan with a little lard or dripping. Fry the batter in small round cakes, brown lightly both sides. Cut the remainder of the liver in slices, dust it with flour and fry it. Lay the head upon a dish, place the hash round it, lay a slice of liver and brain cake alternately on the hash all round.

Onion Flavour

Take several large onions and peel. Put them in a saucepan with a little salt and flour and a small piece of butter to prevent burning. Cover closely and set by the fire to brown and stew gently about 2 hours. They will be quite soft and with the addition of a little water will yield a rich gravy to fry potatoes with or flavour any dish.

Icing for Tarts

Beat the white of an egg to a froth, spread with a brush or feather on the top of the tart and then dredge white sugar upon it. Return the tart to the oven about ten minutes.

Gingerbread

A quart of molasses, tea cup of butter and tea cup of cream. Two teaspoonfuls saleratus (bicarbonate of soda), tablespoon or 2 of ginger. Take as much flour as you think the molasses and cream will wet, rub the butter thoroughly into the flour, crush the saleratus very fine and put it into the cream. Now add the cream and molasses and ginger to the flour and knead it into a dough of proper consistency to roll out. Soft gingerbread is made by mixing three teacupfuls of molasses, one of melted butter, one tablespoonful ginger, 4 well beaten eggs. After mixing these together add a few handfuls of flour, then a teacup full of cream with a teaspoon of saleratus dissolved in it. Add flour to make it just thick enough to stir it. If milk is used instead of cream add more butter. Beef dripping is very nice for part of the shortening.

Sausages

Proportion your meat half fat and half lean cut fine, then to 100 lb meat add $2\frac{1}{4}$ lbs salt, 10 oz sage, 10 oz pepper. Warm the meat and mix them in thoroughly and stuff them.

Instead of skins make linen bags, say as large as a man's arm, and put the sausage meat in. Hang up to dry, slip off the bag from as much as is needed and cut into slices for cooking.

Calf's Foot Jelly

Take two calves feet well cleaned, break them in several pieces and put them in a saucepan with three quarts cold water. Boil slowly till reduced to about three pints, strain it and let it stand till cold and take off the fat carefully. Put the jelly into a saucepan and along with it the juice and yellow rind of three lemons, two stalks of cinnamon, half a bottle of sherry wine, the whites of 8 eggs well beaten with the shells broken, and white sugar according to taste. Mix all together and boil 20 minutes.

Take it off and let it settle with a cloth over it a few mins., then pour it through a jelly bag made of clean thick flannel. It will take some time to run therefore hang the bag near the fire, cover it and let the liquid run slowly into a jar. If not quite clear run it through again then pour it into the shapes.

Bread

For four or five persons where the baking is done only once a week take 21 lbs flour. Put it into a pan large enough to hold double, make a deep hole in the middle of the flour, pour into it half a pint hop yeast having previously mixed the yeast in a pint of lukewarm water and well stirred. Then with a spoon stir into this liquid as much flour as will make a thin batter. This will leave a large part of the whole mass of flour dry with the batter in centre. This is called setting the sponge.

Sprinkle on the top of this sponge a little dry flour, then cover with a warm cloth, either flannel or thick cotton, and set by the fire in winter or in the sun in summer. The leaven will then spread to all the flour. Let the whole stand till swelled and risen so as to crack on the outside, then scatter over it two tablespoonfuls of fine salt.

The next step is to make into dough. Take 4 quarts soft water as warm as milk in summer, a little warmer than in winter. Add by degrees to the flour till thoroughly moistened, stirring with your hand. Now knead with your fists till smooth and stiff so that not a particle will stick to your hands. On this depends the quality.

Then make the whole mass into a lump in the middle of the trough or pan and sprinkle over with flour. Cover with a warm cloth and if winter place near the fire. It will swell in an hour or less and be at its height.

Now make into loaves for baking and put these on well floured tins or earthen plates and put immediately into the oven. To tell when the oven is too hot sprinkle a little flour on the bottom. If it burns black at once wait until it cools.

Pickled Cabbage

Pull off the loose leaves and cut the cabbage into shreds with a sharp knife. Sprinkle a little salt in the bottom of the keg or jar, then put in a layer of cabbage. Sprinkle this with salt, peppercorns, a little mace, cinnamon and allspice. Then add another layer of cabbage and then the spices as before. Continue these layers until the jar is full.

Heat your vinegar scalding hot, put in a little alum and turn it while hot on the cabbage. Turn the vinegar from the cabbage six or seven times, heat it scalding hot and turn it back to make them tender.

HARRIET FLETCHER'S (15) RECIPES

Dock Root Ointment

Cover a quantity of dock roots (after washing well) with water and boil for an hour or more. Strain off the liquid.

Melt a quantity of lard, minus the salt, to equal the amount of water. Stir them together, adding a teaspoonful of boracic powder, and when all is well blended put aside to set in small jars.

This is a good healing ointment.

Pannikin Pudding

A pannikin resembled a tin mug and measured one pint. This recipe was found when altering an old house at Upper plain, Masterton, on the section believed to have been Edward Farmer Eaton's original 1854 Small Farm forty-acre section later occupied by Edwin Meredith of East Coast and followed by P. Nathan. The recipe is included through the courtesy of Mr B. Iorns, Masterton.

2 pannikins of flour
1 pannikin of suet
½ pannikin of sugar
4 small teaspoons of soda
2 teaspoons of acid

1 pannikin of raisins
½ pannikin of currants
a little lemon peel
1 nutmeg

Mix all ingredients together and stir stiffly with a little milk. Cook in same manner as soda plum pudding. To make a smaller pudding use a teacup for measurement instead of pannikin and half the quantities of soda and acid.

FROM THE RECIPE BOOK OF MARIA TUCKER (47)

Pig's Head Brawn

One pig's head and set of trotters left in salt for one day. Cover with water in large cast iron pot and boil with few cloves and peppercorns for about three hours or until the meat is tender.

When ready strain off the liquor and cut meat from head and trotters into small pieces. Place in bowl and season with pepper and salt, finely chopped sage and thyme. Cover with the strained liquor and place on top a plate smaller than the top of the bowl. On this place a 2 lb weight, leave till cold and then turn out.

For a larger quantity a shin of beef can be added to the pig's head and trotters.

RECIPES USED BY METTE KIRSTINE NIELSEN (32)

Men's Promises—Easily Broken

Mix 3 egg yolks mixed with sufficient icing sugar to make a stiff paste. Add a little baking ammonia. Bake in manner of meringues.

Chocolate Meringues

Mix the 3 whites with enough icing sugar to make a stiff paste. Add a little baking ammonia and cocoa to give chocolate flavour, or cochineal for pink ones.

Bibliography

Bagnall, A. G. and Petersen, G. C. *William Colenso*. Reed, Wellington, 1948.

Bagnall, A. G. *Masterton's First Hundred Years*. Centennial Committee, Masterton, 1954.

Bannister, C. *Early History of Wairarapa*. Masterton Printing Co., 1940.

Castlepoint Historical Committee. *Early Castlepoint*. Masterton, 1940.

Groves, H. G. *Early Castlepoint*. Wairarapa Times-Age, Masterton, 1940.

Hatton, L. *When Gisborne Was Young*. Logan Print Ltd., Gisborne, 1969.

Harper, B. *History of Country Women's Institute*. Whitcombe & Tombs, Christchurch, 1958.

Jury, O. *The Story of Glendower*. 1951.

Lambert, T. *The Story of Old Wairoa*. Coulls, Somerville, Wilkie. Dunedin, 1925.

Mackay, J. A. *Historic Poverty Bay and East Coast*. Gisborne Publishing Co., Gisborne, 1927.

Manson, C. and C. *Pioneer Parade*. Reed, Wellington, 1960.

Meredith, E. *Reminiscences of an Early Settler*. E. H. Waddington Ltd., Masterton, 1898.

Rafter, P. *Never Let Go*. Reed, Wellington, 1972.

Roe, R. *Early Days in Wellington, Westshore and Eskdale*. Daily Telegraph, Napier, 1929.

Rosevear, W. *Waiapu, The Story of a Diocese*. Paul, Hamilton, 1960.

Williams, F. W. *Through Ninety Years*. Whitcombe & Tombs, Christchurch, 1940.

Woodhouse, A. E. (ed). *Tales of Pioneer Women*. Whitcombe & Tombs, Christchurch, 1940.

Unpublished Papers

Bibby, M. G. (diary).

Colenso, E. (diary).

Eaton, E. G. (diary).

Haigh, H. *Ross Family Notes*.

Hamlin, J. (diary).

Jackson, E. D. *My Scandinavian Forebears*.

Lysnar, W. D. (diary).

Ramsden, J. *Nairn Chronicles*.

White Family History

Index

(Figures in bold type indicate illustrations)